The Cycle of Life and Death

The Cycle
of Life and Death

A Magnificent Journey

Thea Terlouw

1st edition

July 2019

Obelisk Books

More about the author can be found on the website:
www.obeliskboeken.nl/thea-terlouw/

1st edition, July 2019
ISBN/EAN: 9781085927284; NUR 720
Original Dutch version, Copyright © 2018: De Cyclus van Leven en Dood

Key words: spirituality, philosophy, religion, near-death experience, NDE, dying, death counselling, suicide, reincarnation, extra-terrestrials, Atlantis, Pleiades, Arcturus, Sirius, Adromeda, spiritual guides, guides, dimensions, spheres, light spheres, city of light, coma, euthanasia.

Content

Foreword

The one certainty in life that we carry with us during our lifetime, like a millstone round our necks, is death, which is imminent for all of us. In our current society, based on economy and technology, death is not only a taboo, but also undeniably the most important of all fears we face. Other fears often derive from that. Death is the most dreaded disorder. Moreover, there seems to be no answer.

Insult to injury, Western Society today dismisses everything that matters, where might is right. Provided you are lucky enough to have the means, happiness can be made or bought, unlucky if you cannot. Life needs to be enjoyed without the burdens.

We hold death at bay for as long as possible, because we are defined only by our brains... there is nothing else... or is there?

Fortunately, the ever more rapid technological advancement is now leading humankind towards robotisation at an ever-increasing pace, and we are happy to spend our billions on the development of artificial intelligence. Man is imperfect and urgently in need of improvement.

Technology will save us and with genetic manipulation coupled with a variety of pills if need be, we make every attempt to extend our life as long as possible. Fortunately, we are almost there. The question whether this is sensible or only useful, whether it is wise or only 'smart' is of course irrelevant. From ethical or moral point of view, there is nothing to gain.

We rather live than die. We are not interested in our planet nor in the billions of have-nots. We consider it the inevitability of death will be here for some time to come. More technology perhaps?

Does the above ring a bell? Then why hold this book? Does it worry you or make you deeply unhappy? Did you recently suffer the loss of a loved one, a relative? Are you terminally ill, fed up with watching the world's misery on television? In other words, have you been confronted with your own mortality? Do you wonder "What's the good of it all: what comes next?" Did you live a righteous life so far; do you regret making some wrong choices perhaps?

This book is about the realisation that we all came from somewhere. That besides the many lives here on Earth we have also been elsewhere in the universe at times. It provides an entirely different way of looking at things.

Not one we are usually taught nor one which is discussed often. When we were young, we remembered this. Then we went to school however and were educated. We went to work as was expected, we met our other half, became a two-income family, took a mortgage, had children... We were busy with the daily madness, the insanity of this world. Until somewhere along the line, for whatever reason, we were faced with the question: "What about life and death?"

This book contains a wealth of information, knowledge and wisdom from people who have passed before us, who have made the transition from their physical life to what 'comes next'. It contains their own interpretation of their lives here on Earth, their transition and the time they now spend in their 'reality', claiming to have come "home"

There is hardly a better way to discover the meaning of life on Earth than to realise that there is no end to that life but merely an end to a temporary stay in this physical world as we experience it.

With this book Thea shares her experiences together with her guides and all those who contributed with their personal life stories. For all of those who hold fears or who are simply curious. This book is a real page-turner, and to reread certain passages for example just before going to bed. After all, each of us has contact with what we call 'the other side'. This happens especially during our sleeping hours. Many of us will not realise that, and put it away as 'only' a dream. That does not matter, since the contact and the exchange do their work anyway.

Thea's special talent is her capability to contact the other world at any time. A talent she would have preferred to get rid of as a young child. It took her many years to learn how to deal with it and make it work not only for herself, but also to the benefit of others. She will never claim it to be the 'truth', but shares it with us as an experience. After all, everybody has to discover, feel and reflect. What suits you? That is the essence of our earthly lives.

You may ask for help, as help is readily available for everyone in this End Time. "Seek and Thou shall find", and this book has found you, or do you think you found the book?

I hope that it inspires you, reassures you, allows you to let go of unfinished business, become physically, emotionally and spiritually whole. We wish you and your family a wonderful journey and hope this book will help you with that!

Team Obelisk Books

The Cycle
of Life and Death

Children about 'the past'

'Granny can walk again, where she is now.'

Grandmother had been in a wheelchair for fifty years.

An 8 years old boy

'When you are dead, you go back to heaven,
They come pick you up,
You come upstairs,
You meet people, who are already dead,
Others who change again,
Become alive to go back to Earth'.

A 6 years old girl

'When you were still my baby...'
and
'When I was a grown up and you were small...'

A 2 years old girl

'Daddy, when I was big and you small,
You always sat with me on my lap.
When I was daddy, you were still a child.
I have chosen a good mommy, don't you think so?'

A 3 years old boy

Quotes from *'Vroeger toen ik groot was'* -
Far reaching memories of small children.
Joanne Klink

1. Margaret

Thea: It was a moving experience at that special place by the water, when she first appeared to me in spirit. First, I heard her deep warm voice, which I would have recognized out of thousands. Everyone who knew her would remember her voice, because it was so special. After I recognized her voice, I saw her appearance in my mind, through my third eye. I am not surprised; because when I am working on a reading I see everything as clearly, as if I were there. I have always had that ability, but hid it for a number of years, but has since returned stronger than ever before.

My entire stay in Ireland was a revelation, because so much happened to me. I saw myself in previous lives in that country, happy times. A memory of a former life is not always pleasant, but I know from years of experience that these images never come past without a reason. Old, negative parts are rapidly purified that way. It is part of me, so I have worked with it throughout many lives. I later visited areas in Ireland I had previously lived even though I never had that desire before. I know of so many places where I once lived, but these parts of my being are sealed, having served their purpose. I saw these memories as a precious asset. They gave me a lot of insight in who I am, in all my positive and negative experiences, and they have shaped me into who I am today. An educational journey taught me a lot.

I often met people who felt the need to go back to the villages and towns where they once lived. They would carefully set out a track sometimes going back as far as Russia. I never had the need to do that. The fact that Ireland always appeared in my dreams was a reason for me to go there. Going to Ireland was food for my soul. I never expected to find Margaret there. The fact that I had no premonition about that made it so special. I cried tears of joy. Here is what I wrote down.

Margaret: Hello, dear Thea, I am so happy that I managed to make contact with you. I have been looking forward to this moment. It took some time before this was possible. A lot has happened during the time following my transition. I think it's great that you found this place in Ireland. It was a journey of confidence. Pieces of the puzzle fell into place and you were directed to this place where energy is very high and pure. Preceding this period you went through an important phase of growth. I was with you when you and the two men from the hostel, John and Robert, went looking for the stone circle you dreamed of. Since coincidence does not exist, the right people were together at the right time. When the stone circle was found, you got an experience from ancient times. In front of your mind's eye, another landscape unfolded in a clearing in the forest. You realised that you had known each other for a long time. All three of you saw Druids in the circle, images from an earlier life, a distant past. It was moving to see three people, who had only known each other for one day, stand hand in hand in this magnificent scene. Words were unnecessary, even when each of you went your own way again later. Words will not do justice to an experience like this.

Something beautiful happened there; something was healed and a connection restored. You will not forget the light that went through you and which you were all able to see. John is an expert on the subject of ancient sacred sites and has often protected them. At soul level, I know these men. I was happily surprised I could be present at this moment. I like the fact that you never feel surprised, that you are like a child on a voyage of discovery, in silent wonder.

At our first meeting at the summit of the green hill, I was as touched as you were. It was my first time to make such a contact. Everything came together at the right time. Our deepest wish has come true and it is all so simple. Down by the cliffs, a dolphin appears regularly leaving traces of light in the water. This dolphin has a task to heal the people who feel attracted to this place. It is not a myth that children are healed here. Dolphins belong to a species that are attuned to a high spiritual level; they come from a higher dimension. I watched you meditating, high on the cliffs near that piece of eroded rock. You had forgotten about the dolphin and you were lost in time. You spent hours there aware that something special was happening. You felt how energy changed, was raised. You can from now on hold on to this new frequency. When you opened your eyes, you saw how the dolphin jumped up into a white aura. I saw it too. From this other dimension, I can see much more, a rainbow of colours in and above the water. This being emits pure love. I can see why people are attracted to dolphins and whales.

Dear Thea, please keep experiencing life as a child, in pure wonder. Once people had a spiritual experience, they often start meditation expecting similar experiences. I have studied this in detail. Meditating just to experience that thrill again. I have studied many kinds and ways of meditation and prayer, which was very fascinating. For me the most delightful one remains the open, silent meditation, in connection with the great Light, or whatever you choose to call it. Connecting with the Light and with all the people who are tuned in at the same level.

On Earth, I was not aware of such a thing as spiritual greed. I think an even better word is 'spiritual materialism'. Your teacher and now mine, Leviahnarah, taught you that word. He also showed me what it is. I was amazed to see that in some places it has taken on huge proportions under the influence of certain energies. There is a growing amount of people who meditate and in different ways, but all from the heart with the same goal.

These worldwide connections during this period of transition of the Earth from the third to the fifth dimension are important. These people lay down a solid foundation on which the entities of light can build a solid house. Without all these people, that would not be possible. All those sincere meditating and praying people create very powerful fields of light. At some distance from the Earth, you can clearly see that the Earth is getting lighter and lighter. Entry gates, portals that were closed by dark, dominant forces for many thousands of years are now being opened one by one. The Harmonic Convergence of 1987 was a major breakthrough in that respect. Big changes became visible then. Together with Ohan and Leviahnarah, I was able to watch these developments through the holographic screens. The fall of the Berlin Wall was a very distinct turning point that could come about through the change of energy on Earth, an increasing light flux and a changed, higher collective consciousness. The foundation that is laid is growing and shows a solid base whereupon the forces of light can build. I hope to say a few more words about it in this book. The changes are happening so fast. With the increasing light, everything that is still unexposed in the world becomes exposed. This applies both to the yet uncovered parts in humankind, to all aspects of Earth's civilisation. Nothing will remain hidden any longer.

You see that we are growing towards a light-consciousness and whoever wishes to be fully engaged in this is busy with his or her purification processes. Sometimes it concerns very old vibrations of past lives. This purification covers an entire cycle of 26,000 years. People who prefer not to go along and still need the energy of the third dimension - living in duality - go to a world where they can do so. My father's house has many rooms," Master Jesus said. There will always be those who still have a need for power and other corrupting desires. They have not yet worked this out sufficiently and still want to experience that.

They will be incarnating elsewhere in the cosmos, until they are ready to grow to a higher dimension.

For many people the process of purification is difficult, I know that from my own process with cancer. However, no matter how heavy this road was, I succeeded completely. Everywhere on Earth, these kinds of processes are now taking place. Many people experience chaos in their inner world and are confused. The pouring in of the light emphasises those unfinished issues that our Higher Self thinks should be purified. All parts of our soul-being, all with their unique experiences on Earth, seek wholeness to be able to continue their journey.

There is a spark of divinity in everyone and when the sometimes many layers of concealment fall away one goes searching, touched by the light. On the way home. To wholeness, inner peace, abundance and spiritual richness. Every human being longs for this from the depths of their being. We all come from the same light source.

After I had made my way through the spheres, and reached my place of spiritual alignment, I followed a long training in the Hall of Wisdom. That training included how to pass on the material to you in the right way. It was in fact a refresher course, because I now know that I have worked in this way with people on Earth many times, in other incarnations. The whole process was like opening old shutters. I now know that I did this work together with you. I passed it on and you were the receiver.

It was wonderful to be back in the Hall of Wisdom, a sense of homecoming. Like a sponge, I took everything in. You will understand that after my death on Earth I did not go straight to the Hall of Wisdom. That went very gradually, but since I had already done a lot of work on Earth, it flowed through easier and quicker. I was already aware of so many things.

Dear child, you prepared me so well for my death and my new life here. I also have a strong feeling, that your absolute conviction and belief in life after death will be a great support if you are as sick as I was. When you hear that your life is over, many emotions pass by. From this dimension, I will tell you about my process, and what other people here told me, went through. I concluded that there are as many different ways of dying, as there are degrees of consciousness.

No longer in earthly life, only now, do I fully realize how important it is to live consciously. To heal and transform old fears, just as you taught me in the years of counselling preceded by years of intense reading esoteric books, as you know. I also realize that spiritual healing is a natural process that can last many lives because man is lazy by nature. Unfinished business, negative vibrations from previous lives, complete cleansing requires effort and is often painful. Many people prefer to avoid that pain.

My study in the Hall of Wisdom taught me that an increasing number of people try to consciously break the wheels of karma. You and I belong to that group, and fortunately, we both know many people who have the same interests. I can now assure you that this search for truth and wholeness is more than worthwhile. What I love most about everything is the experience of Light and Love in which I can live. I so enjoy having got rid of my old, sick body. It once served me as the temple of my soul, I was allowed to work out a lot with it, but now it is so wonderful I no longer have to live in that heavy, tormented body.

A few times, you told me that you felt that my time to leave had come. You were right. Twice there was the opportunity to go; both times, it was in my sleep at night. My mother came to fetch me, but I was so busy and refused to come along. I thought I still had to help a number of people on Earth, pray for them, and ask for physical and spiritual healing for them. Repeatedly I found a reason not to leave. Twice I asked you for a reading and twice I was told that in the advanced stage of my illness all I had to do was to think of myself in order to die in wholeness and peace. Sometimes you apparently have to live to be 86 years old to continue living with blinkers on, while your body slowly surrenders. I learned that once you are attuned to the light, you can do much more for others on the other side of the veil, a lot more than I thought I could do in the last months of my life. I am proud to say that I had so many extremely sweet people around me during the years of my illness. That was a great gift. During the last period in the hospital, there was a growing awareness with my daughters, a growing light. I could see how different they were and yet they had so much in common. We grew closer. With my granddaughter, I always felt that seamless contact where words were no longer necessary. Three women I can look at with pride and love.

Once you are here and read your book of life, you will discover the purpose of your incarnation and of your specific family ties, at least with those people who are involved in your process of growth. I completely resolved certain issues from a previous existence for which I was partly to blame. If you read your book of life here so consciously, it is an hour of truth. You see every aspect as it is, life after life. I too was lazy, and in my life immediately before I was

Margaret, I left many opportunities untouched where I together with others could have solved karma. For that reason I seized the opportunity during my life as Margaret to work out a number of issues at an accelerated pace, through cancer.

I am grateful that my old material body offered me the opportunity to work out all the remaining karma. It is like a fire that burns you clean, like a purification process. I read my book of life, watching holographic images, as you predicted. It gives me the chance to look at every aspect of my past life and the lives before that, at my own pace. Nobody forces me to. It is presented in a loving way and it is up to you to do something with it should you wish to.

Thea: We know that since a while, different laws apply and that from that moment onwards, everyone is obliged to read the blueprint of their past lives. This has to do with the End Time in which we now live, the transition period of the Earth and its people to a higher dimension.

Margaret: Indeed, there were people who, life after life obstinately refused to look at their book of life. I, however, made good use of it when I passed on. I processed things in complete peace and sometimes, when I felt the need, I went to the healing chamber for a while, a day or afternoon in earthly time, choosing the light that suited me at that moment.

The last weeks of my life, I spent in hospital. I managed to live in my own home for quite a long time thanks to the loving homecare I received. How hard these people work! Most of them are extremely loving and dedicated. I would like to thank them all for their good care, but they will not hear me like you. Maybe when they read this book they will remember me. If you are so sick and helpless, personalised care is very important. Such healthcare is increasingly being eroded, not only because of budget cuts, but also because some jobs in the healthcare sector are so poorly paid. It is work that is looked at with contempt by some and unjustifiably so. Their work should be better rewarded! You realize that when you are gravely ill and so dependent. These loving people are priceless.

Right now, you are writing these words down in that beautiful booklet that you have received from Hanneke, as a gift, the sweetheart. She hoped that we would write together as we had planned; she will be one of the first to read this book. To pass on to you what it is like here was always my desire and intention. You are a medium and your readings are like waterfalls of events from previous lives, down to the finest details. As you write, you see the images passing by, like a holograph, as if in a movie. Very vibrant and colourful. It looks a bit like reading the book of life. When you describe previous lives, it is as if you are actually part of the holographic images.

Ohan took me to a place in the Himalayas, where you received your nightly lessons from master Lau-Me. You told me about it. I was taken to this place where you and likeminded receive their lessons. It was a beautiful space. As I pass this on to you, I feel your happiness when you think of this place, about Lau-Me, the large space built high up in the mountains, with only glass on one side and the enormous holographic screen on the other. This space is built in another dimension and Ohan, one of your spiritual masters, takes you there at night. Documents you will be passing on to people will be discussed there and worked out.

It is responsible work to pass on parts of one's book of life. I was allowed to be present once, together with Ohan. Leviahnarah prepared a big reading together with you. It was for a psychologist. People ask the spiritual world very special questions and some of them so profound! Of course, it gives a lot of insight into the consciousness of the applicant. Leviahnarah taught me that every reading adjusts to the level of awareness of the applicant. That is why sometimes it may seem a simple reading to you, while at times a very detailed and complicated one. The aim is to prevent damage to the applicant. I know that you are always aware of that.

The readings are made with the personal guides of the applicant. Mostly these people are stuck in the rational field of mainstream medicine and psychology and their spiritual guide inspires them to explore a different path. They might end up with people like you who can look beyond the veils of the third dimension. Luckily, there are an increasing number of people like that, waking up and I think they are desperately needed. It has helped me enormously to understand things that were hidden from my own vision. Ohan taught me how each reading contains certain keys. An open and honest story about a previous incarnation sometimes contains more than one key, releasing something in the subconscious.

It can revive old issues, processed and understood in the here and now. The insight you were allowed to give me in my past lives led me to process and transform certain matters. It has accelerated my personal process tremendously and that appeared to be necessary, because I had so little time left on the earthly plane.

My days in hospital provided me with great inner peace, necessary for me to realize it was truly time to go. I enjoyed the complete treatment. Of course, nurses never have as much time for patients as is probably needed, but it was good. The absence of the immense stress associated with being sick at home was so wonderful. In the hospital, I felt less isolated, because there is always some activity around you. It had a reassuring and relaxing effect on me.

No matter how lovely it was to be at home, amidst my own belongings, the long hours of being alone in a state of need weighed heavily. Being capable of doing simple chores like changing your bed, doing the laundry, bathing and going to the toilet is an enormous wealth. You only realise this once you cannot do so any longer. Then consider incontinence. Your great desire to clean things when there is no help available. I found being incontinent, confined to my bed, very difficult and perhaps even more difficult to accept, than the fact that my body had cancer. When I struggled with it I could share it with you. You commiserated, because your own mother became incontinent in her old age and you were familiar with the conditions. I was always afraid people could smell me, despite the good quality of the incontinence material.

The fact that I would deteriorate mentally was also a haunting picture for me. I learned to accept my physical deterioration step by step. You have no choice lest life would become unbearable. You stimulated me to follow certain thought processes that were fully in line with my own interests. One day you told me about Elize, my personal spiritual guide. You described her. I cried, remember? I always loved playing Für Elise on the piano. How beautifully things interlock. In this way, as my process continued, I gained more and more insight into these wonderful patterns. You reassured me when I expressed my anxiety about the hospital or - even worse - a nursing home. Eventually the hospital turned out to be my liberation. There I could surrender to the flow of things. I finally had the time and inner peace to think about my impending departure.

I had the feeling that the suitcases had already been packed before the trip and all I had to do was wait for the train to take me to my new destination. You know, dear Thea, there was no fear, only a deep desire to go. A complete resignation descended upon me and I decided to go along when my mother appeared again. I know now that third time I had no choice.

My daughters went through their own processes at a high pace. Also with regard to their relationship with me. Most people think that when you are so sick in bed, you are also mentally dying. Some people, also in nursing, talk to you in a way as were you an abandoned child, or even backward. I remember being clear-minded; my perception was sharper than ever. As my body slowly died, everything became more beautiful by the day. It is important that loving people surround you, and I have been fortunate enough to experience that. A heartfelt kiss, a stroke over your head. Someone who holds your hand in peaceful silence, loving and real. As a dying person, you see through all the pretence. It must be terrible to get unloving people to your bed, as I have often heard in this dimension whilst doing research for this book. In countless conversations with others to gather as much information as possible about the passing and the spiritual world that awaits afterwards.

My experiences in the last phase of life were beautiful, like pearls on the road. Sometimes I was outside my body and picked up thoughts of those who love me. Apparently, the same goes for coma patients, who also perceive all the thoughts around their bodies. For me they were short moments. Moments with a golden edge, briefly without pain, without the obstacles of a sick body. That was wonderful. Being outside your body is a blessing, especially when it is so sick and in great pain. At moments like that you realize your body is not everything and that you are immeasurably more.

That gave me increasing confidence for the coming journey. Your words sounded very frequently in those days. Where I am now I realise how important terminal care can be. You meditated in front of my picture and you prayed for me. Those days I experienced what it is like when people pray for you. They call upon the workers of the Source of Light, the angels, the people from the realms of light spheres. It was an experience. I was reassured that what I did every day for the sick and the needy was good and done wholeheartedly. When you pray or meditate, always do it with your heart or don't do it at all. Habitual prayers are powerless.

In my last days, I had a very beautiful experience. I would drift away, was in pain. It was quiet around my bed. Then I got a vision. I saw you walking along a brook of water; the weather was nice. You sat down on a large stone, half in the water. You were all alone in that place. You opened your hands in your lap and started praying for me and for other people. Then, I really felt what it is like when someone does that for you wholeheartedly. At the same time, I knew that more people did this for me, and knowing that brought great peace to my heart. Now that I am completely immersed in my new life, I know you were truly there. Thank you, as well as all those sweet people who did this for me, out of selfless love. To experience that with the people around you is a true God's gift.

When I describe the hour of my death it is important to know that such an experience is different for everyone and depends on everyone's own spiritual alignment. I only describe my personal experience that is related to my spiritual alignment. My fear had disappeared and that is very important. I hope this happens to everyone who passes. A few days before I finally passed away two women appeared. A small blond woman wearing a soft blue tunic and a darker woman in a purple blue tunic. At first, they were there only briefly before leaving again. I know now that the last three days before my journey they were waiting together for the hour of the transition.

One woman was my mother. I recognized her first. You told me that people in the light spheres looked younger, like in the best years of their lives. My mother looked like forty, so did the other woman. She was my grandmother from my last incarnation. They mothered me on my deathbed. Every so often, they would stand very close to me and held one of my hands. That was so wonderful. I probably had a blissful smile. What a delight when they are there for you. Every now and then mother put a hand on my head making me float away on little clouds. I felt like a child being cared for lovingly. How valuable were these moments. The spiritual became more important, whilst the physical body interested me less and less during those moments. I had surrendered to the birth process into the spiritual world. My two sweet, light mothers next to me were my midwives, along with my guide Elize.

When the hour of death came, you appeared. You stood at the end of the bed and just smiled. You saw me come out of my body and you saw a spiritual doctor break the silver cord. You stood there shining my child; I will never forget that image.

Thea: I have consciously experienced her death in spirit. Leviahnarah took me with him. This often happens when you work with the dying. These are precious moments given to you. I saw how a butterfly came out of its cocoon. From the sick, tired body a radiant being emerged. I was deeply grateful that I could see this. It is a miracle to experience such a death.

Margaret: It became clear to me that this was also an unforgettable experience for you. What followed next was the shining path after death, something you often see in your work with people who are still earth-bound. It is always special. My dear mothers and Elize took me to a shining path that appeared. I experienced everything consciously as was my deepest wish. I looked back once more at my physical body and thanked it sincerely for the services rendered.

We crossed a crystal bridge. A whole range of beautiful colours passed me by. It was a conscious journey. They took me to a large gate where a few people were waiting for me. A dear friend who had died a while before from the disease ALS (Amyotrophic Lateral Sclerosis). She looked young and radiant. Next to her stood a man. He stretched his hands out to me and touched me for a moment. There was a sense of recognition and joy. I saw them again later, at a time when I was also more aware of what happened and who were there. The man was my husband - he had passed away a long time ago - and it was a warm reunion. I was lovingly welcomed and taken to the healing chamber.

A woman in a light tunic with long trousers welcomed me there. I remember the modern style of her clothes. She had a sweet face. I was in the healing chamber for a few weeks, rated according to time on earth. A very special experience. The bed I was lying on had no legs. It floated a little above the ground. I was first positioned in a golden-blue-green energy. I let go and floated away in that lovely light. When I woke up Elize was there. I only had to think about her and she was there again. The power of thought sets everything in motion here. I was so happy with her loving presence. That guidance is so important.

My cancer process was fully worked out on Earth. I only needed that recovery period, in total spiritual rest. Dying is hard work, just like a baby has to work hard to be born. Loving help with such a process makes the process easier. I am deeply grateful to my family and friends for their loving help. If I would wake up for a moment, I watched in amazement how my hands and feet had gone slim without wrinkles or spots. It was a game, getting used to that new life, that young, subtle body. At moments like those I did not think about Earth anymore, that only happened later. I once woke up and saw an enormous alabaster vase on the ground, creamy white, containing beautiful white roses. I looked at it with admiration. Between the roses, there were little blue flowers. Then suddenly I had to think very strongly about you. You always said: 'Margaret, when you have gone over, I will send you a large bunch of white roses for the new beginning'. As always, we joked about these things. Then I said to you: 'Just add some little blue flowers to it, for the book we are going to write together'.

After all, we had no idea whether our mutual desire to write this book would actually become reality. Elize told me the flowers came from you. I know you teach this to many people and it is wonderful to receive such a floral greeting. Spiritual flowers do not wilt. Later when I left the healing chambers for my own house that was ready, I took the flowers with me. They now stand in the corner by the large window and reach all the way to the ground. A few months later a beautiful red rose came from you, it is still there. By then we had not made any contact and did not know if that would happen. You bided your time.

A few people sent me spiritual flowers and I cherish these sweet gifts. It is a wonderful opportunity for contact without expectations. A kind of acceptance of passing, without expecting anything in return. Nobody on Earth pulls at me and that is a very rich feeling, because I often see that happening to others, who are not released by those they left behind. That is a big obstacle in one's advancement in the spiritual world. Sometimes I went out of the healing chamber to walk with Elize. A man visited me occasionally, admired my roses and later went for a walk with me. He became my guide to teach and show me all these new things. Elize introduced me to the power of thought, telepathy and teleportation, and it turned out not to be that difficult. It was a surprise to be able to see her now. On Earth, I was aware of her presence as a spiritual guide and sometimes I saw a glimpse of her, a lovely appearance of light. Now we were sitting there in full glory, outside under a huge tree, on a green bench. We were only radiating towards each other.

Elize taught me to visualize a cup and then a drink. I chose grape juice. At first, I could not hold the thought, so the juice fell to the ground. It took a while before I mastered it. We do not eat here as we are used to with our earthy, coarse material body, but we absorb the essence of the fruit. I was offered a drink the other day that was delicious, a kind of spicy mead.

With Elize I walked through the gardens, in a sloping landscape in which I immediately felt at home. She told me about the new life. We walked past large, elongated gardens with lavender. The colour was deeper, more intense than I had ever seen on Earth and the smell was delicious. Close to all the healing chambers that are everywhere here, you will always find lavender gardens. Essential oils from lavender have a healing effect and therefore there is lavender in those places where people make a new beginning. I know that many people have a certain fear in the beginning, but only because they have absolutely no idea that there is something so beautiful and loving.

We walked through the rose gardens. I saw roses, three times the size of a peony, so delicate in colour and so perfect in shape that I kept looking at them. Roses represent a very high love-vibration. I have cherished that beautiful energy. Sometimes such a walk was so overwhelming for me that I had to go back into the healing chamber for a while to take the spiritual rest I felt I needed. Invigorated and full of energy I continued later.

I also saw others, accompanied by their guides. Most of them radiated bliss, free of physical pain in the heavy physical body. The wing of the healing chamber where I was staying was specially made for people who had cancer on Earth. Some people require a longer stay in the healing chamber to complete their processes. Elize told me that many helpers were oncologists or nurses on Earth. Many spend this period in different light chambers at the frequency necessary for their total recovery. Time does not exist on this side.

It is pleasant to lie in the colours that are custom-made to your being. There is always gold in the healing chambers for cancer. That gold is like an all-pervading mist, which is located within a blue-green space. I became part of those colours, was absorbed by them. What a blessing to be there. After my transition, I arrived in the third light sphere, but my spiritual alignment was above that. It takes time to transform and to be able to go a step further. A person could not bear this much light at once. The third sphere was already such a revelation to me, the beauty of nature, the beautiful flowers I saw there, the variety of birds and butterflies, the smells and colours. The green colour of the heart chakra is present in everything here. It has a calming and healing effect. My final destination turned out to be in the sixth light sphere. On Earth, you have no idea of such a thing, and perhaps that is for the better; in that way you will be working on purifying your body and mind without prejudice and pre-defined limits.

Elize accompanied me to my home. Remember you told me about the houses you had seen during your visits beyond the veil and their enormous diversity? Everyone creates what suits him or her. You once sent me a beautiful picture of a small white stone house, overgrown with beautiful roses. Joanne's house, with the large chestnut tree. How many times have I looked at that picture and drawn strength from it on my sick bed.

Yet my house looks very different. You create what suits you at soul level before arrival. My new life here is focused primarily on the healing of my being. The house is beautiful, very spacious and with a beautiful view. Seen from above it is somewhat dome-shaped. Completely closed on one side and completely open at the front. I can, if I feel the need, shield the space from the outside world and obscure it. I enjoy the pure simplicity of this design, the space inside and around it, the peace. In my home, there is a comfortable sleeping area where I can retreat if I feel the need to unwind. Day and night rhythms do not exist here by the way. The sleeping space is in soft colours, a bit peachy, very pleasant to rest in. In the spacious living room, you will find those colours too, with here and there bright colours that I chose.

I have a beautifully shaped chair that floats a little above the floor and can move in any desired position. Elongated, so I can see outside and enjoy the landscape. Flowers are everywhere. I had such a need for that after my years of being ill and my secluded life in my earthly home. I missed the beauty of nature so much. Around my house is a field of small white flowers. On the edge are white and pink roses. Again those very large ones. Bigger than peonies. I cannot describe the beauty of this place with earthly words; there are simply no words for that. I enjoy it and cannot get enough of it. Around the house are huge white chairs where I usually receive my visitors. There are beautiful tall blue flowers in large bunches together. In front of those are small low-growing flowers in different colours. A beautiful place.

Over the hilly landscape hangs a silver haze permeating everything. The spiritual alignment that you chose as your goal when you die. My transmutation from the third light sphere to this place was a wonderful and happy process. We can go to all the spheres below, but not automatically to higher spheres. I know that this is only possible in a special protective cocoon reserved for special occasions only. People like you, who pass things on to the people on Earth, are transported in such a cocoon to get to know the spheres.

I read my life book, slowly, at my own pace, first with Elize and later in the Hall of Wisdom, focussing on what I had intended to do during my illness on Earth at soul level. That is to pass on to you what it is like on this side, hoping that the living will benefit from it. That is to overcome the fear of death. Death does not exist. We are like butterflies crawling out of a cocoon to rise up brilliantly.

I have met many people with regard to this book. I discovered that everything happens according to a plan, an "agreement" between you and me and with many others who all had the desire to take away the fear of death and dying. When I started my study in the Hall of Wisdom and received training to make contact with you in the right way, sources of forgotten knowledge opened up to me, entries to the previously known. Little by little, I faced all the facets of my life before incarnating as Margaret. While searching I discovered our old connections, the times of cooperation of the spirit, friendships on Earth. I discovered that in a life in the seventeenth century I could play the violin beautifully and had a gorgeous singing voice. In a life after that, I played the piano and you were my piano teacher. That took place in Vienna. We were dear friends. Until your early death at the age of 42 we were inseparable and I could do for you what you did for me now.

You died of tuberculosis. Your mother could not cope being with her dying daughter. Together with your father and twin sister, we took care of you. High in the mountains where your twin sister had founded a sanatorium, together with her husband, who was a doctor. It was a special time, all together, full of emotion but that last year was wonderful. I played the piano by the open doors while you and other guests were lounging outside on the terrace. These were very special moments. Leviahnarah, one of your spiritual teachers as well as the one who convened the readings, was then your father and your twin sister your granddaughter Eva of today. How beautiful everything fits together. You can see these things through the thousands of life readings you have passed on and you understand and know from your own experience how beautifully things interlock. Fortunately, more and more people today gain insight into these kinds of processes, of themselves and others.

In the Hall of Wisdom, I met people who sang in a choir. We chatted and I joined their choir. I really enjoy singing together. How wonderful it is to do that. I also get piano lessons in a building where they practice fine arts. Many community buildings here resemble ancient Greek buildings. Simple in their great beauty. My interest is mainly in the music of Chopin and Mozart. I go with friends to concerts. The music is not comparable to the music on Earth. Almost impossible to describe, so beautiful, so pure, it affects me in my deepest being. I now know that I was involved with music in different lives. All these pieces of knowledge I thread together like beads, expanding my reality a little bit every time. An enormous wealth. Most people work on their last incarnation, whereas

I work on more than one incarnation. It depends on the extent to which they have processed their issues from their last life. That is why I am now so happy that in my last life I have tackled and worked through my unfinished affairs. Processing old matters and acquiring awareness goes deeper if you do that during your life on Earth. Now I also understand why so many different therapies were introduced to Earth. This way there is a way to heal for everyone.

In the Hall of Wisdom, I got to know your teachers and guides well: Ohan, Leviahnarah, Edward and about 4 others. You told me about their sense of humour. I have experienced that now and their humour is indeed heart-warming. I could use that at such a moment. As I learned more and more, at a pace that suited me, I began to gain insight into my past lives and I could see how our connections worked and how old they were. We have worked together many times.

Like in the life, you know as that of Anne Marie, in Berlin at the beginning of the nineteenth century. Leviahnarah was your brother at the time. Together you worked on pamphlets, small writings for a gnostic society. In those years, I passed on a book to you from the spiritual world. Collaboration between a person in the spiritual world and a person living in the material world. This book was then distributed under a male pseudonym throughout Europe. You travelled a lot with your husband, who attended conferences as a neurologist and gave lectures in other places. Even though the Inquisition had officially been abandoned, persecution of dissidents took place on a large scale with often intense consequences in that life.

The Gnostic societies, spread all over Europe, have been very important in preserving messages of light, until it was safe to come out in the open again. During your travels with your husband, you transported the copied writings in a secret space in your carriage. It is wonderful to open the registers of past lives and with the necessary amazement, you start to connect the dots, slowly increasing your understanding of the magnitude of your being and what you have done. At this point, I also understood why I felt so sure we could accomplish this together; we did it before!

Is that why it is so easy? It is as simple as making a phone call. You can ask me things and we communicate. When I read my book of life, I see so many beautiful things, but also my obstacles. I think it is so important to report that nobody here judges or is judged, except perhaps by yourself. If you have hurt or injured other people, you feel and experience that in yourself during such a review, and wished you could change or balance it. Sometimes it is nice to see how during a lifetime when you have hurt people or have inflicted terrible pain you have solved it during that same life. I think that is good news to pass on and that we are actually always doing the balancing act. Between fathers, mothers and children this happens very often. If only we would pay attention, you would see that these possibilities are always there. We so often are unaware of the possibilities that are being presented. More and more people are consciously working, cleaning up and improving their lives and with that, they create new fields of light due to their larger and intensified light consciousness. With their conscious growth they take many people with them into something we could call the formation of a morphogenetic field. It is also called the hundredth monkey effect.

In the Hall of Wisdom, I was shown how the growth processes of many people, both individually and in groups, are progressing at a high pace. They in turn take many people with them into that new, lighter consciousness, which is wonderful to see. I myself learned to develop my previously acquired talents. My first contact with you went smoothly and naturally, as if I was talking to you on the phone. Your talent as a channel has of course been actively used for years and is constantly developing. In Ireland, where you wrote these words, many people still live in fear of hell and purgatory. Yesterday I was with you for a moment when you meditated in that beautiful old church. There I discovered the thoughts of fear in some of the people who were praying there. With fear in their body, they still go to confession here. In the same Ireland there are still a lot of dogmas, but an increasing number of people, like all over the world, are outgrowing these things. A young generation is looking for the truth, wanting to be free from the imposed doctrines of the Church. Gently we are going in the right direction. As I see it here, this awareness and the choice to be free may go faster than many people think. I must say very honestly that I had no idea that so many people, often not visible to the outside world, are searching and sometimes growing slowly, sometimes at a high pace.

My new life on 'the other side' is a great pleasure after my long illness, after all those years of cancer, pain and sorrow. I have learned that you have to respect your body - the temple of your soul - and take very good care of it, and I honestly have to admit I have not always done that properly. I see many cancer patients here who also need to acknowledge this. People who have already healed on Earth have learned to say 'no' more often and take better care of themselves. The more people learn to listen to their feelings, the better they do.

Contact with your soul is the only way in the right direction and brings you where you would like to be in your life at soul level. If more people listened to their feelings better, more issues would be solved during their lifetime and in a shorter time. It is not always pleasant what you come across on your path, but it is what needs to be healed in yourself.

Often only then, can you clean up and heal old and non-healed parts swiftly. This way you can achieve a level of wholeness, making life a lot more relaxed with a sense of harmony and increasing light. Not everyone is equally receptive to this and thus many opportunities to heal remain dormant. I can now oversee my own path, my own choices, to transform my old karmic aspects at an accelerated pace.

About living and dying

When you die,
It doesn't happen because you were ill,
But because you were alive.

Seneca

2. Doctor Carl

Always studying and working

Margaret: While reading in my book of life I came eye to eye with my careless treatment of my own body. Through holographic images, it is as if you are in that moment. You see, feel and experience everything in all its different aspects. You feel the pain that you inflicted on another person or that was inflicted on you.

I came to the shocking discovery that the man I loved so much and who left me for someone else I alienated myself, by my inner attitude. This happens mainly unconsciously. Now I am getting insight in the role I played in this. I saw how I was dominated by my immense fear that he would leave me for someone else. So where does such fear come from?

Looking back further, I came across another life in Bali and saw that it was I who left my husband. I left the man I loved in that life in Indonesia for another man. I abandoned him and he was very distressed. So what I did to him came back to me in another life. I had to experience the 'law of cause and effect'.

Thea, you know how the 'law of cause and effect' works through all the readings and memories of your own past lives. During my life and with your guidance during my dying process, we have worked on the supreme forgiveness for that man and for myself, for every unresolved aspect of my life, including events during the years of war in Indonesia.

I am glad I started practicing forgiveness, because that takes a lot of time. Time and again, you stumble upon a new layer when you start processing things. You always think you are there, but then you find yet another layer. These karmic aspects have now been fully resolved.

The discovery of the past life, which I now fully comprehend, made me decide to attend dr. Carl's lectures. There I met all kinds of people who are looking for a different approach to life. dr. Carl was a cell biologist during his last life. He showed us how everything works here. Learning, studying and how easy it is here. You concern yourself here with just the things you want to do, things that really move your inner self, otherwise it is a useless exercise.

Dr. Carl teaches in such a natural and self-evident way that you would wish everyone could receive such an education. A man with a lot of humour and the necessary self-mockery. Most of us really need humour as most people think that the spiritual world will be very boring and serious business. It takes us some doing to forget about our upbringing and religion for we are ill prepared for the humour of this place.

Dr. Carl's lecture hall is very special and I want to tell you about it. The Hall of Wisdom is a beautiful building with pillars and a Greek facade, marble staircases leading to wide open doors. The floors are made of marble, or in mosaic that is laid in intricate patterns. There are courtyards, many rooms all around, and enclosed lecture halls with enormous holographic screens. Outside the gigantic complex are several amphitheatres with round marble stairs that also serve as seats. Lots of green all around, in an undulating landscape. Flowers everywhere. The Hall is built in horseshoe shape with a plateau in front and behind it a holographic screen.

Dr. Carl likes to be in nature, he says, because he has been very busy all his life. Always studying and working. He hardly ever went out and neglected his body. He would usually be terribly stressed, lacked sleep and ate badly and irregularly. Rarely did he see the sun. Taking holidays, he found a waste of time. His wife and children did not see him much and when he was doing research, he often slept in the laboratory. We all know such stories from people around us. Now I hear the stories on the other side of the veil in the fourth dimension. His honesty is a true delight; I love it.

That impressed me the most, Thea, when you were with me in my last hours: your honesty and openness. That in your work you also dared to show your own pain and vulnerability. Many therapists behave as if they were God Himself, perfect and invulnerable and consider it a weakness when someone shows their own pain and weaknesses. Here that is perceived as strength.

Dr. Carl dares to tell about his deepest feelings and that openness is wonderful. He leads by example so that his students dare to do the same. Jokes are made on Earth about methods that 'teach you to love yourself'. Yet these methods have reached many people and made them think about how they feel about themselves in life. They provide the most important elements, allowing you to train yourself to appreciate yourself. Only when you learn to love yourself you can start loving others in a completely new way. The many different possibilities of 'being', that the Earth offers provides something suitable for everyone's talents.

Here in the fourth dimension I learned to see that often the cause that prevents you from loving yourself and others is in an earlier incarnation. The people I meet are very open about these issues. Acts committed in an earlier incarnation can create a certain kind of guilt, as happened to me after my life in Bali. Something like this will have an effect on your next life, blocking you to love yourself. Unloving behaviour that leaves you with pain in your cells.

Dr. Carl showed us clearly on the holographic screen how our states of mind, our negative and positive beliefs, are visible in our cells. Scientists on Earth are also paying more and more attention to this issue. I love it when he shows holographic images at lectures like this. You become part of the experience and that is why you will never forget what you have seen. He can make everyone laugh with a remark or a joke in spite of the very serious topics that are often discussed, or, ask him to discuss. Talking about it later makes us laugh all over again. I enjoy that. My last years of life were certainly not without humour, but really laughing intensely, with my whole being, that was a long time ago.

I meet many people here who are willing to share their story with me to contribute to this book. In the Hall of Wisdom people of all races and colours of skin, meet each other. I enjoy the unity in diversity. If only it could be like that on Earth. I have had lessons from a Hindu man, dressed in a beautiful silk tunic. I always look at him when he elegantly crosses the square with an animal like, smooth stride. His clothes have the beautiful colour of spices. In a small group, I learned from him about certain principles of reincarnation, which were in line with what I already knew on Earth and in earlier lives.

There is also a black man here who I find very impressive. He has a great robust appearance. He teaches the doctrine of the soul. I enjoyed his lessons. My inner knowing on Earth fitted in nicely with this. He is a teacher of great distinction. Many people come to him who struggled with apartheid deep-rooted racism for quite a few subsequent lives. Among his pupils are former followers of the Ku Klux Klan who persecuted other people in the first half of the twentieth century for their race and the colour of their skin. In a future life these people, as a karmic lesson, incarnated themselves with black skin and underwent the consequences of their earlier actions.

I have listened with admiration to their profound experiences. Earthly racists should realize that their souls have gone through all different areas, incarnated in all conceivable races and peoples. According to this impressive man, many people have learned meanwhile how things really are. However, there are still large groups of people who hold on to their old, racist beliefs.

As they say, "it is difficult to teach an old dog new tricks", and sometimes a disturbing experience is needed before a breakthrough can be made. Many, however, repeat themselves. We are such a tenacious people, learning only slowly and with great difficulty. This way, we kept the wheel of karma turning for eons.

3. Sophie

And the ultimate urge for freedom

Margaret: I also especially met up with Sophie concerning this book I was going to pass on. Whoever opened his or her book of life for me did consciously do so all hoping for a fast awareness on Earth. They all want to do their bit to raise awareness of these matters.

Sophie: 'In my last life on Earth I experienced the consequences of a series of earlier lives. In a life in the early 18th century I was a beautiful woman and very rich. I lived with my family in a large country house in Germany. My father loved me and I had a huge influence on him. I discovered my influence on men at an early age with a gesture, a certain pose and sweet talk. I practiced that on my father and when I was older I put that into practice and went on the manhunt.

My father was blind for my power games and spoiled me rotten. That was not beneficial to my character. My greed grew bigger and bigger and nothing was ever enough. My father was used to it, because my mother was exactly the same. It determined my whole way of dealing with people. I lived on the energy of others. Some of them avoided me getting very tired when I was around.

In several previous lives, I had developed a pattern of greed and very egocentric behaviour. That continued in that life in Germany. Usually it is the man, but here I was the hunter and my behaviour was considered amusing in the circles that I belonged to. I did not care much about what other women thought of me, and their gossip only made me laugh. I thought they were pathetic creatures forced into pre-arranged marriages, and saw how unhappy they often were. During this life, my urge for freedom was so extreme that it changed from positive to negative. In earlier lives possessions like jewels and gold, paintings and houses, gave me a feeling of independence. Being dependent on a man to me was the worst thing that could happen.

I have experienced a lot of misery with a number of forced marriages and there were lives where I was no more than a servant, the slave of the house, without her own life or own opinion. I was only there to serve and nothing else. It was terrible also to be used sexually.

That all escalated in the life in Germany. My desire for freedom, my contempt of men all came together at the height of my incarnations. I played with men, as they had played with me, only to throw them away like garbage.

Well, you only had to do that once in those circles but I attracted them like bees to honey. I mainly played with their feelings. Not with one man, but with dozens. I took so much energy and treated their love for me with so much disdain that two of my husbands died of a heart attack. I was rude, unloving and cruel. My wealth and beauty was all that mattered. That I harmed other people did not bother me. I unconsciously took revenge on what had been done to me in previous lives. It was my preferred pastime to deal with other people's love in this way and I hurt a lot of people. It was a type of violence, with major consequences.

When I was 44 years old, I had broken many hearts of men who had fallen in love with me, who loved me heart and soul. My body was beautiful on the outside, so to speak, dazzling. I gave birth to three children during that life, no more than that. But I was incapable of loving the babies; they ruined my beautiful body and that was more important to me than anything else was at the time. I employed a wet-nurse and a nanny, and after that, I did not care for them. Occasionally the children had to make their appearance in the drawing room and I would play the mother-role. At times, I did not even know their names and would casually wave at them. They would come to me anyway, happy as they were with a moment of attention from their mother.

I was not there when they were sick. I had no nurturing feelings or love for them. The same was true for my four husbands. On their sickbed these men were alone and forsaken. I never visited them, with the excuse that my delicate constitution was not able to withstand the sick. After their deaths, I acted the mourning widow for the world to see.

I passed, very lonely and attuned to a low astral atmosphere.'

Margaret: The spiritual violence she displayed in that life took its toll. Because she had damaged so many people, she needed to work that out, bit by bit, sometimes in very short lives. Thus, the spiritual violence and her tremendous unloving nature returned in Sophie's life. The previous life she had died in Germany with a self-hatred towards spirit and body. She cursed her old and wrinkly body. When also her mind, her quick tongue, her great attraction for men had disappeared, there was nothing left to her. Therefore, her spiritual attuning then brought her to a lower astral atmosphere. She continues:

Sophie: 'In my life as Sophie I had to bear the full karmic burden of that life in Germany. I encountered each of those men through incest and sexual abuse. I craved for people to love me. I dreamed of that all my life. I kept falling in love hoping for a lasting relationship. They played with my feelings and me. Eventually I ended up as a prostitute and had three children during that period. No matter how sweet and caring I was, my children preferred my older sister and my mother to me, as they were the ones who cared for them because of my work as a prostitute. They also lived with my mother and sister and as they grew older, I saw them less and less. I felt very bad that I was not interested in them at all. I often felt like a stranger to them. It was a tough journey, but for me it was the only way to break through these old processes I carried with me through so many lives. The covers and veils were shaken off and I returned to my core being, the being of light, my original self.

I was killed in a stupid car accident. I drove far too fast because I was angry with the children. That was after I had visited them. From one moment to the next, I was thrown out of my body and hovered above the car. It was strange to see my body lying there. I did not realize I was dead. When the ambulance crew put a sheet over my face, I began to doubt.

A light being appeared, but I refused to come along. During my life, I joked about such things. Several attempts were made to show me the way to the light, but I brushed them aside.

I found my mother's house, walked around the rooms, and tried to make them understand that I was not dead. They did not see nor hear me. I walked right through my mother when I wanted to give her a hug. The light being came and asked me to go with him I had nothing left to do there I was told. I turned away.

In the corner of the room was a chair that no one was ever allowed to sit in, the chair of my deceased father. I sat there for days. I saw my mother crying and I felt her sadness. Her grief was enormous. I could perceive her thoughts. My sister, too, was truly sad. My teenage children were indifferent and said awful things about me. They felt abandoned. They were angry.

I went along to the funeral and wandered around everywhere. A friend of my mom's was there and supported her through this difficult day. This friend was a sensitive woman. During the service held for me in the auditorium, she felt my presence and her thoughts reached me. She asked me if I wanted to follow her. I ended up at a meeting in Harmonia in Amsterdam. There were more people like me. There were several light beings, but I did not want to have anything to do with them. I avoided them and focussed mainly on the people in the room. I felt their genuine intention to show the light to people like me. It is odd I was inclined to listen to this material being, rather than to those friendly light beings. That particular moment something cracked inside me; their words and thoughts felt so real and pure. Then I allowed help.

A man appeared wearing long trousers and a blue tunic. He looked like my father in his younger years, which is probably why he caught my attention all the time. What I did not and could not know then, is that people in the light spheres become younger. They go back to the age they felt most comfortable. I knew nothing at all, and had always thought that there was only hell and heaven the way I knew from church during my years at school with the nuns. Something made it possible for me to wander around as an earth-bound soul though I did not know what

The woman who worked as a medium now turned to my father and me. She told me my father was there to pick me up. She spoke words that touched my innermost being. It is still difficult for me to describe that moment, but I joined him. One of the light beings came along with us.

I made the choice to go along and I entered into a state of unconsciousness after which I woke up in a healing chamber, a special section for people who die very suddenly, like in a car accident. I spent a long time there, at times awake and my father would be there again. Later on in between my periods in the different healing rooms, he would take me into the gardens. Together with the light being and my father, I read my book of life part by part.

Father was also the father during my life in Germany. We saw how he had always given his daughter everything without teaching her any norms or values. We were able to laugh about that now and the fact that we wandered around in oblivion and in darkness. Looking back, I needed that good humour. The light being showed me that it had not always been like that, not during the lives of my father nor in mine.

After some time studying in my book of life, I arrived at the lives where those negative aspects were not present yet. Harmonious lives lived both in simplicity as well as in wealth. At some stage, I was able to share my prosperity with others. I shared my money and belongings with people who had less than I had at that time. I had often worked for minorities, especially women and children. My concern for children must have been enormous in those times. The structure of my soul and my experiences were in harmony.

Independence turned out to be very important to me. This important aspect in life kept re-occurring. I saw lives during the oppression of women in China, long ago. I always tried to improve the situation for the group I lived in. My commitment was always absolute. I enjoyed revisiting tribal life in the America's long before white men set foot ashore. Sometimes in a harsh society, but one in which I, as a woman, had been appreciated and had held a valued place. I have learned a lot during the lives with the different Indian tribes.

I looked for moments when I had lived as a man but I could not find them. It turned out that that change of man-woman was much further back and not even on Earth. My origins from the Pleiades were revealed and I saw myself coming to Earth together with many teachers and parents. It had been my own conscious choice. My task as a mother became clear to me and the eons of lives and work became visible. My job was to create a proper foundation for children and young people. I had done this during my periods on Venus and later on Mars, for soul groups that were due to populate the Earth later. During those times, I returned regularly to my home world.

Like an inquisitive child, I went back in time, step by step, and slowly my whole being became visible. With every step, I began to understand a little bit more about myself. As an apple cut into small parts, I looked at every part of my soul and its accompanying learning processes. I saw how many populations from the stars came to Earth and how intense were their interconnections. I made this journey together with my father, who had been my father in multiple lives, but also in other connections with him and my soul group.

I started to recognize a certain kind of loneliness that I had often felt in places where I had lived. I investigated my desire for independence and discovered that the place where I came from before my earthly lives, male and female beings were considered equal, both important. Freedom also is very important there and I learned that these beings as a people have fought a long and difficult battle against the dark, dominant forces from the cosmos. That was before they went to the Pleiades, on Lyra.

Just as we would later experience duality on Earth with all the opposites that go with it, I had experienced that at Lyra before that. Now each of us was free to choose to incarnate here for a longer period. We descended from a higher dimension to serve Earth and its people. We belong to the Family of Light and often serve as light-bearing beings in dark places. I saw how many of my people chose such lives and I felt admiration for them. I had lost my way, a stray sheep that had lost its herd. In Egypt, the need for power overwhelmed me. I had only experienced harmonious lives until then. Originally, women had their own, highly valued place in ancient Egypt, equal to men. Women could hold any position they had talent for. However, when the change came and the masculine became dominant, I saw how women were forced into slavery.

I descended deeper into the material world, sometimes in deep darkness. Difficult lives. One day, when I chose that side of the spectrum, I made a deep fall as an initiate. I started on an experimental path that was new to me. I never before felt any desire for money and goods, but when I myself was oppressed and exploited by men, it became a path of freedom for me. I learned a lot from it.

My journey back into the light was long and difficult. Thank God, I never chose for black magic, something that trapped so many in that period of increasing darkness. There are many facets to power. Their way has been so much harder. It keeps pulling you down. You need to be so incredibly strong to fully get out of that trap.

My experiences as Sophie, a karmic accumulation of old habits, are now dear to me. With what I went through, I became a real expert. Prostitution was clearly a learning curve. That choice lay at the centre of my desire for freedom. I worked alone, from my own home, and decided for myself who I would deal with. I did not get involved with alcohol or drugs. My deepest wish was to be independent.

Those issues have become quite clear to me now and I appreciate their value during the course of my life. I regularly meet souls of the Pleiades here, souls who, like me, have been linked to Earth for so long and have been incarnating here since our arrival at the beginning of the Atlantis period. It is always wonderful to meet soul mates; that goes for every human being.

About ten per cent of our people have made karma and most of them have solved that in this time. We work hard towards the time of the great change, the increase of energy, in which all soul peoples will go along. My energy now focuses on children and their healing. Souls who often opted for heavy karmic aspects, in order to speed up the balancing of old karma. That goes fast now.

I keep telling myself that these things will no longer be important in the fifth dimension. There will no longer be any karma.'

Margaret: I spoke to her often after my lectures with dr. Carl. She had already processed a lot on this side. Once she was in the spheres of light, she worked on her book of life. The insights she gained in doing so boosted her growth. Her progress was very fast. Her three children arrived in the spiritual world and they found each other. Souls who have been connected for so long, life after life. After the karmic processing on both sides and the joint reading of their books of life, they regained their bond with each other. Now there could be love between them and they enjoyed it. Right now, she could scarcely believe who she once was.

There she sat with me, a sweet open face with long dark hair with Dorothy, her daughter in both lives, next to her. Counted in Earth time, she has worked for many years in the children's sphere, especially with those children who were mistreated and abused during their last lives, both mentally and physically. Her eyes shone when she told how love had changed her, how she found her Self again.

Sophie: 'At some stage I had a heart of stone and if I wanted something I would aim straight for my goal. I just took, unable to give back. In that dark period of the soul I hurt and injured many people, betrayed their deepest feelings.'

Margaret: I felt admiration for her frank story. Dorothy works together with Sophie in the children's sphere. The other two children continued after the period of reflection, each going their own way. One of the three, the boy, is now with his father. The other chose to incarnate again. Sophie's children were adults when they arrived, but in relation to Sophie, I can use the word 'children' here. Shortly after this conversation, Sophie took me to the children's sphere.

4. The Children's Sphere

Torn away from youth

Margaret: Children of fourteen years and younger who die on Earth go to the children's sphere. There they are looked after by extremely kind people, often by family members of the children, souls who are connected to them. Grandfathers and grandmothers, fathers and mothers, if they preceded them in the afterlife. Once on this side and in a light sphere, adult people take the age of their choice and spiritual attunement. Usually, the choice is made for the period of life on Earth during which they felt the most powerful. I myself now look like the Margaret on Earth of about 35 years old. In the beginning, in the healing chamber, it was strange when I looked at my rejuvenated, subtle body. Especially my arms and legs, which I could see easily. Like everything here, you get used to that quickly. Children grow up in the children's sphere to become adults. It is such a great place. If only all people who lose a child would know this in their hearts.

I came into a garden with beautiful trees in full bloom, a garden of the most diverse species and full of delicious fragrances. I saw pink and white blossoms. Between the trees were toys. Swings and merry-go-rounds, like in a regular playground on Earth. There was a patio, actually more of a large, open gazebo, with easy chairs like those that I have seen before. I saw many toys in bright colours. The whole spectacle was a feast for the eye.

Several gardens led to the open part of the garden with the gazebo the playground and all the toys. We walked further into the gardens. Sophie took me to her pupils. We walked up a hill and once at the top she pointed at two little blond boys with half-long, curly hair, playing in a large garden. They wore clothes made of very flexible material. It looked like silk shaped to their body movements.

Next to them in the field was Dorothy, the daughter of Sophie. She waved at us and pointed at the boys to Sophie, who kneeled and called them holding her arms wide open. The boys started running and flung themselves right into her arms. They put their arms around her neck. She walked with a boy on each hand to a large spacious house. I followed the whole bunch with amusement.

Sophie told us that she lived here with Dorothy and the two brothers. We went inside, the sidewall entirely open and looking out on the sloping gardens. All kinds of multi-coloured flowers you find on farmlands. It was a cheerful view. Inside was very spacious and almost futuristically furnished with very comfortable sofas and chairs. At the large window stood a sky-blue chair with many books around it. In another corner of the spacious room was a large table. Further on was a glass extension. There is no glass here like on Earth, but a substance that looks like it. This was the domain of the children. The long narrow table along the wall was full of drawing stuff and brightly coloured building blocks. The wide semi-circular bench in the corner was full of stuffed animals. I thought it would be a great place for children to play. It was messy, as you would expect in a children's room.

Sophie sat down in the blue chair in front of the window and pointed at a seat next to her. A bright red coloured wingchair with wide armrests completely enveloped me, I fitted in perfectly. I was most comfortable. I saw how the children went outside again with Dorothy. They continued the game they were playing before our arrival.

Sophie: 'The parents of these two children had a serious car accident, and the whole family was killed instantly. It was a French family. They stay in a special healing chamber, the same kind of chamber I had been in. A place for people rudely pulled from life. That help is very specific like there are tailored forms of care for every aspect of life here. These two children must stay together until they are reunited with their parents. This is expected to happen very soon. Then new children will come to live with us.'

Margaret: One of the boys came running into the house and gave me a hand. He took me to the side of the big house. I gazed in awe and saw the open structure I had seen earlier on, conservatory-like all very light as if you were in the middle of nature. The shapes of the house and the garden seamlessly joined in a harmonious, organic unity. On one side of the house was a huge white aviary. Not closed with wire or netting, like on Earth, but rather a canopy, with sticks sticking out of the back wall. From the living room, you could see the birds at the corner of the house. On the edge of the roof was a large white bird. It reminded me of a cockatoo with upright feathers on its head, except this one had a straight beak instead of a curved one. Two smart little eyes looked at me. I had no choice but to feel love for this animal.

The little boy stood in front of the bird and stretched out his hand. Very carefully, the animal stepped on his arm. It was a beautiful sight, those two together, that blond little boy and that big bird. They understood each other.

He communicated with the bird and the animal seemed to like his loving attention. Sophie took us further inside and there I saw two birds, again as big as a parrot, but without a crooked beak. They looked like birds of paradise and maybe they were, adorned with a beautiful plumage hanging upside down from a stick. One of the birds stepped carefully on her shoulder and the other on her hand. She passed the latter on to the other boy who had joined us. For me it looked like a kind of bird festival.

Sophie explained to me that the birds were free to come and go as they pleased. The bird on her shoulder flew away and we watched it go until it disappeared from sight. The boys each walked through the garden with a bird on their shoulders, until they also flew away. I saw the children playing some sort of game with red and blue pieces on the lawn with Dorothy close by.

Sophie: 'Children like this always get one-to-one care. In this period they are never alone, always together and with one of us. They are certainly not ready to play with the other children in the patio; that will happen later. We enjoy their presence and let everything flow as smoothly as possible. They felt we were honest with them when we told them about their parents and that they were in hospital, just as they had experienced. You cannot lie to anyone here; the truth is seen and felt. They accept their temporary stay in our big white house as completely natural, as only children can do. We make it as pleasant for them as possible'.

Margaret: Sophie took me to the large garden with the gazebo surrounded by flowers. It was a large garden with several children playing together and bordered by wide rosebushes giving it a nice intimate atmosphere. At long wide tables on a mosaic floor several children were drawing and painting, while others were busy with a kind of watery substance that they could model nicely. The children were of different ages and skin colours. It was a pleasant scene, a quiet place to work. The children were focussed with concentration on their faces. There were a number of easels in the room and there were children at work.

A man with a large flappy leather hat on his head sat at the head of the table. He looked at me with a broad grin but did not come out of his chair. It made me bashful. Sophie showed me a wide wooden bench, under the trees, so I could quietly watch the children's activities. A while later the man strolled towards me and introduced himself as John, constantly wearing that wide grin. He was tall and lank, his blond curls sticking out from under the hat. A real artist by the looks of it and I know I thought it was a funny idea that he had retained this unique image.

A long silence fell. Then he sat down next to me in a way as if we had known each other for years, but he did not say anything. He stretched his legs out in front of him. He was wearing jeans and boots. Every time I stole a glance there was that broad grin again. Therefore, I rather just kept looking at those painting children. A girl of about ten years old came up to us and handed John a thick drawing sheet. She had painted beautiful flowers and John said she was a natural talent. I was glad he finally said something.

Then he began to tell me about the girl with an enthusiasm that took me by surprise. He beamed when telling me about her special talent to paint nature. The girl had meanwhile walked back to her easel and continued her work. John was still there for a long time with a broad grin closely following the children's activities. Later he got up and walked past the children, looked at their work and spoke to each child individually. I saw the communication between them and the warm contact with the children.

Sophie and I walked further along the hedges of wild roses. The two boys were now playing on a sloping meadow. Dorothy sat under a tree and looked at them. There was a big light dog, a Golden Retriever. He ran like crazy and the boys ran after him.

Sophie: 'That dog has been severely mistreated during his last life. Here in this place between the children he is completely healed of the loveless treatment on Earth and is a healing factor for the children in this part of the children's sphere. These children here have all been subjected to physical or mental violence in different ways.'

Margaret: She pointed at a white-painted, wooden house with a wide veranda in front of it just past the green hill. The kind of house one would find in the southern states of America. I saw a big guy in a rocking chair on the veranda with a little girl sitting on his lap.

Sophie: 'She lives with the man who was her grandfather on Earth. She needs one-to-one care and he can give it to her. She died of AIDS. She was eighteen months old when she arrived here after being seriously neglected. Her mother was a crack addict and had abandoned her baby in the hospital of a big city in America directly after she had given birth. They took care of the baby in the hospital for a while, but then she had to go to a special home. There she was terribly neglected, both physically and mentally. Her grandfather waited for her here and now takes care of the child completely. She is about three years old now. As you can see this man does not look like a grandfather at all. He is not an old man but has the appearance of a forty year old.

All this was generally anticipated, including the addiction of his daughter. Nevertheless, before her incarnation there was still good hope that she could overcome her addiction in this life. He did what he could do to help his daughter, whom he loved dearly.

Overcoming a strong addiction is hard, some succeed, and others do not. Not yet. She struggled with it during several lives. The little girl consciously chose this incarnation and for this mother. Their souls are closely related and have been interconnected for so long, in different lives, through love and suffering. It is a soul that carries a lot of light within it with a high frequency of love from the heart.

The life plan that lay prepared carried a big promise. It was an act of love to incarnate with this mother. The mother experienced the pregnancy as if it were a dream, but crack is a terrible drug and that pulled at her like a magnet. She promised her parents repeatedly she would stop. A few times, she was admitted and she did her best to end her addiction permanently but was unable to. When her father suddenly died, every reason for her to fight for herself seemed to disappear.

After her father left the healing chamber, he became her guide something he had been in several lives previously, also for other people from his soul group. He is a wise soul. His daughter became more and more oblivious of the spiritual impulses given to her from the spiritual world and became like a ship adrift.'

Margaret: How many AIDS babies will have died like this? The children's sphere has special places for cancer patients, for example, and for victims of war, famine and disasters, for sexual abuse. For every facet of life, there are special healing chambers. I was lucky enough to be able to die with loving people around me. That was truly God-given.

5. John

Child with the children

Sophie: 'John, the painter, died in total solitude. He had AIDS. His partner died a few years before him and since then lived in a lower astral sphere, one to which he is spiritually attuned. John continued to live in solitude in rural California. He painted and made a living with it. When they diagnosed AIDS he deliberately chose to not be treated with experimental drugs, as his friend and partner had done. In the same period, other friends and acquaintances also died and he saw a lot of misery. Since that time in the eighties so much changed.

John had a tough time, refusing to go to hospital once the disease set in properly. The whole process did not take long with him. He wilfully chose for a fast, natural death without life-extending medication. He would take it as it came.

John rapidly grew weaker as his body often could not keep food in. He meditated and prayed a lot and had a strong faith and an inner knowing of a life after the material death and was convinced he would be reunited with his friends. He died of pneumonia, in all solitude.

After his transition, he immediately went to a special healing chamber in the light sphere, one especially for AIDS patients. On Earth, it took a week before someone found his soulless body.

In John's youth, many bad things happened. He was beaten and abused by his father. Often just for speaking. He used to be a talkative, smiling child and open towards others. He became so contorted that he spoke less and less and became more and more silent.

Now with the children in the children's sphere, which was his greatest desire, he himself became a child again. He plays with shapes and colours and teaches children to draw and paint the beauty of God's creation. The children love him. Maybe precisely because he does not keep nagging them about all kinds of things. Everyone here accepts his silence. We love him and the loving way he deals with the children. He is always available with his attention and energy when a child asks something of him. They laugh a lot and do crazy things together, spontaneously like only children do.'

Margaret: Something big appears from the shrubs: a huge, grey, Irish Wolfdog. He walks towards John and crashes down at his feet. 'They are buddies', Sophie says.

Sophie: 'There are dogs and birds with the children here. Here at the site there are no cats, I have never seen one. John's Irish Wolfdog went the same route as the other dog you just saw. Neglected, abused and starved, the animal died. John and the dog found each other in a very natural way, a love connection at soul level.

John regularly visits his friend, together with a spiritual guide in the middle twilight sphere. He does not want to be helped, not by John and not by others from the light who try to help him. He is very bitter and blocks increased light. He never believed in an afterlife and was convinced that death was death. That there was nothing after death. God was dead to him. A bitter man with a large dose of self-loathing. Hard drugs were one of the causes for his condition. People of the light do their work in the shadow spheres and never lose courage. They all know that one day their help will be accepted.

John has a firm belief in his friends' healing, he has seen that so many times. In the meantime, he works very hard at his own healing, the severely damaged child in him. The children love him, you see that and he enjoys them. Here it is really impossible to pretend to be anyone else but yourself.'

Margaret: John put his big, leather floppy hat back on. The children want to take turns putting on the hat and he does not mind. The enormous grey dog slowly walks between the tables and stretches out on the sloping lawn. A girl of about four years old walks towards the dog and puts all kinds of flowers in his rough coat. His head looks like a flower garden but he does not seem to mind.

I walk up to her and ask whether she enjoys decorating the dog with flowers. "Yes, I always do that," she says. She takes a ribbon out of her hair and ties it around his neck. The dog looks friendly towards me and seems undisturbed being fiddled with by the hands of the little child. He actually looks pleased.

I walk back, up the slope, to Sophie and Dorothy. They take me to the big white house. There we drink a thick red juice that tastes much better than strawberries. It was really made from strawberries, Sophie assured me, when I reacted a bit surprised. Let us face it, on Earth, cultivation methods, the frequent use of pesticides and the pollution of the environment, completely alters the taste of food. Strawberries on Earth often have a watery taste or no taste at all. Wild or homegrown strawberries slightly taste like the ones here.

We do not eat here, we rather absorb. Sometimes I enthusiastically shout 'heavenly' when I am offered something very tasty, and Sophie laughs very loudly because of it. I experience everything so much more intensely than I used to do on Earth; the colours, the flavours, the music, the beauty of the flowers.

I take my leave and walk along the path with the rose hedges. I walk past John's workplace; he raises his hand and greets me. John gave Sophie permission to tell his story for this book. His story touched me profoundly. The people I meet all seem prepared for my arrival and every encounter feels as if it was meant to be. Nothing is a coincidence; all things are connected.

I met Sophie again at the Hall of Wisdom, on our way to dr. Carl. She said she would introduce me to Anne, who wants to tell me her story.

Tomorrow we will continue Thea. I can see you are getting cold. We have been writing for such a long time now. Ireland is not really a country to sit in the grass to write for so long. So, bring something to sit on tomorrow.

I see high waves splashing against the cliff in a rainbow of colours. I perceive the energy of all things and that is truly a wonderful sight. The energy of this region of Ireland is magnificent.

The horizon

Life is eternal.
And love is everlasting.
And death is merely a horizon.
And a horizon is nothing else than
A limitation to our perception.

Rossiter W. Raymond

6. Anne and Pieter

The nurse and the doctor

Margaret: I meet Anne, sitting on a wide wooden bench under a tree. She cuts an imposing figure that impresses me. Her large dark eyes give me an open look. She is tall for a woman, yet graceful. We chat about dr. Carl and his lectures in the Hall of Wisdom where Anne also went. She has become friends with Sophie and visits her regularly in the children's sphere. We talk about the white house with the birds and the beautiful garden. I ask her if she would like to tell me her story.

Anne: 'During my last life I was an obstetrician and thus strongly connected to babies and birth. Events in previous lives determined that choice. I only worked, studied, and took too little time for myself. In busy periods, I did not take good care of myself, eating badly and sleeping little. Nowadays, there are the multiple partnerships of obstetricians that allow them more time to look after their health and wellbeing.

There was no place for love in my life. In my youth, I kept the boys at bay and concentrated on my studies and it continued to stay that way. I had shut myself off from personal love. I kept my heart closed to boys and men. I opened my heart wide for babies and pregnant women. I would see very loving couples in my work and then there was a deep longing for a life partner, someone with whom you could share your love and suffering. I daydreamed about that. When a man would make a pass at me, I would be as tight as a drum.

At the age of forty, I met a very sweet man, Pieter, who took a lot of doing getting to know me. I sometimes went out for dinner with him, but rejected every further contact. He was a general practitioner and I had met him through work my work as a midwife. A sweet, gentle man with a lot of compassion. He put me into contact with a therapist who could help me with my inhibitions. I went to her twice. She was a nice woman, but I was too scared to face my obstruction. She also 'did' regression therapy. I was not sure what to make of reincarnation and it was rather a far-from-my-bed show, I had never been interested and it did not really appeal to me. I also found it a frightening idea to have to relive all the misery should something like 'previous lives' exist. In hindsight, I know that it could have healed me, regardless of whether I believed or not.

Pieter did his best for years to conquer my heart, but I reacted like an oyster that clams up and is hard and impenetrable. Eventually he gave up. More than ever, I threw myself at my work. I died of a heart attack when I was 56.

When I arrived in the fourth dimension, I discovered in my book of life and through the holographic screen the actual causes for this and that it originated in the two lives immediately before this one.

You may well wonder why I suddenly regarded those previous lives as very normal. Yes, that is right. With the spiritual attunement I had now, it was all quite normal. Longer ago, before my soul was shrouded, I had also found that quite normal. Moreover, once you are in a certain frequency or sphere of light here, it all becomes quite normal and as a logic consequence, you want to investigate how things fit together. You work on those puzzle pieces at a pace that suits you. You get help without being judged. You judge yourself and believe me; we are sometimes very hard on ourselves.

If it would get too much for me, I withdrew into my home and took an indefinite break. My home is an oasis of peace, no piles of books, and no more bookcases everywhere. There is a huge oleander just outside my house. I can enjoy the view for hours. I created the lounge myself using soft cream tones. No bright colours and stones everywhere. I love them.

Time does not exist here, but if I need a real rest it may be, that I 'sleep' about four to five days of earthly time. I can really enjoy that intense undisturbed rest. During my last incarnation, the phone and babies who wanted to be born ruled my life. That is the reason why I also relish that real deep peace, now and then. I know it is necessary, because I am back working full time.

My processing period is completed. I did so at a fast pace, so it did not take me long. This is different for every human being, because every life is different and every human being knows his unique backgrounds from his past lives. There are collective processes that we work out together as a soul group, but in that play individual differences too. Everyone experiences things differently.

I discovered that Pieter gave me sufficient opportunities to heal an old trauma in my life as Anne. At that stage, I had not done so in between lives. After a life during the First World War, I just wanted to be left alone. I had died full of bitterness resentment and anger. I attuned to the upper twilight sphere and did not let anyone help me; I was out of touch. I had kept on refusing any kind of vision. That was still possible back then. With the transitional laws of this end time, however, every human being is obliged to read his book of life and all the help you can imagine is provided. Therefore, processing is faster and insight is gained into how and why.

Allow me to tell you about life in the First World War. In 1914 I lived in England and was a nurse. I had chosen to work at the front, thinking I was doing my duty. It was hard work. There was a French military doctor, François, whom I worked with closely. That is the Pieter of today. My name was Elisabeth then, very English and I came from a conservative Victorian family. Actually, I was an exception when I chose to work at the front in that dirty war.

At the time, I shocked my family with my decision and caused them a lot of grief when I was reported missing. They spent a lot of time and money in their attempts to track me down, but in vain. My family were never able to bury me; they never had a chance to say goodbye to me.

With François and a number of other colleagues, I went out to pick up the casualties. Hazardous work. At some point, we reached a place where many people lay injured. While we were busy helping, the Germans opened fire and I saw how François and my fellow nurses were shot. It all went very fast. I was taken prisoner and transported to a large country house.

Several of the officers checked me out, like cattle at an auction, which was a very humiliating. One of them picked me out. There were two other women, as if paralyzed, just like me. I could only think of the colleagues who had been shot dead and I decided to choose my own ending. I attempted to escape, but nobody bothered to shoot me. I had expected them to shoot me in the back when I ran through the large garden. They managed to catch up with me and unharmed, they took me to the manor. They gave me two rooms with every imaginable comfort at my disposal, even a private bathroom. Attempts on my part to seek freedom were unsuccessful. I did not eat, wanted to die, but was forced to eat my food. I became the bedfellow of the highest officer who forced me into sexual acts that I experienced as rape. I was particularly furious about the fact that one human could do this to another. I detested the man and that did not change, no matter how nice and polite he always remained. He adored me and that fact made me provocative. I swore at him and did everything I could to scare him away or, if necessary, to make him kill me. He never got angry or furious. He let my anger rage itself out calmly and took what he wanted.

I became pregnant and went through a hell of emotions. He even admired my pregnant body.

My resentment grew, as did my anger. The officer said that he wanted to take me with him after the war, that he would take good care of my child and me. It was an insane situation. In all his acts, this man was a robot, cold and unloving. In his own way, however, he loved me and made plans for a marriage before the baby was born.

When I was more than six months pregnant, I miscarried. I was alone, locked up in the two large rooms where I had lived for so long. I was scared, called for help, but no one heard me. Everything went wrong. The baby was born and shortly afterwards I had a severe bleeding. I hovered out of my body and saw myself lying down, the baby next to me in my arms.

More than anything else, I felt anger at what had happened. Not that anybody could have done anything about this bleeding, I know now. I remained connected to my body, although the silver cord was broken. I saw the officer enter the room and find us, covered in blood. I could see his true, sincere and deep sorrow. I had never wanted to assume that he had come to love me. He sobbed uncontrollably next to my soulless body wrapped the baby in a clean sheet and buried it in the garden with me present in spirit as you do when you leave the material body. I saw and felt his sadness and pain, and perceive his thoughts.

I saw him walk into the garden and pick roses. How he laid the flowers on the little grave under the trees. He sincerely mourned the loss of the woman and the child. My body was buried in the estate's large garden where there was a small family cemetery. He was there regularly to put flowers on my coffin and cry. That is why my family members never found me again.

After my last life, I discovered that in the life before that of Elisabeth's, I had acted very unlovingly as a man. I was Edward, found myself in an almost identical war scene and I did the same to a woman during one of the Napoleonic wars. Together with my spiritual counsellor, I looked at that life processing the information that came to me. I saw very clearly, what I caused with my possessiveness and greed. That I had not given her the care she so badly needed. That I had not understood the necessity to assist her, so she died causing her and her child's premature death.

Ignorance, oblivion leads to so much human misery. My experiences have made me aware of that. During my own, isolated existence during the First World War, I became aware of the importance of care during pregnancy and birth, something I had sorely lacked myself.

I died as Edward attuned to the highest twilight sphere and let no one help me. Not long after, the Council of Karma and my spiritual counsellors decided to incarnate Anne. That would contain everything to achieve processing and transformation. I was privileged to accomplish a lot in that life. In blueprint of my life was the intention to become a midwife and this came from my lonely experience. It is a pity I managed to dodge the proffering of all those wonderful moments. I ignored literally every possibility that came my way during my youth and college days. It was foreseen I could have healed everything in a relatively short time. My rage and bitterness towards men unconsciously kept playing a role. It was a conviction that had cemented itself.

Four years after my death as Anne, Pieter arrived here and had lived till the age of 63. I greeted him, knowing he was coming. I knew by now how everything worked and I finished processing and transforming my affairs. This was a while ago and after our journeys upwards, into the light we are working together.

I invite you to our house Margaret. Many people choose to still live independently even after having entered into a love relationship chose to share a spacious house now that we had found each other. I took my oleander with me on my journey through the spheres.'

Margaret: I promised to accept Anne's invitation. Her big brown eyes looked at me in a friendly way. She took me to a part of the children's sphere where babies arrive. The children's sphere is comprised of many different departments with different functions and backgrounds. I entered a green space with twelve newborn babies. It is the colour green that you see a lot in nature; warm and reassuring. They were not in a floating bed, like adults who have passed but in beds made of a transparent material. I saw more caretakers here than in the other healing chambers where I had been.

A small, somewhat stocky man came running towards us. His head was bald with a rim of grey curly hair all around. He had the same open mind as Anne. His bright blue eyes took me in warmly. I was shown around in different rooms. Here and there were smaller rooms with very specific colour tunings for each baby. It was a wonderful, serene atmosphere. Love, pure love surrounded these children. We went to a wing with spacious rooms for four babies each. We walked in and there were four babies; two dark and two light. I looked at them.

They were sleeping so peacefully and it moved me deeply. These were babies of crack-addicted parents. All four children had died of Aids.

At one of the beds stood a big dark woman. She came to me and introduced herself as Ellen. A big smile appeared on her friendly face. She was a nurse and personal caretaker of these children. The children still 'slept' most of the time lying in a pink-purple energy, very soft and delicate. It reminded me of an amethyst I had seen. I felt very special to be there.

Ellen grabbed my hands and said that she thought it was important to show this, so people would understand that all babies, no matter how they die, are well and lovingly cared for, whatever their spiritual attunement. Everyone here wants to let the physical beings know that there is another side and that every person is well cared for, no matter how spiritual he or she is attuned.

Ellen said she always believed in a spiritual world. The people she belonged to in her previous life were members of the black human race and originated from Africa but now lived in America. They would cry when a baby was born dating back to the time of slavery. If someone died however, his or her send-off was accompanied with special music.

Ellen smiled broadly and said that the latter was still a great tradition. I am told that there is a new trend growing within the Aids community to give parties with drinks and snacks to say your farewells in a different way. Maybe someday someone can tell me about his or her personal experiences that I can then pass on.

We walked on with Anne and Pieter. They showed me a room with only one child. Died of cancer. It lay in a blue-green energy, permeated with gold. These colours are difficult to describe. A golden mist is probably the best description. I myself was in such a room. It was very special and it stayed with me for a long time, as also this touched my own process. I left the room in silence and longed for the seclusion of my own home. We walked out into the soft, beneficial light. I told them I wanted to go to my own place, said my goodbye's to Anne and Pieter with the promise to visit them in their combined home. Moving is becoming easier and more natural. You think of the place where you want to be, and then you move yourself with thought power. I was in great need of a period of profound peace.

Thea, do you remember that you told me about these things when I was still sick? We used to joke about this. That sense of humour helped me then. My teachers, who were also your spiritual teachers, taught me a lot. Ohan, one of them, showed me with holographic images how they took you to all spheres during the years of your education and development. The bottom two deep black spheres had started to dissolve by then.

Thea: I have seen images of those two lower dark spheres where souls that had been there for many centuries were stuck in a deeply darkened consciousness, some of them already for eons. It was horrendous to watch. There are now five lower spheres and three twilight spheres, and above them seven light spheres. Between these spheres are transitional areas. Of course, the seventh sphere is not the end. In the context of this book though we concentrate only on the spheres I have just mentioned. Here, as well as on Earth, a lot is changing and these changes go very fast sometimes, with a lot of things obtaining a higher frequency. Amazing things are happening on Earth and that has everything to do with the increase of vibration in the entire cosmos, causing shifts in different degrees.

Margaret: I have witnessed how you travelled to higher spheres. You were in both the lower and the upper levels, together with one of your spiritual teachers. Ohan or Leviahnarah would put you in a light cocoon in order to protect you against attacks from the lower region but also to protect you from too much light in the higher frequencies. I found it very extraordinary to see and it was very clear to me how well trained you are in your work. It disclosed your own source of knowledge and unlocked pre-existing knowledge. You gave me permission at soul level to witness these parts of your development. People in the light spheres are so eager to share their own experience and learning path with others, which is far from usual on Earth. Yet all that is going to change quickly. Sharing knowledge and experience will unite us and bring us further.

I am leaving now to go to my sphere of attunement, using my own thought power.

I am in dire need of spiritual rest and once in my healing room I will chose for a white golden frequency. We will continue tomorrow.

7. Hans

Margaret: In the Hall of Wisdom, I met a man during the lectures of dr. Carl. He studies the integration of peoples. In earthly time, he had been working on this for a number of years. Through his own soul-experiences, he felt the need to study this more deeply.

I always notice him in the square in front of the lecture rooms together with a group of people from his field of study. They hang out together. What strikes me immediately is the 'unity in diversity' of this group of people; they are all very different. I see all kinds of races together. It was decided to keep the physical features of the last or second last life. They talk and laugh with each other.

Hans is a very big man, not only big but also broad. He has medium length, coarse, curly, dark blond hair. When he laughs, and I often see him do so, his entire face beams and his blue eyes shine like stars. I had known for some time that I would talk to him about his soul's journey. Ohan had already told me a few things and gave me the time and liberty to prepare myself for this. Part of his past, I would have sharply condemned on Earth and before I could talk to him, I had to deal with that. The remnants of an earthly existence. The interview took place in the first period after I had just started my work.

It was a good thing to contemplate the issues that would be covered. At the large square, he asked me to listen to his story, because according to him it was important. We met in a garden, adjacent to the open fields. A place where people go because of the beautiful view. There were small comfortable seats, all white. The place reminded me of an old-fashioned tea garden.

There we walked around a bit first. Hans told us that these were the places where people go for a chat, or just to enjoy the view. We looked for a place under the trees. I did not know where to start but Hans put me at ease by starting the conversation himself.

Hans: 'In my penultimate life I incarnated in Germany. I was born in 1910 in Bavaria and had a wonderful childhood. When the First World War started I was four years old and eight when it was over. I cannot remember much of that. My grandfather was a high officer, a proper metal-head. He came from an old Prussian family of almost exclusively soldiers. It was the tradition that the men went into the army.

Grandfather died in Belgium during the war. My father came back, but was wounded, rancorous and disappointed. Two of his brothers had perished and many of the men on my mother's side of the family had as well. We were not exactly a joyful lot at home. My grandmother was very resentful and would do everything she could to make her grandsons go into the army. That was essentially the world she knew and grew up in and was well connected in that environment. She was proud of her heritage and the lineage of the soldiers.

When Hitler and his National Socialist Party emerged, my parents became members. I was brought up with the stories of war, the horrors, and the heroics. I also wanted to become a hero. Many little boys wanted that. We were stimulated from all sides. My parents made sure I became a member of the Hitlerjugend. That was quite normal and I must say, we as children enjoyed what we did there. As children, we knew nothing about war, power and brutalities. All sorts of activities were organized for us and I enjoyed it.

I was a real outdoor child; camping out was a treat for me. I lived in an environment that prepared itself for a large and powerful Germany. Through the educational and the employment systems people were made to believe they were working towards a good cause. My parents were convinced that they were raising their sons for something huge that was about to happen. As the thirties progressed, all my family members became fanatical supporters of Hitler. I did not know anything else. That was my world. I know that people outside could not understand why we let ourselves be so carried away. Here, in the spheres, I have seen how that enormous, dark movement became so powerful. The time was ripe.

There was a feeling of hate under the Germans for anything exotic, out of the ordinary and that is how I was raised. There lived a Jewish family in my street but I was not allowed to play with their kids. We did not understand why, and played with them anyway. Outside the village, we went fishing and cycling, and we climbed trees. Boy's games. As a child, you like someone or you do not like someone. I played with the two Jewish boys outside the village at our playground. We formed a close bond. However, very gradually, everything changed. I got older and within the Hitlerjugend, the thumbscrews were tightened. We made certain choices and gave way to energies that encapsulated us. A kind of numbness followed, making us indifferent for everything that happened, a kind of euphoric intoxication too, which led from one thing to the next, like an organic growing process.

As was expected of me, I became a soldier. My two younger brothers also joined. I was destined for bigger things and the family background definitively played a big role in that. My grandmother and my parents harboured great expectations of me. My cousins went the same way. My entire education and training was aimed at a military career. In a relatively short time, I climbed up to being an SS officer. I saw the construction of the concentration camps and the construction of barbed wire fences. I was convinced that we were doing the right thing. Part of my work was administrative; everything was meticulously recorded. I travelled a lot and spent a lot of time in Berlin in a large office.

I was transferred to a concentration camp in the last year of that life, when I was 35 years old. Masses of people in the most appalling conditions populated the camps I had seen built. That was in the northeast of Poland. When the Russians arrived, they positioned me together with four other officers in front of a fence and executed us. A neck shot for all 4 of us. It was over before I realised it.

I stayed earth-bound for over a year, Earth time, and wandered around. In those days, I learned a lot. I saw the misery; the oppression caused and how badly the few left in the camps were doing. I stayed close to my still living colleagues and that is how I came to Germany in spirit, but earth-bound. I felt the misery that had descended upon many people. I observed their thoughts and listened to their conversations. There was profound doubt amongst many about everything we had lived for. The ones who returned to their families in Germany were not believed when thy told their stories about the concentration camps.

I hung around with a friend, a man I had been a close friend with. I hooked onto his aura like an octopus and went wherever he went. He shared his stories, which were also my stories, but people did not believe him. Nobody believed that thousands of people had been driven into the gas chambers, nobody believed in death camps. I always heard the same thing: "They were labour camps, because our men had to fight".

My friend travelled to his parents in Dresden where he discovered that his house and his family no longer existed. Many earth-bound people, like me, wandered around in the flattened city. Terrible things happened there. I stayed with my friend, in his aura. He searched the whole city for news of his parents and sisters. He became more desperate by the hour, and my presence in his energy field did not help. A lot stirred in me too, as the extent of the whole drama started to sink in. Our ideals were wiped out.

I exhausted my friend with my aura lift. I withdrew a lot of energy from him. Eventually he went looking in southern Germany. He dressed as a farmer; ever vigilant for fear the Allies would discover him. He travelled through forests and fields and once I came to familiar territory, my hometown, could I leave him with his fear. I searched for and found my parents. Their grief was enormous, all three of their sons were killed and both my parents were convinced they had died for a good cause. My grandmother was also firmly convinced that her grandsons were great heroes. Only one of the nine grandsons had returned. In her house on the sideboard, she had a collection of pictures of all the men who died. Both from the First and Second World War. It was an altar with images of saints, flowers and candles. A symbolic image I carry with me into this dimension and shall never forget it.

The absurdity of it all began to penetrate. I stayed around her, looking for something but did not know exactly what. I know that my spiritual guide inspired me to do these things. In the period shortly after my death I learned more than during the whole of my life of thirty-five years. Grandmother felt a hatred for everything different and a discovery like such, feels far more intense in the spirit than in your material body. I tried to talk to her, because to me my subtle body felt as real as it had been before. I began to see that we had let ourselves be carried away in a compartmentalised reality, because outside there was nothing for me. I did not know any other reality.

They buried my body in my hometown, just like that of my brothers. The youngest had died in France, the middle one in Belgium. I hung around my parents who visited the graves of their three sons every day; their three heroes. Many people came to this large cemetery and I could make out their thoughts in my earth-bound condition. How different they were. There were people who saw how insane it all had been and I immersed myself in their thoughts. They thought back to the years of a life lived in numbness of being lived. Others thought of the fears they had, because they did not want to be involved with Hitler's National Socialism and his henchmen, but were forced to join at some point. They expressed their fears at the cemetery, because also their sons had been sent to war during those last years, some of them mere children. There were those with a deep sense of guilt. They had been much more aware of what was going on than I was at the time.

One man in particular caught my attention. His grief was immense. His thoughts were not filled with hatred towards the Germans, nor towards the Allies. He sat there on a bench immersed in deep prayers. His daughter, son-in-law and their two children were laid to rest there. He had helped them go into hiding when all the men had to go into military service. They all worked for the Resistance movement and his daughter was on the 'wanted' list because she had helped Jewish children go into hiding. The man was an anthroposopher. When that entered his mind, I had no clue what that meant, I really had never heard of it. Sitting on that bench, he repeatedly relived the moments he took his daughter and family to bring them in the care of other anthroposophists. He had been a teacher. Two years passed before someone betrayed the family in hiding and they executed them in the town as a terrifying example.

The man on the bench never stopped thinking back of the moment he found his daughter and her husband and children dead on the pavement. He knew it had almost become a compulsive thought. I saw the images he saw. I followed the man to his house, attracted by a soft light that the man emitted. At home, he meditated in silence. He reflected on his loved ones that were now in a better world; he thought of other spheres and light. This man carried huge knowledge of life after physical death. I was particularly fascinated by his lack of hatred and resentment in his thought world. At soul level, this man chose to let someone like me into his energy field. Nothing happens by chance. I was given the opportunity to see other truths when he reflected on the war period and the years before in his inner silent world.

My truth about my upbringing and my life was certainly not his. He read Rudolf Steiner's books and I could follow his thoughts. One evening, two women visited the man. That was the end of my apprenticeship as a terrestrial soul. They meditated with each other; in a joint prayer, they remembered their dead. They talked about them as if they were still alive somewhere. In their minds, they were in a place where it was good. One of the women felt my presence and told the man that he had an aura lifter and told him she saw a statue of a man in the uniform of the SS. He said that he suspected it, because he would often feel a certain chill. They lit a candle and put it in the middle of the table. The woman tuned in and made contact with me. That was crazy. Never before had anyone felt my immaterial presence. She started talking to me telepathically and she told me a lot about the spheres, about other places than Earth. She encouraged me to ask for help and she kindly offered to help me with this. I agreed.

I will never forget what happened then. My grandfather appeared, that old metal head. It was a younger version of him, as if looking at his a childhood photo. He was the same age as me at my time of passing. She told us that people on the other side of the veil adopt the age during which they felt the strongest. He would take me with him, it was time to go, the woman said. Without hesitation, I went along, after which I saw another male figure appear, but I soon slipped away in a state of unconsciousness. I went to the sphere of my attunement in the lower astral spheres. Later I could see that my earth-bound year had taught me so much that my attunement had changed a lot since the moment of my passing. Then I was attuned to the sphere of deliberately killing other people. My consciousness had now increased; I did not yet go to the light, but to a shadow sphere where people approached me with kindness and help.

Thanks to the anthroposophical man and his visitor, I was able to accept the help provided. I realise many people are quite adamant in refusing any help when they arrive in a dark sphere. I still had a long way to go before I could enter the light spheres. Of course, I was not yet aware of the spheres above mine, but I was willing to look at the past and was assisted in doing so.

Victims from the past life were introduced. We would see each other again in a next life. I underwent schooling. Even in the twilight spheres there are places where you can learn. I read the book of life of that last life in Germany and when I finished that I went back further to see where and when I had lost my attunement to the light. We never actually lose all of it. Every human being carries a godly spark in him. Mine was encapsulated, obscured, by aberrations in earlier lives, making choices with major consequences.

Because we can see everything later in our book of life, I studied all the experiences of that earthly period in great depth. After my next life in Yugoslavia, I have used my book of life in the groups I visit.

My earth-bound period of over a year is a document that I am offering to the people who are studying war, violence in general, racism, political ideals to which they want to force others to commit to and lack of love in general. These are all people who have gone through that, one way or another. Whether those past lives are as far back as two thousand years ago with the advancing

Roman legions and the armies of the Greater Austrian Empire, or at the time of the battles of Napoleon or the American Civil War, it does not matter. Time is irrelevant.

We are now purifying a long period of about 26,000 years. During that period, the exhibition of heartless behaviour is hard to fathom for the human brain. From the state of light in which I find myself now, after all the karma I have experienced it on occasion stuns me to see the terrible mess we have made of such a beautiful planet. All those battles, all the wars, the insatiable need for power. How many times were people allowed to let themselves be manipulated by kings and rulers, landowners, the Roman Church? Everywhere in the world, people are persuaded to serve their country and fight for a higher cause. It is clearly visible from here what that has led to and then often purely to the financial benefit of a handful of people. Not all humanity's wars maybe, but most of them.'

Margaret: Hans got up from his big white chair and walked along the edge of the garden. He seemed emotional. He lost control of his feelings for a while. His thoughts were so immersed in his own experiences that he could not hide them from me. I sat still and thought about the extraordinary stories I had just heard. I experienced the war myself, in Indonesia and shortly drifted back to those moments. I had processed all of that, together with others who had had similar experiences and wished to do the same. It was okay and I understood. Understanding your own processes gives you inner peace and tranquillity.

Hans returned with two large glasses of rosy fluid. I truly do not know where he got those so quickly; I did not see him get them. His creation was delicious, slightly sweet and reminded me of lychees. We sat together quietly and let the previous moments sink in. He looked at me and his broad smile lit up his serious face. It had a contagious effect. He could read my thoughts; I did not manage very well trying to hide them in those days. I had dreaded this meeting. We kept silent for a while. Then Hans resumed his story.

Hans: 'I incarnated again, this time in Yugoslavia. From early childhood, I was aware of the intense feelings of racism in my new country of birth. My parents and grandparents had clear-cut ideas about the different ethnic groups that populated Yugoslavia. I chose to become a nurse and worked in psychiatry. My incarnation took place quite soon after the Second World War, in the early fifties. Masses of people with my background incarnated quite quickly. I belonged to the generation of baby boomer born directly after the war.

I worked in psychiatry for more than twenty years. Hard work under difficult conditions. I put my whole heart into it. I thought I had become a patient and loving nurse. I felt responsible for the people in my care. Many of them had been my victims in my previous life in Germany. That usually happens unconsciously, when you live and work in the here and now.

I died not long ago during the hell of that terrible war in former Yugoslavia.

My country went to war and as a Croatian, I ended up in a Serbian camp. A long year of heavy and intense suffering followed going through starvation and thirst. I was tortured several times, leaving me more dead than alive only to recover slightly to having to go through the same thing again, but worse than the previous time. I was aware of officers being present at my interrogation. They showed no emotion at all I noticed. They were just standing there, while I cried out in pain. Eventually I died at the edge of a mass grave. I saw the officers who gave the orders to shoot us and I had a moment of déjà vu of me standing there in another life, also emotionless.

I died instantly and my grandfather picked me up, it became sort of a habit. A good one though, because I was so happy to see him. I went to a healing chamber in a light sphere. I had evolved so much that my spiritual attunement transferred me directly to a light sphere this time. That is a law you cannot change. You are simply pulled towards it. I had already travelled a long way through the different spheres before.

I have become an assistant in the healing chambers for the people badly damaged by persecution and war. First only people from Yugoslavia and now also from other countries. It does not matter where you come from and from which race. I am an expert by experience and I am mainly concerned with the severely damaged among them. I am also very conscious of the great clean up that is going on worldwide; the karmic healing that is taking place everywhere on Earth. I am committed with all my being to the great change on Earth and everything living there. With my whole soul being, I'm committed to the healing of people. All people in the spheres of light are very aware that big changes are taking place. The birth process of the Earth to a higher level of energy and vibration. From the third to the fifth dimension. Everyone is contributing consciously to the making of the Earth into a light world.

Our negative experiences in particular and the fact that we are familiar with every fibre of our being with the evil and the complete lack of love on Earth makes us extra cognisant and determined to put in every effort. There is an atmosphere of hope and expectation in this work. Humankind is working out so much residual karma. Many adopt the karmic remains of loved ones and relatives, of connected souls, to work out. An act of love to the soul group, the monad and itself. Whole groups and countries accelerate this endeavour. In the new age, there will not be any more karma. The people who cannot or do not want to flow over to that higher dimension will incarnate to another third dimension, planet. For those who still crave power and the abuse thereof. They can do so there. There are galactic convalescent homes for some souls. No soul is ever lost. All souls will return one day to the Source of light and love.

We are noticing the strong effects of the forming of the so-called morphogenetic fields described so beautifully by the English scientist Rupert Sheldrake. Twenty years ago, relatively few people believed in reincarnation, but we notice that an increasing amount of people is accepting it. In today's day and age, more people than ever before are willing to consider this as a real possibility. This is true for many things relating to our transforming consciousness. Unfortunately, this also applies to negative group beliefs.'

Margaret: I pondered over my last life as Margaret, and my commiserations on the events in former Yugoslavia. Ohan, my spiritual guide, appeared and the three of us went to a part of a sphere where only souls from these countries end up. Ohan explained that when they exit the healing chamber it could be confrontational for many, because all groups come together. All the different nations and factions related to the old Yugoslavia. Ohan showed me around and told me about the different people and their backgrounds. He showed me the special rooms created for groups to work in, processing past lives under optimal conditions. There are beautiful healing chambers for the purging of old karma.

Lord Kumeka, whose name will be returning often in this book, employed large groups of helpers for this. Without exception, all masters from the various hierarchies. The help from the light realms for the total purification of all negative vibrations on Earth is tackled at a very large scale in this end time; during the end of a cycle. The people of the former Republic of Yugoslavia have worked out a massive amount of popular, group- and personal karma together.

That karma was very old and most definitively not built up in only a few lives. There were connections that originated from the destroyed Maldek world.

Many cosmic populations came to Earth of course as part of the greater plan to get populations to live together on a planet. In the cosmos, all eyes are on what is happening here. Many souls chose to work out very old negative energy together in a relatively short period. These people feel highly supported by the entities of the angelic realms that are committed to helping to transform the old. They realize that they have to do it themselves, but all the help and spiritual support make it a lot easier for them to work on that.

Many people went through huge growing spurts because of their lives in Yugoslavia. Many lived several lives in a single lifetime. By sharing their experiences what they once did to others and to each other, they paved the way to the light. Regrettably, this is the way it has to go. Fortunately, for some souls this was never necessary.

Despite the fact I was told and shown, it remains a mystery to me, and I continue to find it inexplicable that people go to war with each other time and time again, fighting over a piece of land. It is incomprehensible to me that so much blood continues to flow. Ohan said that there are places in the cosmos where people have been fighting for eons, where wars are part of existence. Now that things are shifting in the entire cosmos, with the accompanying higher consciousness souls are looking for ways to find peace in themselves and with each other.

Ohan: 'Be careful pointing a finger at people who, in countries such as Yugoslavia, are working out old processes. You do not know what processes you yourself had to go through. People that react vehemently when witnessing violence or any form of loveless behaviour might do so because they need to overcome unprocessed parts of their own life, often with great difficulty. Never judge another being even if their book of life were open in front of you. Every soul meets with negative and positive experiences on the path of its soul. You have no inkling as to why that soul made certain choices. Hans is such an example. He chose to live in a place where he served a lifetime in a difficult profession such as psychiatry. Generalizing is very dangerous. People who choose such a profession do so for many different reasons. Servitude and compassion towards a suffering human being can be one of them. Not necessarily does there have to be a troubled history in a previous life. As long as there are those, who keep on judge others harshly, without love, it is good that lives remain closed. It is the here and the now that matters. People, who grow in consciousness and look for the truths behind the veil, are also less likely to judge.

I am shocked by the euphoria that surrounds newly awakened people. They often think that by following the light, the light in the here and now, they have become saints. They are unaware that in so doing, they are sharply condemning everyone who thinks and acts differently. There are phases in the awaking process and only by travelling one's own path towards healing and awareness, can one understand earlier mistakes. Do not judge yourself either, but be aware of your ignorance at the time. Do not get stuck in those old feelings, but look ahead. Realize that every step we take as an individual also adds more light to the whole. Guilt halts your growing process.'

Hans: 'It is inconceivable how people are fighting each other, century after century, each for their own truth. As you continue to grow in your light, you see how insidious the madness is of some traditions, feeding the rigid attitude of one people towards another. It means the holding on and the maintaining of hatred, of decimated and crumbled principles, dreading change. I have studied anthropology and you learn how hate can fester and passed on over the centuries, from generations to generation. The rationale behind it always seems to be self-importance and power. Take a beautiful, large country like Yugoslavia, where people can easily live next to one another in peace. Peaceful periods were also known there, only to be drawn back again into the all-consuming hatred of nations against each other all over again.'

Margaret: Hans went on to talk about the arrogance of the Serbs he had experienced and gave examples of this.

Hans: 'It becomes almost inconceivable, that we all come from the same source of light. During my life in German, I too was brought up with that arrogance, pre-conditioned to believe we were superior and destined to create a higher and better race. My attitude towards other people was gradually poisoned, drop-by-drop. They became like a stream and affected all those children who received the same upbringing as I did at the time. It finally became a torrent of hatred that would lead to a terrible war. No respect for the uniqueness of the other and intolerance towards integration. People that are part of such a society are often unable to transform old vibrations and were attuned to hate even before they incarnated. I visited many of them in that sphere of hatred. It is a horrible place where all souls are attuned to hatred also there with the different grades.

We do this work with many people, and we all deliberately chose to do this work. Some of us have gone through hate ourselves in previous lives and have completely transformed it. If you, as a soul, ever found yourself in that state of hatred, it leaves its marks. Your soul being will never forget that again. In spite of that, there are still souls that keep on walking into the traps they have set for themselves and need long to recognise these and manage to avoid them.

We try to reach out to as many people as possible, but a descent in that dark sphere, even being there for a short time, requires a lot of patience and training. Whole groups regularly attack us, sometimes at once. People of the light will continue to visit the darkened souls relentlessly, hoping to achieve something. However, one has to ask for help oneself and that has everything to do with the sacred free will of man on this planet Earth.

One call for help suffices to get them out, all that is needed is just one glimmer of light consciousness. Then the way home ensues and that way, little by little more light can penetrate their consciousness. One by one, old grey veils are discarded, like peeling an onion. The buried soul-spark will start to recognize things from when it was still completely in the light and the way home will become visible. The encapsulated and often tough soul can change because of the admission of light. It may look like a hard lesson to learn, but only when a human goes through his own negative actions will he be capable to avoid repetition.

Conceit and feelings of hate are the source of much evil on this Earth. It is often the underlying reason for man's other negative expressions. These are therefore the most difficult to clean up. It all depends how deeply hate and pride is embedded in a person during his different lives. There are many degrees. The deeper the hate and egotism the heavier the effect and the longer it will last. That is why a soul can sometimes consciously choose for an accelerated karma process, effecting a quicker transformation of fixed vibrations into the light. I know this from experience because, with the help of the Council of Karma, I consciously chose for such an approach myself.

First, the Council of Karma always looks for the gentle way to let a soul learn its lessons, which may take many lives. Every soul chooses its own, unique way to dissolve its karma but because man, by nature, is disinclined to invest a lot of effort into this process, a lot remains unfinished. One manoeuvres skilfully around the difficulties and challenges of life. Some even choose suicide to escape the challenges of life, but that does not solve anything. You will then return to a new body, to learn the same lessons for the soul.

With the 'great change' happening, souls choose this accelerated path. My Higher Self wanted that, I realised. I am experiencing how beneficial it is to work out that deep-rooted lovelessness, and will never again say I do not 'know' what I am doing. Anyone who dares to look at his or her own negative experiences in life with an open heart may see what kind of lessons need to be learned. These lessons only become evident at a much later stage and they cannot always be made out with the left side of the brain. You can get there however with introspection and the right hemisphere of the brain. Somewhere in your deepest source, you can always find the answer.

There are people who ask for insight, before going to sleep and put their question in the 'lap of the gods', as they say. The world of light will always honour such a demand. Working with dreams takes some practice, but a growing number of people find their answer this way. They wake up with a clear 'knowing'. Others find their answer in prayer or meditation. It does not matter how you find your answer but the most beautiful thing is to source it from your strength, independent of a human intermediary. One is inspired to do it oneself, to stand in one's own power and from there get the answers to life's questions. In this way, the field of life stays clean and no energy and interpretation of someone else is interfering. Those days are behind us. Trust it! Any human being can learn this. Every human being carries this power within himself, we have just lost that connection in the course of time but we are back on track to learn how to connect, it belongs to everyone.

Margaret: Hans arranged for me to meet Achmed, the man who was his friend and teacher. I promised to come. Right now, I needed a light bath. There are places, connected to the healing rooms, where you can 'park' intense experiences. You just stroll in and by using certain methods you can choose the frequency and colour that suits you. I went there with Hans.

You can choose to lie down or stand up. I preferred to lie down. Hans had gone. Beautiful colours and designs dominate this place. Everything looks like glass, in natural colours and appears to be open, which it is not. These spaces offer all the privacy you need and I enjoy the respect and the way of interaction. How wonderful after so much earthly misery. I look forward to meeting Achmed.

Actions

I own my karma,
Heir of my actions,

Born from my actions,
Related to my actions
And have my actions as a referee.

What I do, right or wrong,
Of that I'll be the heir.

Buddha

8. Achmed

War for the 'right' religion

Margaret: Hans brought me to Achmed. The place where we meet is in the first light sphere. Here are churches and mosques, villages and towns, there is light. Here man has transcended his veil henceforth starting the conscious way up to the light. Here people want to look at what they left behind and slowly release the opinion of that past. They want to balance out the negative actions they took on Earth. There is still a very clear memory of pain and sorrow, of the suffering because of the fight for the right religion. Here we still need the familiar shape that is associated with a religion. The outer shape of churches and mosques are required here. Many lives were lived within this framework.

Whoever lives here has released hatred from his consciousness. The sphere of hate is four levels below. There is however not the inner freedom of consciousness yet that God is omnipotent, that He is in all of us, as a God-spark. Here is often still the belief that God is a man on a throne. Many here are disappointed when they find out that their conviction that God is light and that you cannot see or touch Him proves to be wrong. It has everything to do with consciousness. The greater the consciousness, the more light one can carry. The higher one gets into the spheres, the less need there is for outer shapes.

In the spheres above the level from where we are now, there are open temples, where people, according to their needs, can 'be' in their own experience of God. There are always beautiful flowers on the square stone of rock crystal or pink quartz. The temples themselves are made of alabaster, marble or crystal, depending on the frequency of the sphere often surrounded by semi-circular marble benches. An ambience of supreme simplicity and beauty. Sometimes people just sit there, alone or together. I do so myself on a regular basis. I enjoy the beautiful garden and the serenity of that place. When I discover a place like this, I always take a moment to meditate, to connect with All-That-Is. People sitting around silently feels good. Nobody tells you what to do or believe.

In the churches on Earth, people are not free, often confined to a particular form of religion and any deviation severely condemned. The great Master Jesus taught us 'thou shalt not judge'. In many earthly churches, those in power decide for their parishioners the number of children they should bear, whilst they are scarcely able to feed them all. People often live in poverty.

Plenty of mothers cannot to take care of their children the way they would like. Multiple pregnancies and giving birth take its toll on the body. The ban on contraceptives seems an inconceivable rule from here.

In Western countries, change has been a long time coming. Women no longer tolerate being dictated what they can and cannot do. Only a minority in very orthodox circles are still being told what to do. The situation in the so-called Third World countries however is disturbing. It is much worse there than it ever was in Western countries. It is no less than criminal that that the Church bans the use of condoms in countries where so many people die of a terrible disease such as Aids. Ohan told me that many people end up extremely perverted by the rules imposed by their religions.

Here, in this place, people are starting to change their mentality in this area. Those who wish to do so can take part in small gatherings that are in harmony with their own experiences on earth and their desire to change those. Most people are looking for this exchange, especially because they will not be judged here. They look at previous incarnations and what can be learned from it. 'See what is without judging', Ohan always says. There is always loving guidance at hand and I have experienced this as very pleasant. It prevents you from getting lost and from being stuck in the pain, or in big or small feelings of guilt. They are not 'know-all's' who guide you, but light people, who have gone through all the levels during many incarnations. Hands on experts.

Nowadays, more and more beings we call angels are involved in heavy processes. They lead and guide, and do so with the love they are. Together with the experts pain and sadness, inflicted mutually over many lives is dealt with. It is the souls of equal attunement and background that seek each other out. They could have been of the same monad and have come to oppose each other during the course of history. Entire groups of souls are now healing their negative past together at a rapid pace. The new transitional laws make provisions for this. I often see angelic creatures, small and slender, figures of about one metre fifty or sixty, running through life like a cheerful thread of love.

They come from a certain system, never incarnated on Earth and never were human themselves, but they were often there to guide and serve humankind. There are now angels who do incarnate on Earth as New Age children with very specific love tasks. They are of a different origin than the angels I see so often working here. Men see the little angelic creatures as a blessing. In the beginning, people would take on an aloof attitude and one of adoration but once these love beings teach people that they are a part of God and serve the ALL, just like man, they are accepted as helpers on the path to wholeness.

What I find a blessing is that they are so cheerful. On Earth, it is generally considered as very serious. I have seen these angels accompany a group of passed souls from Yugoslavia. The mood was heavy and a lot of shared sadness and mental pain bubbled up. They were enemies when they were still living on Earth. Confrontation with old adversaries is often hard to deal with in the beginning yet it happens all the time. I had been a silent witness a number of times, together with Ohan, here, in the first light sphere. Women meeting their rapists. Executioners meeting their victims. These encounters take place in every conceivable form. Usually not as an individual versus an individual, which is too much and too heavy, but in a small group in a place where one feels safe. The small angelic creatures generate a great flow of love and help people to face this challenging confrontation.

I happened to observe such a confrontation, which was so charged that everybody present was at a loss what to do. One of the angels asked them to tell a positive story and slowly, one by one, they all did. One woman said that she was starving and that food parcels were distributed in their village in the mountains. As a Muslim, she never ate pork. The packages of the various aid organisations included sausages and meatballs. The rescuers had not thought of that. She and her children were so hungry that the cans were opened and the contents eaten with much gusto. She could not read the labels, she told me. Later someone told them it had been pork. Almost the entire village had enjoyed the contents. They all had a good laugh about it. In spite of the tremendous suffering and sorrow, there was laughter she said.

They do not show you that on the news. Two women chuckled, amused by the stories. They were sisters in their last life and had fled from Kosovo. One of them said they needed sanitary towels and got them from one of the relief organization. When they saw the sanitary towels had 'wings', they got the giggles, in spite of their misery. They got different ones every time and each time they giggled together when they shared this story with the other women. I saw the energy of the angelic beings flowing in the direction of to these people and how they joined in the laughter. It relaxed the atmosphere and later Ohan told me that a group connected in pain and suffering, finds great relief in ordinary humour and will be able to move on with the purging process and work things out together. He showed me that this group had been connected for a long time, thousands of years, through many lives.

We walk to Achmed's group, which sits in a circle on a beautiful green softly sloping lawn. All things here are still interwoven with life on Earth. I have seen the houses that, in contrast to the sixth atmosphere of my own coordination, were close together. Villages and towns with streets and squares. Houses, attached and detached, spaced intermittently. In other spheres above, you can see the need for individuality and privacy. This individuality is reflected in the shapes and materials of the houses. What strikes me in the first sphere are the white stone houses with red tiled roofs, overgrown with roses or other climbers. Lovely to look at. On Earth, these people longed for such a place for themselves. I see an avenue with many trees and very wide gardens, with exclusively white houses with red tiled roofs. A little village, small-scale, very cosy. People who were no longer at ease in the big city, and always longed for a nice spot for themselves, will find a beautiful place here.

There are city-like shapes with large churches and buildings. There you can find all you need: a music house, study houses, a Hall of Wisdom, the library, and everything else you might want, just like on Earth. In the sphere of my own attunement, those buildings stand far apart, with each its own spot in its own natural environment. The desires change as souls advance in the spheres. I love being here in this place where I visited dear friends on a regular basis, one of them living in one of those cosy white houses, surrounded by a garden full of flowers.

At this meeting, twelve women were sitting together. Four women wore flowery garments and their hair was covered. They were Muslims from the former Yugoslavia. Four women in airy, cheerful summer clothes, also Muslims. One of them was wearing white jeans with a red shirt, another wearing a fashionable clingy cheerful summer dress. Two more were wearing jeans with a large sweater and there were four women with a Christian background.

Ohan informed me about these things and said that it was a special study group of Muslims and Christians. They had all concluded during their last physical life that waging war for your faith and persecuting others because they happen to have a different perception of God makes no sense. Insight gained in times of great suffering and need. All had been killed in religious battles and saw the absurdity of mutual harassment and massacres. Here they had found each other in a working group. They tried to approach others in order to exchange information. In turn, all these women moved on to become teachers for other people. They help each other with the processing of the chaotic past years. I spoke to several of them and each had their own story about the horrors of the war. I had followed this war with so much horror, like many with me. It was so very recent.

The man who led this group had had centuries of different incarnations in Yugoslavia. He came up to me and we exchanged greetings. A small man with big brown eyes and a very open face. He had unmistakable Turkish features. He invited me to sit.

He was going to tell his story in front of the twelve women.

Achmed: 'Centuries ago I belonged to the conquerors from Turkey. I was an ordinary soldier serving my country. I wanted to do my bit to establish the holy Ottoman Empire in the world. I did everything for my people and my country. Conquering countries and oppressing other peoples was part of life.

I have lived a whole series of arduous lives. Killing, plundering and raping, we went along with the big army. I was famous for my specialty: decapitating people with one big stroke of the sword. It was regarded an honour to be so famous. I obtained high status in many of those soldier's lives by virtue of my skills in battle. I had no doubt that what I did was good, serving my country with heart and soul.'

Margaret: His nice face breaks into a sombre smile and he continues:

Achmed: 'A lot of people lived this way, convinced that they were fighting for a good cause and doing the right thing. It is all about consciousness in all its levels and layers. I never did it for the money. I loved women and I took what I liked in that respect as well. That, too, was quite common in those days. I never thought about the pain and misery I caused. I was insensible. I lived like a member of a clan; following blindly I did what was expected of me. In contrast with other population groups though, I never tortured people,

My consciousness changed when I had to undergo what I did unto others. I incarnated a number of times as a woman and was captured and taken as a war trophy to be raped and killed. In one of these lives, I experienced the consequences of such a rape.

When I had to give birth, the attitude of the small community to which I belonged changed. That child looked like the soldiers who had ravaged our village. Instead of compassion from my neighbours, I was expelled. My parents gave me some money and food and told me to leave with child.

I wandered through mountainous land and everywhere I went I was treated the same way as in my hometown. Repeatedly you face the fact that everything revolves around consciousness and growth. It has given me a lot of insight into cause and effect.

In the 1920s, I ended up in a war with the Turks as an Englishman. I grew up in a strictly Christian family but I saw the folly of fighting for Islam or Christianity for that matter; all leaves from the same branch. As a 40-year-old officer in the English army, sitting on my horse, I was decapitated with a sharp blow.

I know that the vicious circle of hatred and violence has to stop somewhere. After I lost my 'head' as an Englishman, I stayed on this side. In due course, I slowly ascended to the fifth and sixth sphere. Since then I travel to other spheres to teach people and have been doing so since before the WW2, seen in earth time.

Counting in Earth time, I have been in the spheres for over eighty years now. Time does not exist here, but in such a period, a lot can happen to a soul, a lot. I had the choice to stay and I never regretted not incarnating again. My heart found peace here when I saw my opportunities to contribute positively to life on Earth.

I had many lives in other cultures, places where I was able to redeem my earthly karma in between the lives of the Turkish conqueror and that of the Englishman. I did that in small doses. One of them was a life with a tribe in Africa with a specific upbringing. Not a life of suffering, but a hard life all right, which taught me very different values. I became a 'better me' with new standards and values.

I also incarnated with the Aborigines in a period before the whites came ashore and stole the land. They offered many souls a warm heart as well as a thorough training in the 'we'-consciousness. I learned how to take care of a whole group and later on, I took on the responsibilities when my father and grandfather departed that life and had left for the spheres. During that incarnation, my vision of death changed drastically. I am grateful for those wise old souls; they helped me to reform my soul being, not with violence, as so often happens, but with love, wisdom and insight.

Life immediately before my life as an Englishman took place in India. Long ago, I had travelled through that country as a conqueror and a soldier. With my present views on things not a life to be proud of, but I had the chance to balance things and I did. That is what is called the soft road. I incarnated as a woman in a wealthy family. I married a rich man and he incarnated with the clear intention in his blueprint to balance negative vibrations. I cared about the fate of the poor and oppressed, and recognised their misery from my own soul experiences. My husband too. I derived a lot of positive inspiration from above to tackle things. Thank God, I noticed them and acted accordingly.

At the end of that Hindu life, I set up a hospital with highly qualified doctors who practiced Vedic medicine. Specific care was provided for women and children. Young doctors and nurses were trained. We had a particularly difficult time with the English, often very arrogant and proud individuals, who treated my people as slaves. They became rich at the expense of the poor.

Yet we stood firm and our hospital was an example to others who were inspired by our work. To live in oppression under the English in India was a hard lesson for the soul. We invited people with similar ideas to ours to look, showed them around, taught them the methods, and encouraged them to create something like this of their own. We tapped into funds to give them the opportunity to build a small hospital in their own area. There were schools and all kinds of social initiatives. Our example had a ripple effect.

Small actions can bring about big re-actions. It started out as a small undertaking, as it usually does and I was able to see later in the spheres that what we began, worked through in others and how it continued to spread. I could look back on a fulfilling life, instinctively so especially and completely in accordance with my life blueprint. It was good what we achieved, and it was nice that others continued our work.

As a teacher, I often meet people in whom I recognize many of my old soul parts. My study of anthropology, I am mainly an expert by experience. 'I know how the cookie crumbles' a prerequisite for a job as a teacher like mine.'

Margaret: I asked Achmed why he had chosen an Oriental name, whereas in his last life on Earth he was an Englishman.

Achmed: 'I feel more Eastern than Western. I had many lives in Islamic countries. The connection with that intense English life was necessary to be able to do this work, because it brought me great insights. My youth, upbringing, education, connection with a group, in this case also a military career, was all-important to me. I experienced everything in an intense way. I had very devout parents and grandparents in England. The small church community to which they belonged offered a lot of warmth and love. They took care of each other, in that small village in the countryside, and I learned a lot from that. The compassion from one person to another was very sincere there, without any hypocrisy.

At some stage on this side, I took the name that belonged to that English life, Henry. I took on Achmed and an Oriental look from a previous incarnation, because that was more appropriate for me. Connected souls recognize me in this form. It makes me feel good and it suits me. I discovered later that this was an important choice, because the Muslim community is far more difficult to penetrate than the Christian community is. There is a little more allowance to experience spiritual freedom. It is also easier to challenge and, if necessary, abandon old dogmas there.

Many Christians resort to truths in old gnostic writings, providing them with more space for their experiences. The past few years show just that. It worries me to see fundamentalism emerging within the large Muslim community throughout the world. The consequences of this greatly concern us here. The terrible massacres, which took place in Algeria, among other places, are a disturbing development. It is a result of the increasing clouding, caused by the direct influence of the shadow side, the opposing forces. Many flee from these horrors because it is not consistent with their inner feeling of the Source of Love and Light.

I do not deal with fundamentalists; that requires top specialists. I do keep in touch with them, which is necessary to keep a helicopter view. There is an intensive exchange going on in the light spheres concerning all of this. Here we all serve the same objective. I am only dealing with the territory of the former Yugoslavia right now. We have our hands full with that. There is more momentum and progress in the whole process with the Yugoslav people than with those in Morocco or Algeria for example, where developments are slow and awkward. So much is stuck there and immobile. The karmic backgrounds are also totally different. Yugoslavia - with its different ethnic groups - has amassed a lot of karma over the years. In those regions of Mother Earth, there was a lot of fighting for power, and caused deep hatred between groups.

In Algeria and Morocco, there is a very different, but also severe, type of karma. In that vast mass of sand a beautiful, golden city was once situated stretching for miles. Stories still relay those days. The buildings had golden roofs and everywhere were wide streets, avenues and squares surrounded by the most beautiful architecture of all of Atlantis. The golden city was a meeting place of various cultures and arts. There were huge conference rooms and everywhere there was the sublime beauty of the architecture, not only in the appearance of the buildings but also in the interior decoration. Artists from all over the Atlantic brought the best and most beautiful things they had to offer. A society much more advanced in all areas than the present one. They mastered the technology for clean and inexhaustible energy. Imagery and communication techniques far beyond the fantasy of people living on Earth today. I have lived there and I remember all of this in my present state of being. The land was fertile and beautiful, slightly sloping with mountains on the verge. Remnants of it can still be found. If that huge amount of sand covering it were to disappear, irrigation canals, sewers and old buildings would be uncovered. It would lead to nothing in the here and now.

There, in that golden city of art and culture, incarnated Ahriman, a creature from the high Luciferian forces and powers. Outwardly beautiful and dazzling, made him attractive to many. During that third period and final days of Atlantis, he took the opportunity to establish forces of darkness in the openings people had left in their pursuit of power, with their greed and pride, jealousy and envy, people who were susceptible for it.

The brilliance and the promises deceived people. As a gifted flutist I too, succumbed as Ahriman was like the Pied Piper of Hamelin, and I followed him with sparkling eyes. I fell into the trap, bleary eyed and for a while, I enjoyed the power I sought and found. It was a very educational and meaningful experience for my souls being. A deep darkness took root in that beautiful place.

In the middle of that area is a crystal skull, a very special one. This one will not be found like the other skulls. With light and consciousness, he serves as a counterpart for the waves of darkness that over time constantly flooded these areas. Power and domination, control of the energies of the people who live there.

I closely follow the events in those areas, because somewhere in a distant past I became connected to them. The consequences left deep traces in my soul being. I was cut off from the light and the light consciousness for a long time. The way back to my core of light was long and difficult. I learned a lot on that long, arduous journey through my lives. From the sixth light sphere, I no longer need to incarnate and am completely free to choose what I want to do to express the love of God.

Already on Earth you, dear Margaret, chose to work with Thea in the spheres. You made jokes about it and did not take it too seriously but the intention was there. The basis of this desire was in your life blueprint, as both of you have sensed. From the sixth sphere, you, Margaret, also are completely free to express God in your own way. You tap into your soul past as a spiritual counsellor, as a spiritual teacher in Atlantis and in the temple and mystery schools of Egypt. You passed on books to others. Tasks you both had on the Pleiades connected you and you both did the same work many times. All the ingredients were there to make your education go quick this time. I use my old gifts and talents to connect. To make people reflect on what is happening on Earth within the mutual, often old, disputes, wars and hatred between different groups of believers.'

Margaret: Achmed stretched his body and strolled around in the big garden house. It is an elegant structure of wrought iron, curved upwards like the shape of an onion ending in a large graceful rose of gold. Everything here is of such great beauty. I left the group with Ohan and Hans, impressed with Achmed's total commitment.

Hans: 'One feels deep respect for his love and commitment to change the things that 'are', without him judging. He has been working a long time with small groups of people who want change. Achmed's influence, and indeed of all those other experts has proven indispensable. Anyone who incarnates again takes those lessons with them into their new life plus the desire for change and bring an end to the spiralling violence. Visits to Summerland also offer new lessons to bring to Earth to put them into practice. Collected inspiration in Summerland is used in one's often-difficult everyday life.

Inspiration could mean the placing of flowers in places where violent crimes were committed. Sometimes there are thousands of flowers in one place.

The media pick it up and that way draw the public's attention to it when they see it on TV and its energy touches them and they start thinking about this kind of thing. This may seem like a trivial example, but it really boosts the awakening of those whose consciousness was still dormant. That kind of thing works in many ways. People who lay flowers usually do that wholeheartedly and that expression exacerbates the energy flow.'

Margaret: I am going to my house, get some spiritual rest, and just do nothing for a while; absolute bliss. Silence, nature, in my own place. After that, we go to Summerland, the place where people living on Earth can go at night.

9. Eagle

Power over life and death

Margaret: Achmed took me to a specific place in Summerland, where there is very busy traffic between human beings living on Earth and the etheric human beings on this side. The power of thought took us to the fourth sphere and there was Summerland at my feet. We strolled through the huge garden, although it was more like the size of a park. There were large trees in a gently sloping landscape. We arrived at a low gate, which Achmed opened for me with a courteous swing.

Achmed: 'Fences are not really required here, but sometimes people like it if some areas are fenced in, such as this beautiful rose garden. It gives a sense of seclusion. I love this garden wholeheartedly. These gardens have a healing effect on those who tend them and hold old negative vibrations. It's a garden with a high, healing vibration. The people who care for these gardens often heal from old negative vibrations, just being among the roses.'

Margaret: Everywhere I looked, I saw roses. It reminded me somewhat of a southern French garden with overgrown, low stonewalls, romantic benches between the flowerbeds and small groups of chairs under the trees. Between the beautiful rose beds, I saw blue lavender. It is impossible to put into words what the scents and colours are like here. Fragrances here are so different from those on Earth, much more intense. They are touching my whole being. As if they have more dimensions. I saw a bed of huge white roses, bigger than peonies on Earth. Each leaf had a very thin, pink edge. I found the colours, the smells, and the energy breath taking. I had never seen so many different roses before.

Achmed let me go ahead and ambled between the flowerbeds comfortably. I saw him walking towards someone with short grey hair and a beard looking forty-ish. I walked up to them. With his arms wide open, he welcomed me. Achmed introduced me to Eagle. His last life was in the Netherlands. He showed me around the rose garden and I had the one surprise after the other. There were climbing roses, hollyhocks, and huge peonies, bigger than I had ever seen. I quietly took in all this beauty. It was vibrating through my whole being and I realised what this garden could do for people. We walked to a gazebo that had wide wicker armchairs and looking very English, ornately built with arches and coils.

Achmed: 'This is one of the places where I receive people from Earth and teach them, if their soul being so desires. Their spiritual guides bring them to us. Many people who come here during the day feel the influence and inspiration of the lessons and exchanges that take place here. They try to harmonise with other people, with other opinions, e.g. about faith. I have often been their teacher and facilitator in this process before their present incarnation. This contact is maintained by the nightly visits to Summerland. Together we work on necessary change. Changing old, blocked processes is hard and difficult work. People have to initiate those changes on earth, out of their own free will. We merely inspire from the spiritual world.'

Margaret: This is where four rabbi's and five imams meet on a regular basis. It is moving to see how these people try to unite find solutions to problems on Earth in their country. This group had previously been together in between two lives. They learned a lot from each other and chose to stay in touch in this manner. It is remarkable that none of these men, in their physical existence on Earth, want anything to do with 'passed on' material. Only what is written in the very old books is the truth to them. They strongly reject any new passed on material in the here and now.   Once in Summerland, outside their physical body, this is not an issue any longer.
Eagle often joins in when the groups meet. They discuss life issues that are of mutual interest. They welcome him; such an exchange is quite common here. I love coming to this rose garden, and at times only visit Eagle just so that I can be amongst these beautiful roses. I like meditating under the trees, further on by the walls with the climbing roses. They remind me of our garden in England, but also of a life in Syria some time ago, but time is irrelevant here. These are experiences of a part of your being that fuse here as you rise higher in your light.
Eagle made himself comfortable to listen to the story he asked Achmed to tell. Right from the start when I went to visit people in the different sphere things looked prepared, like a piece of the puzzle falling into place. The completeness of it all never ceased to move me. On Earth, I had the growing

experience how in the flow of life things fell into place in an orderly manner. To discover the sensation that you are in a maelstrom to your destination is a great gift. Many more begin to recognise the signals they are offered on their life path. They make use of those signals to find out what their soul being and life blueprint have in store for them and see the wholeness of things, even the less pleasant ones that come their way. It resonates in your heart when the significance of it is discovered, often much later. Here I experience this very strongly in the light spheres. I love the general awakening and the growing consciousness at a fast pace. The development to sense the offered and make use of them.

Eagle looked at me with a smile. After all, thoughts are shared here, provided you want to share them. He said he liked listening to other people and their stories. For him, the rose gardens in Summerland made him ecstatically happy after years of being indoors.

Eagle: 'I was mentally and physically handicapped in my last life. As I got older, I became impossible to handle and placed in a home. I was wild, smashed things, I raved and ranted. I kicked and hit my mother when she tried to touch me. She was longing to hold me in her arms as I realise that now, but I loathed being touched.

I realise that she was all love for me and had consciously chosen this life before her incarnation. My years as a mentally handicapped boy were anticipated in my mother's life. She was born a few years after the war. There was very little time between her life before that and the next. In her previous incarnation, she had died in a concentration camp during the Second World War. As a young woman, she had gone through a lot of suffering during that period. Her karma made her experience what it was like to be completely at the mercy of other people. To be powerless in life.

At the soul level, she had chosen for this experience in order to really be able to work out old negative vibrations and to balance her energy. She had the choice of a fast, violent road, or a slow, more gradual road that could last a lifetime. She deliberately chose for the first option, to go through it all in a relatively short time, because she saw that the tough way was the right one for her.

It may sound strange that a soul being would make such a choice, but in the spiritual world you can see all your soul parts and assess your own lessons very well. She estimated that she could learn the lessons her soul needed in a relatively short life. You do not forget what you did to others in your unconsciousness or callousness once you underwent the same thing. Not many make the same mistake after that. Those mistakes are then lived and lived through.

In a whole series of previous incarnations, she was a very arrogant creature looking for 'power'. The power she possessed was severely abused by her. In both male and female incarnations, this being had no empathy for those in his or her power. Many fell victim to that. In a male incarnation, this soul was a slave trader and brought shiploads of people from Africa to America. In those days, compassion did not exist. It was a lucrative business.

Many of his victims perished, like rats. This man, this soul part of her being, enjoyed the power he held over so many people, who to him, were no more than cattle he needed to transport to the plantations in the new world. In his opinion, he contributed to the development of that world. He did not consider himself bad or unloving.

He was also a religious man and attended all services on board. He prayed to God. Convinced they were acting in accordance with 'God's intentions'.

The plantation

In another incarnation, she lived as a plantation owner. A hard-working executive who, after the death of her husband, took over the management of the large company. Leadership was her great talent and during that time, she developed into an extraordinarily powerful person. She did not love nor held any respect for other people, not even for her husband and children, of whom I was one. I was her eldest son who had to succeed her. Her marriage was one of pure calculation. Marriages were often arranged in those days and women had no say in it. You could say that in her early childhood she had set eyes on the large plantation with the beautiful house and therefore on the only son in the family. She manipulated everyone, including her father, and in doing so, she naturally steered towards her goal. In her childhood, her family paid visits to the plantation and she would imagine herself as the mistress of that house. She made sure to marry the son.

A white nanny racist raised her children racist as she was and that is how we were raised as well. To the slaves on the plantation, she was loveless and cruel. Her behaviour cost many lives. She punished the slaves severely for minor offences, such as taking some food from 'her' field purely because they were hungry.

She had a satanic pleasure in dominating others and watching them suffer. She enjoyed attending a beating with a leather whip, ordered by her, carried out by her supervisor when one of the slaves was punished. She cruelly beat down uprisings. In doing so, she arbitrarily grabbed a few people from the group, who were publicly punished posing as an example, often resulting in death. She made it compulsory to watch.

Her abuse of power caused her an especially heavy karma. Complaints made by the slaves were not heard, she laughed them away. The superintendent and white slave drivers frequently made themselves guilty of sexual abuse of the slaves. They were cruel men, who not only abused the young women, but also children, both boys, and girls. She refused to do anything about these practices and openly tolerated them, which in turn led to great excesses within the slave community. She was a dictator without any human feeling. Her soul spark was veiled in darkness. Her heart chakra was cut off. There was no place for love in her heart. After her death, her spiritual attunement brought her to a deep dark sphere of the astral world.

I succeeded my mother and completely followed in her footsteps. I continued her reign of terror and when the hour of my death came, I went to the same dark astral sphere as my mother. My life was in many ways a copy of hers. I had reached an advanced age and all the time she had remained in that darkened, unconscious state. She rudely rejected all the help that was offered to her in that past period. She cursed the light beings who offered her help.

Things did not work out for me. At the end of my life, I had doubts. My sons were different to me. During my lifetime, major changes took place on the plantation. As an old man, I sat on the porch and watched my sons do things in another way. In my last few years, houses were built for the slaves. My sons removed the slaves' necklaces with which they were often kept, as well as the branding, which I had introduced entirely in line with my mother's rule.

I sat there and there was nothing I could do. A stroke felled me by and spoke with difficulty after that so my loud, dominant voice was not heard any longer. In fact, nobody listened to me anymore. We fought and I would call them names in my inability to do anything about the situation. My daughters-in-law brought in slaves as cooks, house cleaners and housekeepers. Eventually a black nanny raised my grandchildren. I was furious and blamed the whole family, but no one listened to me. They took care of me, without love and respect. I sensed that lying on my deathbed. When overcome by pain, I frequently left my body. At that time of my life, I finally learned a few things; pondering over the changes I had seen taking place. The plantation flourished and there was singing and laughter amongst the slaves.

My son fired the supervisor and some of his white men when he caught them raping one of the young slaves. He did this in front of all the slaves. My sons built a large white barn that would become a little church for the slaves, a place of congregation for them alone. Slowly but surely, the slaves grew a little more confident about the improvement in their living conditions.

After the Great Civil War, some of them came back as paid workers. While the younger men went to war, their families, women, the elderly and children, had kept the plantation running during those difficult years.

I have seen how loving the nanny was for my grandchildren, and how the cook made me tasty snacks and even fed me, when I could no longer eat myself. She had experienced me as a dictator and knew my mother's regime as a child, and yet this woman did not feel any hatred or resentment. She could also just have ignored me.

On my deathbed, she washed and cared for me or sit at my bedside and sing songs when I was in pain and could not sleep. These songs were of great beauty, the vibration of which stirred my being. They brought a vague glow of light into my consciousness and gave me something I had not known in a long time. My nurse told me about the light from the other side and did so with so much inner conviction that I started to long for it. Her songs were half-sung, half-hummed; very therapeutic because death terrified me. I know no, that in between many lives, the terrible lower astral spheres were always waiting for me. That subconscious, inner knowing struck me with terror.

When I was outside my body, on my deathbed, I could see everyone's feelings and thoughts. The slaves who took care of me did so with sincerity, without hate or resentment, doing everything they could to alleviate my suffering, to ease the pain and to prepare my road to the spiritual world. How consciously aware were these people and how different their spiritual experience from mine. I think there was no better way for me, to understand the nature of those I had prejudged on the base of their appearance, their racial characteristics, for their dark skin. Those people, whom I considered savages, turned out to have a rich spiritual life with each other and within themselves.

Their sung prayers next to my deathbed were real and genuine, while those of the minister and my children were superficial customary prayers, without a trace of sincerity. My relatives were relieved that I was dying which was hard for me to realise. I also say this because many people, sitting next to the bed of a dying person, or someone in coma discuss things that often affect the patients deepest feelings. It may also contain feelings of hatred or other negative thoughts, whilst some people are only concerned with the money and goods that the dying person leaves behind. Even though the dying person can no longer speak, truly everything is heard and felt.

Rather a simple prayer that comes from the heart, than a customary prayer that lasts for days without depth. If you are lying there, it is like a broken record. The same thoughtless prayers recited so many times by people, lacking any sincere feeling.

Dying was a difficult process, partly because my fear of death was so strong. I arrived at the same place as my mother in a low astral sphere; my spiritual attunement brought me there. My mother was inaccessible to the beings of light who repeatedly visited us and offered to help us. I had brought a gift with me that the slaves had given me on my sickbed. A glimmer of light and insight into other ways of 'being'. I soon accepted the help offered to me and ascended a little into the light.

The slaves on the plantation prayed for me for a long time, in the little church that I had cursed so deeply. They must have known the workings of the spiritual laws well. I have felt their help and seized it to get out of that darkness. The beings of light went with me to my mother and finally she could be reached and accepted the help that was offered. She was not to be envied. Together we went to work, with the beings of light. Systematically we started reading our book of life lovingly and patiently. Very carefully, we were introduced into our lives. I felt and experienced every negative action that I took on Earth with my entire being.

Between the holographic images of the last life, I saw flashes of very positive experiences in other previous lives. We saw who we were and how we had descended into the darkness of our desires. I became more and more curious about all this and carried my mother with me. Finally, I saw what the slaves had done for me during the last years of my life, and I learned to see the connections with them in previous incarnations. Lives in which we were all white, but also lives in tribal Africa where my mother and I had a tendency towards power. I saw the tribal wars we waged, the bloody struggle for power.

Very slowly, our light increased and started work as mediators in the company of the light beings and with them, we descended to the deepest dark astral spheres. We could not bring much light yet. To use a comparison, my mother and I were weak bicycle lights in comparison to our accompanying light beings who are like floodlights of a football stadium. They shield their light, or those with a lower vibration would otherwise burn. I have focused entirely on this aid work for some time, especially for people with the same background as us.

The slave trade was once very widespread and caused untold suffering to many people. The earlier slaves themselves needed less help; they generally went straight on to a light sphere. No, the karma lay with the plantation owners and other white workers, men and women who were involved in the trafficking of human beings and the seafarers who transported and abused them. I was going to focus on slavery with people of African descent. I have also met with people who had been guilty of these practices in Asian countries and worked them out with those souls.

After this period, a soft way was considered for us. That is the usual way. Soft, loving methods are a way for many souls to regain their light, but for my mother and me, this concept did not work. The Council of Karma continues to look for tailor-made solutions within the possibilities of the soft path.

We were born again in a beautiful country, in a family with very sweet parents, brothers and sisters. All conditions were there to get more light. It was very difficult for me to see that we, as brother and sister, have made life hell for the family, who were so caring and loving. We have done a lot of damage. The Council of Karma made it a little heavier for us. Too many thick layers on our divine spark made us unattainable. Increasingly difficult lessons followed in lives of oppression and lack of freedom, with loveless parents and educators, lives in which we were dominated by others, violence, hunger and deprivation. There could be short lives with only those lessons our Higher Self thought we needed to learn and become more conscious of. We needed to experience what we had done to others in many lives, in our desire for ultimate power.

My mother chose suicide in one of those lives when she was a black slave in one of the Southern states of America. Slavery had already been abolished by then, but she was drawn to a place where she was no more than a servant and had to do very hard work. There she experienced what she had done to others. She decided that a life like that was not worth living and killed me - her four-year-old child - and then herself. She refused to bear a life like that.

We had a lot to learn before our consciousness changed, going through distressing experiences the likes of which we did unto others.

The Second World War

Then we both incarnated, separate from each other, in the period before the Second World War. When I was 26 years old, I worked as an officer in a concentration camp. There have been several choices in that life, several times. I was at a crossroads in my life and had to make important choices; positive or negative. My parents enrolled me as a member of the Hitlerjugend at an early age and I flourished there. My grandparents - especially my grandfather - disapproved of this and he told me about the Nazis, their practices, and how he foresaw that this could only lead to evil and worse. During my long holidays, my grandfather told me so many positive stories about ways to change without violence.

Grandfather was an anthroposopher at heart. My father laughed at him openly and thought he was a softie. I had many doubts. We lived far from my grandparents, so they could not exert much influence, except during my school holidays. My mother literally brainwashed me, because she thought grandfather's ideas were dangerous. Her son would rise high and gain fame.

I had to go into the army, help to build a great new empire. In the Hitlerjugend I was also brainwashed. I enjoyed the sport, games, and the companionship during the summer camps, also organised specifically for women and girls. In hindsight, these kinds of organisations mainly were downright pitfalls. I became convinced that we had to cleanse our race, and I was emotionally more and more in favour of the Nazis' ideology. Now I know we were caught in a restraining, all-pervading, dark energy. With our free will, we all made these choices.

I was faced anew with such a choice when my grandfather was arrested. I had been in the army for a long time and rarely visited my grandparents. I went to see him and had a chance to talk to him in private. I was shocked at what he looked like, a shadow of the man I had known, with wounds everywhere on his body. He said he was interrogated and tortured. I heard his story but I did not believe him. These things did not happen, I was convinced of that. I had only seen politeness. I was convinced that people were treated nicely. He took off his shirt and I saw the wounds on his arms, chest and back so he could hardly sit. Burns caused by cigarettes extinguished on his back. With great determination, he tried to open my eyes to the terrible things that were happening; I did not believe him.

He did not tell me he was helping Jews to escape and had been doing so for years. Early in that period, he also helped intellectuals who were arrested go into hiding. I only discovered that much later, when I read my book of life of several lives not so long ago. He survived the war and had to go into hiding himself. It saddened him deeply his only grandson made the choices he did.

It is curious to notice how much my soul went through after the time of slavery as a plantation owner and all those lives before that. I experienced and felt so much when finally balancing that karma.

My life as a slave was hard. That was after my mother had taken our lives earlier, and followed by an almost identical life. I was persecuted because I was different and that was terrible. It was in an incarnation as a black man.

Nevertheless, I opted for a military career within the Nazi regime and fully supported it. I could also have chosen a life as a teacher, stimulated by my grandparents who were both teachers. The glitter and glamour of Nazi Germany, which was building up, won me over and I ignored the loving nudging of my grandparents. I now also know how addictive power is, and that is why it is no different from other addictions. An addiction continues to attract you and if you have a moment of weakness, it will grab you again in no time. That is how it was with me.

I did not seem to have learned anything from my karmic demise and the need for power dominated everything. Just a taste was enough for me to completely surrender. I needed to display that power and supremacy. In my work, I was very hypocritical. I never killed anyone myself, nor was I connected to the destruction machine, or so was my belief at the time. I was a man of paper - orders on paper - and my position very powerful. I enjoyed being in control of all those helpless people. It was as if I had returned to our plantation when I had control over all those many helpless slaves, just like my mother.

I experienced the sweet taste of 'power over life and death' again and was attracted like a bee to the honey by those old, not yet fully processed and now reactivated, vibrations. I remember how I enjoyed all this; my life was so much like that of the one on the plantation and the feeling of power and domination I had enjoyed so much.

My mother chose to experience racism herself and incarnated in that life as a Jewish girl. She was so much stronger than I was. In that life as a Jew, she learned all the necessary lessons and made a big leap in her consciousness. Our paths crossed in the camp. When I saw this beautiful woman, I fell in love instantly. That is what got me into a lot of emotional trouble. It was pure soul recognition, two souls who had been connected to each other for so long. I knew what fate awaited her, and that was soul destroying for me.

Only now, did I realise what was happening inside that camp and I started to see everything in a different light. This was offered to me in order to achieve a renewed consciousness. I gave orders to take her to my house, just outside the camp. She hated it and looked at me with fearful eyes all the time. I will never forget those eyes; they are as a tattoo engraved in my soul being. How beautiful she was! I fought with myself, because as a Nazi officer I was not supposed to like a Jewish woman. I forced her to sleep with me, which she had long refused. After a while, she resigned to everything I did to her but that tore me apart deep inside. Never before had I forced a girl or woman into sexual activity; my upbringing played a major role in this. I nevertheless did.

For months, she stayed in my house. She was only allowed to leave the house occasionally to get some air under the watchful eye of a guard. I considered that humane at the time. She cried a lot, I could tell by her eyes, but in my presence, she did not have the courage to do so. She hardly spoke, and there was always that silent reproachful look.

My superiors discovered the Jewish woman during a visit to my house. They were top SS officers. The same day they took her away. A few months later, she died of dysentery and exhaustion. I was torn apart when they threw her into a mass grave. From then onwards I did my work, numbed, more conscious of the madness of things happening around me with every day that followed. I wanted peace; away from the everyday misery I saw I could no longer ignore it.

After her death, I could no longer turn my face from the inhumane treatment and the suffering in that camp. Still, I stayed at my station until a few months before the end of the war. I did not come back from leave and went into hiding in the countryside, with family members who had always been against the Nazi regime. I was accommodated with their staff, got fake papers and worked on the land. I worked and lived like a robot. My family did not know that I worked in a concentration camp, but then again, they were not even aware of these camps because of their relatively isolated lives in the countryside. As the Allies approached, I was taken to my grandfather, who was now in Switzerland. I stayed with him until my death in 1952.

I did not talk about anything and my grandfather did not ask. In those years, everything surfaced and life in the camp was always on my mind as a repetitive motion picture. Life on Earth had become hell. Continually I experienced the events and I could not stop the film. I lived like a robot.

After the war, grandfather returned to his home in Germany and he took me with him. Grandmother had stayed behind in Germany with my mother during those war years. I kept quiet; I just could not talk about it. Everyone was silent, but the film in my head kept repeating itself and was unstoppable. There were so many torn families. My father was also killed in the war. They were terrible years; no fabricated punishment can beat that.

I started to doubt my own sanity even thinking I had gone mad at times. A few times, I was tempted to jump in front of a train. As it raced past, I would jump backwards and ended up along the railway line completely dazed. I did not want other people to having to clean up my remains, I fortunately realized that.   After that, I would return to everyday life. I became an introvert difficult to get in touch with. I wanted to be left alone. Living in oblivion and lying in my bed was something I did regularly those years.

I ended up dying of pneumonia, but actually from my refusal to fight for my life. The medical care was not great, but apart from that, I just let myself slip into a high fever. My will to live was gone and on top of that, there was that enormous feeling of guilt. The Jewish woman from the camp, my mother for many lives, incarnated again five years after her death in the camp, and had a great opportunity to crank up the light in her life to a higher level and she did so completely. She was born in the Netherlands in 1948.

When she was 22 years old, she gave birth to me. I was a severely handicapped little boy, mentally and physically. I could barely speak and moved around with difficulty. At the soul level, I chose to live that life myself. After me my sister was born. My mother was so sweet; with all the world's patience, she took care of me. She was there for me day and night and never complained about her fate. My father took me everywhere and never felt embarrassed. My face was twisted and I drooled. If my father hugged me, he was a bit rough, or when we punched my arm, or stroked my hair but we understood each other perfectly. It was a lot more complicated with my mother. I was aware of many things, such as life in America and other incarnations, where she never touched or cuddled me and left the upbringing entirely to others. In that life, only the result of my upbringing counted for her, and everything else was secondary.

Despite my handicaps I was aware of many things and it is vital that I can tell my story to Margaret. It is a pure misconception someone would be 'mentally' handicapped. The mind can never be handicapped, for after all, the mind consists of pure light! However, there are certain material and intellectual limitations as to what can be called 'normal'. In a way, 'my past lives were on display'. My spiritual guides and my Higher Self gave me everything I could work with at that moment.

I was lying on some kind of platform, a box with collapsible sides, for my safety. All around me were cuddly toys and foam rings so I could not hurt myself when throwing a tantrum. I was smothered with love from my parents and sister, grandparents and uncles and aunts. Love and attention are great healers and at last, I allowed it fully into my life.

I loved it when they sang or made music for me. My parents were anthroposophist and understood the subject of incarnation. They saw it as a mission for the whole family and sought and found the spiritual healing. How that works you do not see until after you have died. I was very well cared for; both my father and my mother massaged me regularly to prevent bedsores. They bought everything to make me as comfortable as possible. My entire life revolved around self-reflection looking at what was. Actually, I had already started this during my last seven years in Germany and Switzerland. My hours working with nature while I was simply reflecting about the past and later lethargic in my bed.

During that self-reflection, there were periods of repose, during which images from previous lives were given to me, lives during which I still lived entirely in the light. My inner God-spark was still without any dark encapsulation and my good deeds and thoughts came back to me. How goodness produces goodness and how it multiplied in the world. I saw how my evil deeds returned and began to multiply.

I still do not understand that I lived completely in the light and in my strength for so many incarnations, only to make such choices for the darkness afterwards. I had had power in Atlantis and I had used it positively for the benefit of the people who had been entrusted in my care. That was constructive and it multiplied. That was in the first period of that era. In the third period of Atlantis - also known as the end time - pride, jealousy and greed began to play a role. The grass suddenly looked greener on the other side and enough was no longer enough. The opposing forces need only little to gain ground. I was dissatisfied and wanted more. It all happened very gradually. You create that opening out of your own free will. We have a choice.

In Egypt a kind of yo-yo effect started. Then I chose the dark, pride, greed and the desire for power only to balance it all in the next life. I see these fluctuations along the thread of my incarnations. I have lived many incarnations in the light, and perhaps the soul needs to know both sides. I have spoken to so many people here, in the spiritual world, and I often listened to Achmed here in the rose garden with a group of people. I am always welcome. So many speak of the crimes they committed, before awareness set in. It is precisely this honest and genuine exchange that is so nourishing for me. People simply cannot pretend in this place, impossible. It is like a continuation of my handicapped life, which was so genuine and allowing me to see and feel in a way I would otherwise not have done.

Recently my mother is on this side and I visit her very regularly. She worked out her karmic issues with cancer, her choice at soul level. During the course of her illness, she changed dramatically. Together with a spiritual guide, I could visit her several times when she was in hospital on Earth. I saw how her energy field slowly changed colour. At some point, she began to notice me. Just for a moment, until she got used to my visits. She knew it was I even though I did not look like a handicapped man anymore. She lay there smiling. She told my father and sister that she saw me, and they believed her.

As her end drew near, I could stay with her for longer periods, and then I would stroke her hair or hold her hand for a moment. She became more and more aware of this and slowly awoke to the spiritual world. It is beautiful to witness that. She was increasingly looking forward to our encounters. Her fear of death had truly disappeared after a near-death experience. This was blessing in disguise for her. The passage through the tunnel to the light, the light beings she met waiting for he. That was extremely beneficial for her state of mind and she found peace. After her resuscitation, her fear of death had gone, and her spiritual growth rapidly increased.

In her last days, there was light and love between us. Just being together in that hospital room was good. I was not supposed to be present at her crossing, but I met up with her in the healing chambers for cancer patients. She was in a deep unconscious state for quite a while in a chamber with a green-blue light, drenched in gold.

Every now and then, I checked on her. She looked younger and more peaceful. On Earth, she lived until she was 50 years old. We had definitely climbed out of our self-created darkness. I was totally convinced of that. Together we had made our long and difficult way back to our light. After she woke up from her sleep, I stood there and there was great recognition.

My mother stays not far from here. She moved into her spiritual home, a light and open building, with lots of glass and flowers everywhere. After a period of illness and not being able to go outside, she too longed for an open house with a view on green hills and many flowers. Her house is filled mainly with wild flowers, which she loved so much in her last life. Lots of lavender and roses. She longed for her dog, who had passed away years earlier. Her wish was granted and I always see them together. A little yapper, one of those black-and-white dogs. She loves him. I notice many have dogs here; some even have two or three. I have not seen any cats yet.

My mother is brought to the rose garden in Summerland on a regular basis. My father and sister at times too. Meetings like that are only possible in Summerland. We discuss all sorts and feel it is good. We celebrate together that the hard work was accomplished. My father and sister then return to their physical bodies, very satisfied.

These meetings between the living and their loved ones in Summerland occur quite frequently. They assume they dreamed that we were all together, but it was true. What remains is a happy feeling and the courage to move on. It becomes a problem when an Earth-living human refuses to go back. This leads to traumas that are not desirable on a terrestrial level. This happens especially if one cannot and will not let go of the deceased person, cherishing the mourning and the pain after the loss and cannot renounce it. After the light and angelic spheres have helped you to cope with the loss, the visits can take place again and there can be peace and acceptance.

Together with my mother I read our book of all our past-lives on Earth with the help of our guides should we so wish. Those light beings make a noticeable difference with their wisdom and their wealth of experience.

Together we often go to dedicated chambers, where the white golden energy of Lord Kumeka can cleanse that piece of our past that we processed. Things are speeding up today.

Since the nineties laws on this side have changed. The Earth is a planet where free will means that you decided for yourself whether you wanted to read your book of life or not. After your death, the last life went past you like a movie and you decided for yourself if you wanted to see and experience all the details. That was the next phase. You ended up in the sphere of your spiritual attunement, which is a universal law. After all, you cannot handle more light than you are, otherwise you would burn.

That is how it could happen that people refused to read their book of life, life after life. The Higher Self, the spiritual leaders and the Lords of Karma, then looked for ways to teach the right soul lessons meaning you were then born in the right place under the right circumstances and with the right people. I often incarnated from the lower spheres of deep darkness to the twilight spheres. In fact, this is not a choice; that incarnation is actually determined by a higher hierarchy. The Higher Self chooses what is imperative for a soul to grow.

Now I am in the sphere where I have so much light in me that I want to look at what is behind me, and I see that self-knowledge is a very important aspect of life. 'Seeing what is without judgment', I am always taught. By reading my book of life and by talking to people with similar backgrounds, I learned a lot about myself and rose into my light. Looking back with my mother, it is deeply tragic that we became so trapped in our desire for power, material matters and domination. With the changed laws of transition to the new age, every human being has to look at his book of life. This has unimaginable consequences. All of a sudden, processes go very fast and people are in a hurry to balance things. Easier too that no one blames you for your soul's past. Every human being walked his evolutionary path. The one person only briefly while the other is stuck in it for a long time unable to relinquish. I learned that very profound experiences - such as my mother's during the Second World War - and mine require profound inner lessons. All the people who have come to light consciousness are unanimous on this.

It is tragic when you are so stuck in that rut of power and violence that only a shocking experience can shake you lose, as was the case with my mother and me.

I understand it is always preferred to first offer awareness through the softest possible method. I have seen that incarnations of children in a loving, nurturing environment could bring about enormous changes. Once the lessons were learned in love, the tougher way became unnecessary. For me that never worked in the past.

I may and can devote myself to my great love in the gardens of Summerland and especially this large rose garden. It is actually more of a park like landscape where people can be together. The roses have a high energetic value and their colours, scents and vibrations work at the heart. They bring about healing and cure me from old familiar wounds of the past and what caused them 'See what is, without judgment'.

Thea: I would like to add something from my own practical experience after Eagle's words. During all the years, I received readings for people from the spiritual world - clairaudient-writing and writing - I have learned from my spiritual guides and teachers, Leviahnarah and Ohan, that certain conditions in a life have facets of either learning or coping. I have seen that the diamond of life has so many facets.

I did many hundreds of concentration camp readings for people who had never seen their family members back wondering what had happened to their loved ones and looking for answers. Knowing that the others are doing well is a blessing for both sides. In this way, people can move on and there will be a certain degree of inner peace.

I did many readings for people who incarnated again after the Second World War and had memories of it and/or related physical or psychological problems. Of all those hundreds of readings, not one was the same. Every life story was different, that is why it is so dangerous to generalize.

There could be hundreds of reasons for a soul to choose such a period. I have met people who worked with premade formats for help in this area. As if a certain disease had a certain cause. I have never been able to work like that, always endeavouring to observe every person opposite me as an unpainted canvas, only then to start working together to find the causes.

From my guides I have learned that generalization is not only the wrong way to go, but is even downright dangerous. Of a hundred cancer patients, all stories and causes are different. Sometimes there are patterns in a syndrome that seem to suggest specific characteristics of karma. I know people who work out karmic aspects in their cancer for a whole group and that is very common in today's age. It is significant that often they are the ones who could never say no, were always available for their communities without boundaries.

Then there are those who choose to use cancer to deal with old traces of karma at a soul level, a relatively quick way, compared to a very long life. From our perspective, it is often difficult to understand why we apparently choose life situations that are tough and challenging.

Especially in connection with cancer, I noticed that the people I treated are going through such a change. Not due to my treatment, but with their inner healing. Of course, this happens with any type of change, but it is striking, how many people with this feature asked for my help. It has always been a privilege for me to help neutralize the negative effects of chemotherapy, radiation and anaesthesia through my hands. I have often seen how beings of light stood around my treatment area and how the colours in the aura changed. People who have undergone several chemotherapy treatments in the hospital often show a deep grey cloud of energy around their heads. I detected it with drug addicts or with people who have a serious drinking problem. In the places where the cancer was, I see dark spots or with the spreading of it, I would see hundreds of dots, tiny ones.

I saw how the beings of light let blue and golden energy flow into the aura.

Like dripping ink droplets in a glass of water, it swirled through the energy field and spread. I would see black spots lighting up, slowly from grey to white.

The healed energy field felt warm again instead of cold above the black spots. Seeing the energy field change in that way, I would assume that the person in question would also change, and the ensuing conversations would prove that. It might take a while before that change becomes visible to the outside world.

With this example, I would like to show that, in my opinion, the disease process changes the person, and although this is undoubtedly true of all diseases, I have never seen it as clearly as in cancer patients. Apparently, this is our choice knowing at the soul level that it progresses us further and transforms old negative vibrations making us ascend into the light.

I have seen the accelerated paying off karma in this process. There is a whole range of possibilities to transform old, unprocessed vibrations. In my readings, I often see that people chose a life with a disability. One particular reading made an indelible impression on me. Someone chose to incarnate with Down's syndrome. She had parents, brothers, sisters and other family members, who in a previous life were persecutors and had no compassion for anyone who was 'different' in their eyes. Some had been inquisitors and she had ended up at the stake, burnt for healing the sick with herbs, a well-developed skill she had. In her life with Down's syndrome, she was all about love and the family loved her. In her short life of just over 18 years, she became the darling of the whole family, giving a number of people the opportunity to let the love of the heart blossom.

There were also people who chose a period in a concentration camp to spread the high degree of light they were carrying. Leviahnarah told me that in every barracks there were up to three such people. They had a function to counterbalance the prevailing darkness with a high degree of inner light. Sometimes they were nurses in an infirmary, or an old woman who took care of the children; such lights were everywhere. Survivors of the camps relayed stories about them to me. They cannot forget them. In other words, there can be many reasons to choose a particular life form. Let us not judge. I witnessed people do that in groups. Let us be aware of the diversity that exists in all things.

Insight into past lives takes us further on the path of cleansing old negative vibrations and 'judging' is not part of that.

10. Healing chambers

And the white gold energy of Kumeka

Margaret: I was a guest of a special group of people. They have found each other during work in and around hospitals, here in the spiritual world. Here we call these places 'healing chambers' and that is how I will continue to call them from now on.

In many spheres, healing chambers are located, each with a particular attunement and task. Some are specially designed for babies and children. People that work there are qualified to do that specific kind of work and often were nurses or doctors on Earth. It can happen, that not until people are on this side, that such a profession is chosen and a very specific training is given. In a certain section of the Hall of Wisdom, a complex of schools and universities in every light sphere, people who wholeheartedly desire such work, can receive this specific training.

Studying here is so very different from studying on Earth. Largely the knowledge you wish to acquire is often already present in your soul being. The reason why people choose to study it in the first place. There are lectures together with groups of like-minded people, but also ways of studying that can best be described as a kind of 'frequency education'. This can be done in spaces where small holographic screens are positioned in secluded corners, and where knowledge flows in via a kind of headphone. Alternatively, the kind of 'home education' sitting in a comfortable chair with the knowledge you are looking for, flowing in. A prerequisite for studying in these ways is a sincere interest in the subject. Without that, there is no point in doing it. The subject of study is always a reflection of what was already developed in the soul.

I was a nurse in several past lives, and although that was a long time ago, there is a lot of practical knowledge available to my soul being. People here follow an inner vocation and choose the work that suits them best. People like John 'the painter', mentioned in a previous chapter, have undergone a certain amount of training. John specializes in drawing and painting and in the general principles of visual arts, representing God's creation in many lives. In combination with his desire to heal his own inner child through service to children, he received a very specific training for this task. The kids love him and he loves them back.

I was in a special kind of healing chamber for some time, because of the cancer I had on Earth. Such a chamber is pleasant, light and airy. Most chambers are without windows, because you go into a kind of sleeping mode. Every person gets the colour and vibration that best suits him or her. It is a beautiful to see a person in such a deep rest, surrounded and drenched in a certain colour. In the former cancer patients' surgery rooms is always a certain amount of gold present. I was in a chamber where the colour blue and green dominated, bathing in white-gold particles. In other chambers, I saw a warm golden haze penetrating everything. The white-gold energy is from the eighth ray of purification. The Chohan or administrator of the eighth ray is Master Kumeka. This period on Earth, his ray is highly effective in all healing chambers. His white gold energy provides total purification of old aspects from all previous lives on Earth.

Humanity finds itself at the end of a 26,000-year cycle, the transition to a new cosmic era, deeply connected to the work of Kumeka. It was only when a certain amount of light had grown in the collective consciousness of humankind that he found access to the Earth at the start of the nineties. Before that, it was not possible to work here. All other rays are connected in this elaborate purification plan.

Kumeka is a brother of Jesus, but never incarnated on Earth. He serves all people on Earth and in the spheres. People on Earth who practice meditation and focus on his help perceive his light-appearance and recognize him with their hearts. People who originally come from other places and whom we call star people recognize it. Through conscious meditations, they soon encounter him. Clear hearers and people who channel have already made contact with him many times. As a result, the star people wake up at a fast pace and are beginning to remember their origins and tasks on Earth. Kumeka shows these people the way in their purification processes, and the channelled messages find their way to the people for whom these messages are intended.

The recognition of Kumeka was a revelation for me too. I too am originally from the stars, I am a Pleiadian soul and I know him very well from those lives. What Jesus meant to us on Earth, is what Kumeka a long time ago meant to the Pleiadians. On Lyra, he first led them through difficult times, until they ascended as people to the worlds in the Pleiades. Later on the Pleiades he was their teacher. It was deeply emotional when I first met him. That was in the period after I had read my entire book of life and, even more than on Earth, became aware of my soul's origins. Seeing and understanding all this gave me tremendous inner peace. Kumeka knows the nature of all-star people from their evolution. He now works in soul groups with the people of Earth evolution. Every human being who has become aware of his tasks to Earth and its people and consciously chooses to ask for his help, receives that help.

This results in rapid purification. Here, too, in the spheres, people are looking for quick, effective ways to cleanse all previous lives. There are special classrooms for that. With the changed transitional laws, every human being must now read his or her book of life after his or her transition, whereas connecting with the white-gold energy of Kumeka, the ray of purification, is entirely voluntary.

These classrooms expand all the time, in order to provide for the immense need of people to balance all their past lives. It is like a wave of deep longing to flow along with the waves of light into the new age. Never before, so much work was done on healing and purification as in this transition period to a new era, in which this Earth will become a world of light. The atmosphere of hope and expectation in these places is highly contagious and hold an enormous attraction for many. Out of these centres, people start working again with newly arrived people in the spheres. Everyone focuses primarily on his or her own soul group creating waves of change in processes previously rigid and laborious. So many people are committed to the changes to the new age.

I meet many star people often working together with countless others from their own soul group. One of their tasks is to help them in their awakening process to who they are, because many have been working on Mother Earth for so long that they have forgotten their origins. Many people in Europe and Asia in particular, are still unaware of that background. In comparison, relatively more people in America are aware of this soul origin. There are also the most channels that, connected to their Pleiadian counsellors and teachers, help people to awaken. They also write books and these find their way around the world. Many people begin to remember this information spontaneously. It is not socially acceptable to talk about it yet, so these kinds of feelings often linger in those people for a long time. For the entire world population, about 4 to 5% of the souls in incarnation come from the stars, of which the largest group returns here regularly since the beginning of the Atlantis period.

That group was stuck in Earth's physicality. They once came as teachers, parents, artists, builders, architects, doctors, healers and so on, with the intention to convey knowledge in the broadest sense of the word. To give new impulses at all levels. Progress was fearful and many of them were intensely persecuted and their good intentions often misunderstood causing fear instead. Their often very open connection with the spiritual world of light - what man on Earth calls the 'paranormal world' - was very often condemned.

Very special was my meeting with a group of people who turned out to belong to my soul group. I was in a healing chamber, on a beautiful spot in a landscape permeated by a white-gold haze. That is where people go who have remembered who they are. First, you have to process the entire book of life of all lives on Earth. Some people need a long time to do that. When the time comes to take the next step, there is a celebration.

At least there was one for me. A real 'coming home', when I already felt so at home. The feeling of recognition can be extremely intense. Just seeing the light beings of the Pleiades caused a stir in my whole self. One of them was Ohan and I remember Thea speaking of him. He was her spiritual teacher for seven years. He taught her who she was and how to rekindle her old talents.

Whenever she was brought here, I looked with her at that opening on the holographic screens. People like her, who are in such an open connection with the light world, have all made their books of life available as educational material and there are books of life from artists, physicians, musicians, administrators and so on. Ohan helps people who can see and hear him on Earth, so that in turn they can pass on a lot of information to fellow souls.

All the star nations who incarnate here have now set up these systems in order to be able to receive every soul in an appropriate manner and to show the way. Tailor-made for each soul at his or her own pace. Once in balance with all this (the process of recognizing and remembering goes fast at this level), they flow out again and become guides for the souls of their group who still live on Earth. This work is very specialized because the souls of the stars who chose to return after the great transition have to balance all their earthly karma. Others choose to work with the people of the Earth evolution. They were always people with whom they were connected in one or more lives. Once the connection is healed, it is particularly moving to see how one is originally connected with each other in love.

The beginning of our stay in Lemuria was nice and fulfilling. It was all worth it, even though it was hard to be pulled so deeply into matter. Many of us descended into dark areas on Earth to help darkened souls regain their light, and those were often hard lives. Ohan has shown us all, during the many lessons, how good the Pleiadians were at that and still are.

I now know that the young woman in the cathedral, who showed Bernard the way to the light when he was wandering around there earthbound, has been doing so for many years. She has practiced for many lives and brought it to Earth as a profound knowledge. Throughout the ages, she taught others how to show earthly people the way to the light. Often in silence and living 'insignificant' lives. More and more people from all soul groups are starting to remember this knowledge, which was once common to all of them. In leaps and bounds, a lot of forgotten knowledge comes back to the consciousness of humankind. It goes fast because here too the principle of the 'hundredth monkey effect' works.

During the last 25 years a great many souls of different light nations have incarnated from all over the cosmos. The time has come that the information about those populations goes public. With the light they possess, they help Mother Earth in her birth process to the light. These souls focus on the light, living inconspicuous lives. To plant their light on Earth suffices. Then there are those who are teachers or writers with a specific task. In the new era, the teachers will once again come from the light worlds and everyone will be able to choose the teacher who fits his or her evolutionary path.

This was also the case in the Lemurian and Atlantic periods, where a method of education was chosen that best suited the soul's individual way forward. One would incarnate in places on Earth such as Peru, ancient Mexico, Egypt or Palestine where a specific teacher would be present after being selected at the soul level. Stone images were sometimes made of their teachers from the cosmos, such as the cosmic Maya, also a Pleiadian people.

Everyone recognises that warm feeling for a culture with whom you feel connected. The earliest times on Earth were beautiful and nourishing, until conquering forces brought darkness upon the Earth. This is a world of duality and we all went through it. With the transition to the new Earth in the fifth dimension, duality will also disappear.

As mentioned before, those who still need for duality can incarnate on another third-dimensional world. This will be a planet that has almost collapsed because of far-reaching wars and pollution and has been uninhabitable for a long time. That is ready to receive its new population, consisting of people who prefer to live in the third dimension. Not everyone is ready for the light world.

Each soul goes through its own growth process, at its own pace. We mean a whole soul group. On the screens, I saw that other third dimensional world in the rooms above the Himalayan Mountains. A beautiful place, with a very special kind of nature and animal kingdom. Because I think it is important, I repeat that everyone is taken care of and no soul is ever lost.

Those who ever came from the stars as teachers, and stuck here for so long, work very consciously in the lower astral spheres to assist souls in darkness to rediscover their light. They teach all those who feel the need to do this work, and many choose to do so because they are aware of its importance. It is nice to see how all souls here work together, once they have arrived in the higher light spheres. The higher you rise in the light, the more the differences disappear that existed on Earth. All the souls from the federations of light worlds work very closely together. All the visible nuances are no problem at all. The Earth alone has such a variety of people, that you can safely say that variation is the keynote of the Divine Plan, coexistence and living together in diversity.

Here in the world of light - on the other side of the veil - you see creatures that are even more different. I like the Pleiadians, with their long, slender stature. They most closely resemble the Dogon, a tribe of black people in Africa. Those beautifully shaped bodies move like gazelles. Their almond-shaped eyes give me a familiar feeling, their beautifully shaped hands with one thumb and three fingers, look very natural to me. Almost all men wear long hair in a tail on their back. The hair is bound together with one or more straps that indicates someone's status. The women also wear a hairband, but their status is indicated either by the bracelet around the upper arm or by a necklace. They earn their status built up throughout many lives. People belong to a certain clan going back for centuries. Someone from the governing clan, can connect with another clan if so require for work and development. I belong to the healer clan and the tasks of that clan are broad and cover all possible areas. This includes, for example, the writing of this book, which intends to take away the fear of death.

There are people who are preachers or pastors on Earth, but who are originally a Pleiadian soul and have their origins in the healing clan. They assist the sick and dying. They have a task as a healer. During the course of many incarnations, they often had souls as apprentices that were younger in their evolution. This could be as a son or daughter, because one can learn a lot from a parent during the rest of one's life. Peoples of very different backgrounds became intensely interwoven this way.

All these different souls work closely together in the healing chambers constantly learning from each other, an interaction that does not stop. Distinctions between all these different peoples are eliminated here but are still to be done on Earth. The work in the healing chambers in all spheres is taken very seriously, with all gradations that are there. We are working very hard. Every person who gained consciousness chooses a task that suits him or her. If there is a need for rest, they will take it. Like the light beings who work on Earth in areas of war and famine, can suddenly choose a period of complete rest in a place of their choice, either in their own home or in a healing chamber. After a while in the light-frequency that suits them, they return to the work floor on Earth, healed and refreshed to continue their work. I choose the light chamber after I have been to the lower astral areas with Jasmine. The peace and quiet I seek then, I sorely need.

I wish hospitals on Earth could be as they are in the spheres, without shortage of personnel and without the enormous workload that is common today. Not speaking of the disgracefully low wages for health care workers. I well remember what it's like to be in need of help. How scarce help is at home nowadays, how limited the time to do the job properly, the enormous workload. This needs to change. That certainly applies to nursing homes as well. Fortunately, I did not have to go through all that when I was sick. I admire everyone who tries so hard in health care. There is one consolation and that is that the people who arrive here are well and lovingly take care of. The unity in diversity here is balm for the soul. I love all those different soul groups that work together harmoniously. I see my own ideals come to life here.

11. The scientist

And the legacy of Atlantis

Margaret: In the healing chamber of Pleiadian souls, about which I wrote so enthusiastically, I met a scientist. He had been in the spiritual world for a long time and had made a long journey before he had arrived in the realms of light. After the healing chambers of Kumeka he could devote himself to a scientific project, together with other scientists. In a specific sphere, scientists meet and exchange ideas.

Scientist: 'I came to Earth at the beginning of the first era of Atlantis. I originated from the clan of scientists and was to contribute to the evolution of the young Earth. My tasks were fixed in my life blueprint and in the contract I had signed. In the early years on Earth, I was still strongly connected to the light worlds. I could fully communicate with them, information flowed easily and it was as normal as eating and drinking.

At first, I still had a very Pleiadian body, tall, more subtle than that of the earthy people and slightly built. Indeed, we were most like the Dogon, an African people. Our skin was light bronze. My hands had a thumb and three fingers. By earthly standards, this may seem like an anomaly, but it was meant to be and my hands were beautiful, slender and graceful. I wore my hair in a long tail on my back. Usually I chose male incarnations, although later, in the third and last period of Atlantis, I lived a few times as a woman.

In the first Atlantic period, I could still regularly go back to my light world. You could say I went to recharge my batteries, just as we do now in the spheres in a light or healing chamber. I was happy with my contract on Earth. I had committed myself to serve as an elder for Earth souls. Souls that came from Maldek to Earth after the huge explosion.

All soul fragments were collected and taken to the seabed of the young Earth, where the dolphins took care of them. Dolphins are our brothers from Sirius and they brought love and healing to these souls. I was part of the plan to look after the parenthood of these souls something I had done many times before in other places in the cosmos. Many of us were involved in this healing plan for Earth, and successfully so. These souls, who had previously lived on Maldek, scattered the Earth to go their way in the evolution.

They had lost the memory of the destruction of their old world and they all set out on a new, promising phase of their evolution. Earth was then a wonderful place to be. I worked as a teacher at the temple schools that we had built, and I enjoyed that beautiful initial period, which lasted more than three thousand years.

My contract ran until the third period of Atlantis, after which I would return. But it turned out differently. I made karma when I became too generous in passing on knowledge. I was naive, because I assumed that the given knowledge would be used for the good of man and planet, in the service of the entire evolution, as we had experienced in many places in the cosmos. We have never before experienced abuses such as those on Earth in that particular period to such an extent. The polarity on this planet was very strong. More than I have seen in other places.

My knowledge I passed on for their own benefit was used to gain power, to oppress and dominate other people, and above all to gather great wealth. Earth is a planet of free will. Many of us made the mistake of passing on too much knowledge and in doing so we made karma. I unfortunately learned the bitter lesson that man chose to use such wonderful knowledge for their deepest evil. Many of us on Earth lost our naivety. It was so painful to see what the people of Earth were doing with knowledge that was beneficial to everybody rather than to the single selfish person who craved wealth and great power. That phenomenon was new to us. No matter how hard we tried to balance the karma we made, it often turned out to be irreversible.

The Atlantis end-time technology was very special. In the beginning, there was beauty, but eventually the whole society ran itself into the ground over the course of the three periods, especially in the third period.

I realised later that had we not passed on knowledge, this situation would have occurred anyhow, but it was unbearable for me that I had contributed to it. My integrity as a scientist was a priority at the time. In our culture, you earn status through purity, integrity, and intentions that are fully attuned to the light. It does not even occur to us to do things any different, that is our state of being. More and more people on Earth, of all soul groups realise this now and start living accordingly! It is the only way home to more and more light.

I longed for my home world and went to one of the temples when my time had come. They took me to the mother ship through a dematerialization room. About 20,000 new Pleiadians would go to Earth after the downfall of

Atlantis, to the next period of the Earth's evolution. Our group of 10,000 souls would return. This would have been a long contract for us, longer than we would normally have entered into. I was homesick for my home world, my cosmic family, after the hectic incarnations in the third and final period of Atlantis.

We foresee things as they come, because they are created by the collective human consciousness on a planet. All I wanted was to go home. Life after life I carried the memory with me of the light world I came from. Even when I eventually carried such an earthly body like anyone else. The memory never vanished. At the end of the 26,000-year cycle, that same memory now returns in this End Time to people with the same soul origin as I or from another star people. It can be very confusing for some when they remember things that do not exist here on Earth and never did. The reason is that we forgot so much. After all, such memories belong to the uniqueness of the distant place of origin.

In that last period of Atlantis, on the mother ship, all the people of my clan helped to dismantle the dematerialization chambers scattered all over the Earth. We made nuclear power plants, some of which were located in the oceans, inoperable in order to prevent even bigger catastrophes, like the one that took place on the planet Maldek, where the whole process with the dark forces had gotten so out of hand that the planet exploded. That was to be averted at all times.

Over the past seven years, the abuse became more and more serious, and many had succumbed to the influence of the dark powers and forces, who were doing everything in their power to fully control Earth. All instruments, such as the ankh and crystal tools, were carried to the mother ship by special teams. For seven years, many of us contributed to these operations doing everything we could. I did it with only one thing in mind and that was to go home.

So I became very homesick. It had been too long, more than 12,000 years of incarnating on Earth. When all people were gathered on the mother ship, on all levels of 'being' and of vibration, a great conclave took place. This happened in a huge hall, surrounded by holographic screens. Representatives of our light worlds in the Pleiades were present too. It was wonderful to see their familiar shapes, to hear of my language. It felt like home again. This meeting at all these levels moved me very much. Most of my group were exhausted from the difficult last few years during which so many awful things had happened.

Over the last thirty years I had been intensely involved in caring for certain people together with a dear friend, a physician. I am talking about 'people' created by the Atlanteans through genetic engineering to serve as slaves. This breed of workers was manipulated in such a way that it needed little sleep and little food. A lot of experimenting went on by their scientists to clone away any sort of feelings in these creatures. They were not allowed to reproduce or show emotion, and were severely punished if they did. The goal was to create work machines.

A very small number of Atlanteans who had different ideas formed a silent underground. They sabotaged a lot, slowing down or paralysing the processes. These pathetic 'people' were taken to the temple complexes of the Pleiadians. They worked very closely together with sister souls, teachers from Andromeda, fewer in number on Earth and still are, by the way. Confronted with all this misery, with the deformed clones, with those people in unbearable pain from deformed gastrointestinal systems, made us ever more determined to take care of them. That society was harsh, harsher than it is now.

Before the start of the seven years of cleaning up of dangerous technologies, I worked in the large temple complex. This temple area was inviolable. It consisted of many buildings, small villages, a huge hospital and was completely self-sufficient. First, we evacuated the large buildings where the older priests lived and built smaller spaces for them next to the temple. In this way, every large space was suitable to receive them. Elsewhere in the area, medical facilities had been created for those who suffered from a disease that in many ways resembles today's Aids. Sufferers of this disease were unceremoniously kicked outside of the immense city walls, without food, drink or possessions and in most cases, left to die of deprivation.

There were corpses everywhere. It was awful to see. They were scattered all over the place, because the dying did not want to die next to a corpse. We used some form of dematerialisation to dispose of the corpses because many of them were in an advanced state of decomposition. The survivors were taken in and brought to safer places.

Special low-flying elite troops of the Atlantic government would hunt at these people. They saw it as an exciting distraction from their materialistic life. With laser weapons, they shot at the pariahs that lived outside the cities. It was a great honour to be part of one of the elite squadrons' missions. The government allowed them to do it.

Properties of expelled people were confiscated, as happened in the last century with possessions of Jews. The disease I was talking about was deliberately spread in order to thin out particular groups of people. The cleansing was successful.

In the last thirty years, the provision of care took on ever-increasing proportions. I often used to go along with the small flying vehicles to pick up people from the outskirts of town. These vehicles had an elliptical shape, a satin-silver colour with sliding walls. An inexhaustible source of energy propelled them, the same energy that would later be rediscovered by Nicola Tesla, which he called Radiant Energy. Today this is often called free energy or zero point energy.

I worked closely with my friend, the physician, and many others in my soul group. We were looking for ways to make life liveable for the people that were the creation of far-reaching genetic engineering and cloning. When all possibilities had been exhausted, we offered them the opportunity to move on to their next existence by means of a specially built dematerialisation room. We applied every other discipline imaginable. Under the guidance of Lord Kumeka - our teacher through the ages who assisted us from the light worlds - we were shown a way to the greatest possible spiritual healing.

Before these people left Earth, we tried to provide as much spiritual assistance as possible. We were always quite clear who was ready for the next phase, for a passage to the fourth dimension. Clones who were able to do so took care of those who were less well off. That happened unsaid and harmoniously. Many died at night in their sleep while others chose the dematerialisation room. There were several of these shelters in Atlantis, and contained a high frequency of love and care. This love and solidarity are carved in my soul being. I will never forget it.

I saw great solidarity, even amongst, what I will call 'Aids patients'. They took care of each other as much as they could. Hundreds of Pleiadian souls worked for these people. Their doctors and spiritual helpers did what they could, working closely together with the Andromedans. The cooperation was wonderful, but the human misery we saw there was terrible. Some of us fell ill working our bodies to the point of exhaustion making us susceptible to the virus due to low resistance whilst new people kept on coming in.

The Atlanteans collected heavy karma through many negative actions during that end time. Later in earthly history, many of the consequences of their actions were worked out in the twentieth century. Many scientists of the time are still busy with genetic engineering and cloning. Together with a very large team it is now one of my tasks to guide them from the spirit. Unfortunately, many of them are not receptive to our positive inspiration and shut off from this energy in their material existence as obsessed as previously. I can assure you that quite a few plans that are being developed closely resemble those in Atlantis. The world's secret leaders direct them but the realms of light will not allow it this time.

Many new incarnations of light peoples came to Earth to serve as catalysts of positive energy, as was our assignment in Atlantis at the time. The people in my soul group, who came to Earth at that earliest stage, remain in the spheres once they have passed on Earth. They stand by the star people as their guides. The federation of light worlds has brought very strong light beings from different systems together.

All these incarnated light beings are accessible to us in the spirit and just as audible as if we were standing next to each other in the material world. This communication may slow down important developments and put them up for discussion. A lot more is open for discussion than previously, and the star people contribute greatly to this. I can divulge that at this stage of the Earth's evolution, the horrors of Atlantis' end-time will not be repeated. This was rendered impossible and is the good news that I can share with you.

Lord Kumeka told us that in June of the year 2000 a golden-white mesh was created around the Earth. This is partly due to the efforts of many light workers on Earth. It consists of many interconnected fine-meshed networks of golden-white light. This will help to work together better in the attempts to let go of duality. This energy is anchored and the process will run more smoothly and balance everything, without 'good' energies escaping from the earth's surface. The energy that is present between the Earth and this web will continue to serve and can no longer be influenced by external forces. It is also intended as a source of energy. It consists of higher frequencies of light and is attuned to, and co-designed by, the light workers on Earth who have made this anchoring possible. The foundation was laid by the people on Earth and can be built upon. It will also serve as a beacon for the coming period.

Many people have waited for this because it was so difficult to balance the controversial energies on their own. By anchoring the light energy, any individual who chooses to go up to higher frequencies will feel carried without fear of relapse into the old. It is all meant to purify and transform and for many there will be a period of renewal, much faster than one thinks. This web is a power source for many positive change processes. These are processes that we also knew in Atlantis, but instead of the negative developments of that time, we now see growth.

During that great conclave on the mother ship at the end of Atlantis, all our hopes were dashed. My happiness disappeared when it turned out that three percent of the large group with whom I had come to Earth had made severe karma. About ten percent had made light karma that could be fixed, but the heavy three percent could not.

In the early days of Atlantis, there were seven civilizations of light worlds, all with missions in their soul being, to work within the evolution of the Earth and humanity. All with contracts to the federation of light worlds with a specific task on Earth. After deliberations with the other members of the federation of light-worlds they decided to leave their people with severe karma. Some chose the cocoons with the dolphins; a handful of guardians would remain. This way there were different choices for those who had become earthbound by karma.

Our people chose another solution. Thanks to a strong 'we' awareness, we opted for 'we came together, we leave together'. Solidarity has always been our greatest asset in earlier difficult times when dominated and oppressed by the people from Lyra. We lived in slavery with these creatures. Our 'we' feeling then enabled us to free ourselves from oppression and exploitation.

So we, the people of the first group in Atlantis, all decided to stay to help that small percentage of souls in regaining their light and repair the damage that was done. The latter was particularly important to all of us and thus that is how it happened. Then 20,000 new people joined us and the long road that would lead to today's time had begun.

Newcomers in our group were builders, artists, members of the management clan and many teachers for all kinds of disciplines. Souls who would function as parents for the obscured, darkened souls, both those of our own soul group as for others. There was a lot of spiritual darkness at the end of the Atlantis period. Thus began a new era, with new blueprints for each of us and for the group as a whole.

For me it was all too much, I could not go back and I could not go on. My homesickness was so great that I became seriously ill. Call it mentally ill. I was put in a light chamber for a long time, a chamber only for myself. I stayed there, more than 300 years in earthly time, in that light chamber in a deep sleep; unaware of what was going on around me. Then, very carefully, I started a new cycle.

I was not the only one, because the end of Atlantis has taken a heavy toll on many of our people. Currently, which in so many ways resembles the times of the past, a lot of work is done in consultation with each other. Like making choices in technology and science, whether to use them positively for the benefit of all people and the entire planet, or to accumulate personal power and wealth. Oil winning business is an example of how it could have been done differently.

I incarnated in South America and found myself in primitive tribes. That is where I recovered from my mental fear of starting that new cycle. Gradually, life after life, I reconnected to Earth and forgot what had happened in Atlantis. Not everyone had lost that memory, but my Higher Self decided that it was best for me. Some teachers, great masters, kept that openness for many centuries and worked with the intention of advancing purification. It was like floating on an ice floe away from my memory and knowledge, of something that had always been part of my 'being'.

I gradually became less conscious living my lives further and further away from my actual life plan. As a very passionate scientist, I did good things and I often got the feeling that my inventions were 'familiar territory' to me. I remained modest and did things in small doses rather than big ones, which undoubtedly originated from my super-consciousness. Later I chose Egyptian society and there I experienced times of great prosperity. When they talked about former teachers who had come down from the stars in earlier times, there was a vague sense of recognition, but I quickly reasoned it away. I was a 'real scientist', someone who rationalizes everything, and weighs and weighs and weighs.

My intuitive abilities remained hidden. I became more and more a man of reason and less sensitive. Those two things had long since ceased to be in accord and no longer integrated, as had always been the case before. The increasingly materialistic worldview slowly drew me in.

In the middle of the nineteenth century, new impulses reached the Earth and the way back to my actual 'being' became visible. I was an insider in the circles of Rudolf Steiner as a natural scientist and all those who were so inspired by the impulse to renew society. I was devoted to the science of the spirit involved in the building of the Goetheanum in Dornach. That period was important to me. I became receptive to the spiritual world and that brought me closer to my core, to who I was. I was there when Nicola Tesla, Lakofski and Royal Rife made their important contributions to science. Their inventions would later turn out to be so brilliant that the Earth's rulers wanted to hide them.

After I died, I opened up to the higher worlds of light and streamed into an area that offered unprecedented possibilities. I chose to stay in the spheres and go the route I felt I had to go.

The years before and during the Second World War I welcomed people, an activity called 'tunnel work'. I was specially trained for this. I focused on intellectuals, victims of the persecution by the Nazi regime in Germany. A practice that took place long before the war. If you did not want to comply with the new regime, elimination followed. People were arrested, disappeared without a trace, and many were murdered in cold blood. I picked them up and took them to the healing chambers. I felt good helping them. Prosecution for my ideas and inventions and my teaching methods to my students and so on were familiar to me.

I was a Cathar and used my knowledge to prepare medicines for the needy during the time of the Inquisition that passed on from father to son. I worked with natural substances and my family was successful in their work. I kept incarnating in the same group of souls. There were many Pleiadian souls among the Cathars and they incarnated together with many different soul groups, all of whom had the same task: to bring light into a spiritually severely darkened Europe. The ruling powers within the church had their own methods to eliminate all light. Therefore, I knew what persecution was. With heart and soul, I dedicated myself to the huge amount of people who perished during the Second World War and the time before that.

Nicola Tesla arrived at that time in the special place in the Hall of Wisdom, where scientists have their own department. It was unbearable for them to realise how many of his brilliant inventions were hushed up, played down or simply thrown out. It is happening constantly on Earth and not unfamiliar to us. Watch what happened to those who brought positive inventions to Earth. Resonance therapy was one of them. There was a strong impulse from the spiritual world at that time to develop clean and effective healing methods on Earth.

Lakofski developed a form of therapy that could cure cancer in a relatively short time. He had much help, spiritually and financially. His devices found their way to many hospitals and the results were astonishing. Royal Rife developed a particular kind of resonance therapy, but his brilliant inventions were hushed up by the scientific world. His name does not occur in scientific literature. Royal Rife died under suspicious circumstances but I know for a fact that he was murdered. They called it a car accident, but they killed him with an overdose in the hospital where he was admitted.

Powerful institutions, such as the pharmaceutical industry, have wielded their influence more often in the last century and here we know they do not hesitate to use tough methods. A cancer patient generates tens of thousands of dollars in general medical care. Big capital forced the hospitals to remove the equipment and the therapies that were introduced to Earth at very low cost were surreptitiously concealed.

Yet, not all is lost. Scientists everywhere have put their heads together and are preparing for change. New Age children in their present incarnation will bring to light what was concealed. Many are looking to find solutions for major problems, such as clean technology for industrial and domestic use, clean energy for cars and so on. The solutions exist, but the powerful on Earth systematically brush them off.

In recent years, these counterforces have always won, but the tide has already turned; this cannot go on. It is a fact, that the wave of renewal cannot be halted. Those who recognise the signs are working on it and the solutions of Tesla, Lakofsky and Rife will find their way back to the people.

The use of alternatives to antibiotics, such as Colloidal Silver, increases and this infiltrates, like a silent, underground river, through the consciousness of the people who experienced it. Those with the right device can make this product themselves and can supply people in their vicinity. In Africa, these devices are distributed and whole villages and communities provide themselves with a safe antibiotic this way, without making them resistant. They are no longer reliant on the drugs dumped by the pharmaceutical industry in Third World countries because they cannot be sold any longer in Western countries, for whatever reason. Low costs in those areas are hugely important. Health does not have to cost a fortune at all; there are so many soft ways to heal. Colloidal Silver is used for both humans and animals. It costs virtually nothing once you have a device like that. Needless to say that the pharmaceutical industry stays mum about this drug.

The change has set in however and what started as an insidious stream is now gradually becoming a vibrant river on Earth, which is unstoppable. At our 'level' we study every possibility to inspire positive and cheap solutions where needed, to pass on the medicine of the light worlds to the benefit of everyone. Here, in the Hall of Wisdom, we are with kindred spirits; no battle for the honour of an invention. Impulses for innovation are constantly given, the reason why inventions happen simultaneously in more places in the world. The printing press, the car and the bicycle are such examples.

The resonance therapy will gain recognition not so much through large-scale marketing, but by word of mouth. It will ultimately find its place in the collective consciousness of the Earth. Fear for these kinds of things is fuelled by the different powers but will be diffused naturally and many human- and planet-friendly technologies will find their way on Earth.

Think of clean energy for cars. At the beginning of the twentieth century, Nicola Tesla drove a car from Detroit to Vancouver on that energy. There was no fossil fuel involved. Where did this invention go? Households and industries could run on the same energy, without polluting the Earth but the energy suppliers had just introduced electricity in houses and industries. What would happen if oil became unnecessary? Wars are fought over oil everywhere in the world. I can give many more examples, but be aware of the inevitable changes. Together with the souls of many light peoples and all enlightened scientists of the Earth's evolution, we are united in our efforts for improvement and change. A change that won't be long in coming.'

Endless consciousness

Therefore, one should seriously consider the possibility that death, like birth,
can be just a transition to another state of being.
During our lives, the body functions as an interface and it has a facilitating function to obtain some aspects of our expanded consciousness...

Pim van Lommel, physician-cardiologist

Author of the book *'Consciousness Beyond Life'*,
about near-death experiences.

12. Coma

Coma, euthanasia and suicide

Thea: Suicide is not an easy subject. In my practice, I notice how diverse the reasons for seeking death can be. In a discussion group with therapists, all dealing with suicide, I discovered even more varieties in this field. There were people from the psychiatric profession as well and their stories impressed me hugely. How desperate or unhappy do you have to be to deliberately seek your own death?

Continually, I had to conclude that many taboos still surround suicide. I asked Margaret at the start of our telepathic correspondence if it was possible to tell something about this. Even though it will be impossible to give a complete picture, it might give us an impression of how people in the spiritual world deal with this and what consequences it will have for future lives. How does one experience self-chosen death? What does it mean for a Catholic not be buried in sacred ground? How do feelings of guilt of family members and friends affect that person? A client asked me the question: 'How is it when a cancer patient consciously chooses to end life at a time of his or her choosing?' This question intrigued me, because I experience this often in my immediate surroundings as well as the question about coma patients, so I presented it to Margaret.

I would like to share my experience with a coma patient. The parents gave their permission for this. These parents got the feeling after a while that their son no longer wanted to be kept alive artificially. Both parents had dreams about him and his request to stop breathing. I listened to their stories, their fears and doubts, without giving advice or giving my opinion. I did teach them to make contact with their son through his hands, in order to learn to rely on the dormant capacities in man to communicate telepathically.

These people taught me much and I saw them grow spiritually in a relatively short period, inevitably connected with intense processes like this. I have seen how these loving parents learned to let go of their son with confidence transforming selfishness into selfless love. I know how difficult the decision to end respiration and treatment has been for these people, but when they made their decision, they did so entirely from the heart and in peace. I saw them radiate it. Four months later, I did an extensive reading for them.

When asked, 'How are you doing?' people often say 'Good', but see I see how great sadness can linger sometimes for 4 to 5 years. I notice grey substance in their energy field. Processing is not a button that you press, but a process that is different for everyone. I got permission from the parents to include their story in the book. To protect their privacy, his name was changed. The reading for the parents contained about twenty pages with very personal information. What follows is a summary of what happened.

13. Peter

A short but intense life

Thea: Peter was a lively young man, but also a dreamer. He enjoyed every aspect of life to the fullest. Sometimes it seemed as if he was in a hurry to experience as much as possible. He preferred to travel alone; walking with his backpack was his best thing. He went all over Europe and beyond. He was a confident person.

He was twenty-four years old when a car hit him whilst riding his bike on the way to a colleague. He was admitted to hospital with brain damage. In the ambulance, he went into a coma and never came out. His parents were deeply affected by their son's accident and spent a lot of time at his bedside. Both the father and the mother had the necessary knowledge and insights in the field of the spiritual world and its functioning.

Despite the great sorrow over their son's misfortune, they believed in the spiritual care around him. They spoke to him, with the inner conviction that he heard them, which he did. They brought a CD player along with his favourite music. The mother, a sensitive woman, said that she felt a reaction when she held his hand. She was picking up his energy.

Peter was in a coma for eight weeks, the hope of recovery seemed to be gone. The damage to his brain and the rest of his body was severe. That is when the dreams started. Very vividly, the father dreamt of Peter. In this dream, he let his father know that he no longer wanted the respirator. The mother had similar, very lucid dreams. At first, they did not dare share their dreams about Peter with each other.

When both came to a degree of acceptance, they told each other their dreams while sitting at their son's bedside. They talked about his life, his ideas and wishes. It was as if pieces of a puzzle fell together whilst talking. In their reading, which took place months later, it became clear how Peter had been able to hear everything outside of his body, their world of thought was also open to him. Both of them had received insights from their respective spiritual guides and so their consciousness grew that they had to let go of Peter. They discussed it with the attending physician and with a good friend, also a physician. They acted out of a deep inner knowing.

Once they had made the decision, they felt a great sense of relief. The mother, sitting at Peter's bedside, felt very strongly that he wanted to see and feel his cat. The next day they brought the big cat in a carrier and put him on the bed in Peter's hands. The father told me afterwards that this had been one of his hardest moments, more difficult than switching off the equipment. 'I let my tears run freely that afternoon,' he told me. They were aware that Peter could understand everything they were saying and thinking being outside his body. The next day, the devices were switched off at eight o'clock in the evening a time that the mother had dreamed about and so it happened, in silence.

I learned a lot from these two people. I did nothing but listening and sharing my experience with them about coma patients. The reading, months later, showed them that they had acted very precisely according to the wishes of their son. Feeling the cat, his warm fur, his familiar energy, had been important for Peter.

Through my spiritual counsellor, he told me that he had died at exactly the right time. It was a given in his life's blueprint that he would live to the age of twenty-four. The accident and the coma were the learning curve and a fixed karma for the parents. In earlier lives, they lived life frivolously. Death was death and existence simply ceased, that was their conviction at the time.

Lack of respect for life and death in general was described in detail in their personal reading. They had asked questions about these aspects in earlier incarnations. Their earlier incarnations had been much and heavy. They had many questions for me with so many life questions following the reading. Their need for self-knowledge was considerable and sincere. How enriching this experience had been for them.

Mother started to focus more and more on helping dying people and eventually became a buddy. Peter gave them a gift so generous that it is hard to see its scope. When they read Peter's diaries about two years later, they discovered at various times in his life he must have had some inner knowing that he would not get old. A boy who lived in the here and now and enjoyed every moment. His diaries divulged a lot.

The father said that he became aware of the value of life and that he was convinced that in those twenty-four years of his life, Peter had lived far more intensely than many people did in eighty years. He remembered the stories of his parents and family about the Second World War. They lived life to the full and with great joy.

Peter went to a healing chamber in a light sphere; he died at the right time.

Leviahnarah told me that many people who choose to end their lives, for example in case of cancer or total paralysis, pass at the time that is set in their book of life. They often consciously choose a day and a time.

The medical world finds it difficult to let go of a patient. Everything is done to extend life as long as possible. In recent years, this has been very clear in oncology. Quality of life is often lost with one cure after another, sometimes with experimental drugs that offer a 1% chance of healing. These opportunities are seized and make the sick bed a major ordeal for the patient.

Many doctors see death as a failure on their part, but slowly we see a turnaround in the acceptance of an inevitable death. Palliative care contributes greatly to maintaining the quality of life for as long as possible making the journey home as comfortable as possible. It has everything to do with consciousness. The way in which people leave this world changed forty years ago. The desire to say goodbye to life is accepted by more and more doctors as a humane desire.

We would certainly like to emphasise here that this wish must come from the departing person himself. Life prolonging actions, deterioration the quality of life, will slowly become obsolete due to a growing awareness within the medical world.

Suffering

Birth, old age, illness, death,
Stuck in what one hates,
Separated from what one loves,
What one wants and does not get,
These are all forms of suffering.

In short, the five-fold clinging to life is suffering.

Buddha

14. Euthanasia group

Euthanasia group in the spheres

Thea: I will let Margaret speak again now.

Margaret: Elise brought me into contact with a euthanasia group and I spoke with some people who chose the 'soft death' for leaving their life on Earth. There are several of these groups here. It seems that there is greater tolerance for euthanasia in the Netherlands than in many other societies. Taboos are plenty, surrounding this subject. I think it is right that euthanasia should be handled with the utmost care, and it is quite understandable people have their objections. Enough reason for further exploration. It will not provide you with the complete picture, but it might give you a glimpse behind the scenes.

Ohan, one of my spiritual teachers for the past period, joins us. We are going to a place close to the healing chambers. Fifteen people have gathered. They form a study group, offer support, and listen intently to the new arrivals. We are in a garden with a large circular gazebo made of wrought iron. There are easy wicker chairs everywhere. It all feels hospitable with a friendly, pleasant atmosphere. Around the gazebo, champagne-coloured roses grow together in small groups. Along the fence, soft pink climbing roses are growing. I looked around in amazement. The peace, harmony and especially the great beauty of these places continue to move me. A masterly hand has been at work here, like in the rose garden in Summerland.

Ohan: 'Places like this are in every light sphere. Everywhere in the spiritual world people arrive and feel the need to take care of flowers and gardens. They enjoy being involved in such a place and heal old aspects of life on Earth. Tending a garden provides a high level of healing but it benefits others as well who enjoy wandering around and find their place of silence. Such a place of great beauty also offers an opportunity to meet each other. These are particularly suitable for this euthanasia group, because many of them have had long periods of illness, cut off from the outdoor life. During their illness, they longed for nature or a garden to be in and that is why bringing a nice bunch of flowers can be so important for a long-term sick person. Flowers have an energy that can be important in a sick room.'

Margaret: Three men and a woman joined the group, doctors in their last lives. The meeting begins. Two new people are welcomed, a man and a woman. They have just come out of the healing chambers and both are from the Netherlands. Everyone seems to understand the reason for my presence. Because of the uncertainty, and feelings of guilt around this subject, there was a collective desire to share their experiences with the readers of this book. They exchange information. New people can ask their questions and anyone with anything meaningful to say can answer. I want to start with the story of one of the men.

15. Robert

Respect for other people's lives

Margaret: Robert suffered from depression a lot in his young life. He was born into a large family, in a small town in America. His family was a member of a Mennonite church community and Robert and his family regularly attended services. His early childhood was quite normal, schools, sports, girls, going out with friends. His depression was of such a nature that he was able to lead a reasonably normal life. His family and friends knew about his dark moods. He would be quiet and introverted and he did everything alone. They accepted it because after a while he always returned to normal life.

He was not on any medication because his parents hoped that his problems would disappear in the protective environment of the family. That is exactly what their life blueprint said. Giving him security, a good basis, teaching him how to deal with setbacks, so that he could process things from a previous life in peace and quiet. The situation in which Robert incarnated was optimal.

When he went to university, he had to leave his hometown and live in a big city. He found a room and his life as a young adult started. He had an aversion for student parties where people drank a lot. Out of the safety of his parents' home, he had to get used to his new situation. His depressions during that time became more severe and more difficult to handle. He would be alone in his room, when most of the students were busy partying and drinking more than was good for them. He soon realised that the parties were not for him and he decided not to go anymore, taking distance from peer pressure.

Contrary to this turbulent student life, his youth had been quiet and very orderly and his gloomy moods were accepted. He could be himself. In college, so many things happened at the same time. His adjustment took time. If his friends had a setback, they shrugged it off with a smile but Robert took those setbacks very hard. He saw problems everywhere. He had to learn to deal with the common setbacks in life, with the small problems and disappointments that everyone runs into during his life journey.

When a girl rejected him, his whole world would collapse. He would mope for days. He carried a permanent sense of guilt with him that was evident in everything he did. He took that along from a previous incarnation with the intention in the blueprint of his life as Robert, he was supposed to work it out and solve it.

He actually unconsciously carried a great sense of guilt with him for his general behaviour in previous lives. He could not and would not adapt to the new life in the big city. His depressions got worse. So he decided to end his life when he was twenty-six years old. He did what he should have overcome. There had often been thoughts in that direction. One day, at a whim, he threw himself off the pavement in front of a bus in a busy street. He died instantly.

The Second World War

His life directly before his life as Robert was at a time around the Second World War. He was too young for military service and grew up when young people started to buy their own cars. Beautiful large cars with lots of chrome. A young man with such a car automatically had many friends. He liked to brag and drive around proudly in his car.

In this life and in another incarnation, he had put other people in mortal danger a number of times by his reckless behaviour. Three people died because of this. He would drink and drive and showed a tough and masculine behaviour.

He was addicted to drinking. He continually put people's lives at risk, with relatively minor accidents, but often with injuries. They took his driver's license away from him after he drove a car total-loss. Two of his passengers had to go to the hospital with serious head injuries. Even though the passengers had voluntarily stepped into a car of a drunken young man, that is undoubtedly true, but that did not make him feel less guilty later on in life.

In spite of not having a license, he still got into a car drunk and hit an oncoming car at high speed. The three occupants were killed instantly and he was trapped in his car. It happened in a remote area with no one around and it took ages before help reached him.

He saw his life pass by his mind's eye and his reckless behaviour exposed. He concluded that his behaviour had endangered many people like his younger brother and good friend, plus all the other friends who had ended up in hospital with head injuries. It was like watching a movie. In the meantime, he could look into the car with the three occupants who had lost their lives. A bloody scene. Two hours he sat like that before help reached him. When the gravity of the situation dawned on him, he cried and screamed, and no one to stop him.

The doctor who treated him had to immobilize him to calm him down. His own injuries were serious and his right leg could not be saved and needed amputation. He went mad with guilt. He recovered from his injuries, but after a long period of revalidation, he was confined to a wheelchair. That could only be a punishment from God for his actions, he thought. Every calamity, everything he did was in his eyes evidence of God's punishment. His guilt became disproportionate. His long stay in the hospital and the rehabilitation centre sobered him up. No more drinking for him, but looking at alcohol, made him feel guilty.

He came face to face with the parents of the three people who died during the trial. Their grief would always stay with him. He turned gloomy and melancholic. Those moods were precisely why he started drinking in the first place. A remedy for his melancholic moods. This would become a pattern that he took with him into several next lives.

He hated the wheelchair, but he did not have the courage to try a prosthesis either. At the age of twenty-six, he put an end to his life with pills. After his death, he remained connected to his body. He experienced the grief of his family, his own funeral and he was taken to a place called Urmani, the place of his spiritual attunement. Those who take their own lives go there. For him, his death was a desire to a flight into the 'nothing' and he experienced Urmani as such.

These people too are taken care of here. Like in the low astral spheres, help is offered but given only once it is accepted with one's own free will. The road that follows from that moment is tailor made.

His help came in the form of one of his victims. This young man, staying in a light sphere, went to see him and offered his help. It was not long before he accepted it. Moreover, there was much specialised assistance from people, now living in the light spheres, who had been alcoholics in a number of lives. They know with their entire being how difficult it is to get rid of an addiction and had gone a long, arduous way to get rid of the vibration keeping them under the control of alcohol. He got help from a man who had run an almost identical pattern in previous lives. Like a boat sailing circumventing every upheaval in life by taking to the bottle.

He read his book of life and saw how, in several previous lives, he had shunned every responsibility, always choosing the easy way out, usually at the expense of other people. Cause and effect were piling up.

Factory worker in England

On the holographic screen, he looked back on a hardworking life as a factory worker in England, at the beginning of the industrial era in the nineteenth century. His wife had a baby almost every year, also working hard at a wool-dyeing factory. She multitasked working and housekeeping under very primitive conditions in a far too small gloomy house.

He did not help his wife and never had time for his family. He reckoned, that was her job. He did not make any effort to change their living conditions, although he had several opportunities to do so like a job in the countryside where he came from, together with his wife, to work as a couple in the big house where he was born. They could live in his father's house, a small cottage with a vegetable garden for their own use. In his arrogance, he turned the offer down.

After an argument with his father, he had gone to the big city with his young bride. He wanted to get rich there to outsmart the farmers of his village. All they did was work and he would show them how much smarter he was. Many people left the countryside for the industrialised cities of the time, dreaming of great prosperity and a better life. A dream from which they would soon wake up once they were in the city.

At the time of that job offer, he only had one son. A reasonably free and clean life in the countryside beckoned. His great pride prevented him from accepting the offer. Ten years later, now with as many as eight children, he had become a bitter man, with a developing lung disease from the dirty work he did. The mortality rate from dust lungs was high at the time.

He ignored the usual problems that every family have to deal with. By looking away, he created his own little world where no problem existed. When family complications would get too much for him, he would make a noisy and violent departure at the expense of his wife and children. He would come home later, heavily intoxicated, more violent than in his sober moments. He would abuse his wife and children purely out of his feeling of incompetence. When his wife died of tuberculosis, he took his eleven children to an orphanage in the city and never looked at them again. He left the city and led a wandering life in the countryside. He worked as a labourer and spent most of his money on alcohol. He lived in remote barns and abandoned houses occasionally poaching a rabbit here and there.

An anxiety attack because of his pulmonary emphysema coupled with a TBC infection, a left over from his years in the factory, resulted in his death.

There was particular anger in him about the past life, blaming everybody except himself. On the other side, however, he saw what choices he could have made to make his life more prosperous and healthy and saw the differences. His choices and pride had taken him further away from his life plan than ever before.

The being of light that accompanied him showed him the consequences of his choices in a series of lives and constantly with the same characteristics that his soul being wanted to learn. Solving everyday problems like everyone else; everyday life, with all its vicissitudes.

He was shown eight incarnations with that theme, with lives in between in order to work out the built up karma. His refusal to conquer minor pitfalls and bumps in the course of his life at the detriment of others often women created a lot of karma. These women married him for love or simply to be at his every beck and call.

Robert looked at his life histories under the guidance of various light beings and people with similar backgrounds. He was steered patiently and lovingly through his own processes to understanding and consciousness, but he could not get himself to accept all of it. Yet he had to learn his lessons and so he returned to Earth.

An added amount of facets were collected by his Higher Self and so everything he had managed to avoid previously came back to him in a more radical way. In that last life, sharp choices had to be made. No more dodging the cliffs, but making tough choices.

South America

He now lives in South America and is the eighteen-year-old son of a man who is the combination of all the negative aspects that he had in different lives. He finds this man lazy, complacent, an incorrigible alcoholic, violent, arrogant who blames his mother and sisters for everything. He is terribly annoyed by the useless and idle behaviour of his father, who drinks away every small issue with alcohol. He is ashamed of his father, sitting there in a chair on the porch.

His mother, brothers and sisters work hard to create the best possible life. He clearly sees that his father does not want to take any responsibility in his life. It is his innermost conviction he does not want to become a victim of his father's behaviour and does his level best to change the situation. Sometimes he mediates in the quarrels and fights and tries to keep his father from mistreating his mother and sisters. He is one of the 12 kids in the family. He loves his mother, but finds it extremely stupid that she refuses contraception, or considers sterilisation offered by certain Western organisations in their country. His sisters did choose that option.

He encourages his younger brothers to study, to achieve something that allows for a better life. He continues to tell his sisters that they should finish school and to seriously consider some sort of education on offer. He is gradually becoming an expert when it comes to exploiting the opportunities offered by certain organisations.

Not only does he encourage his brothers and sisters to take their fate into their own hands, but also many others around him. His father made his oldest sister pregnant and he threw her out in a highly pregnant condition. He also helps her. She now works for one of the regional aid organisations. As his life progresses, he becomes more and more creative in solving the problems that come his way and slowly returns to the man he once was, many lives ago. Unconsciously, this awareness resides in him, propelling him into the completion of his karmic aspects and life lessons. After school, he works part-time for one of the aid organisations. In his family, he is surrounded by souls that he treated so badly in his earlier lives.

His dearest wish is to do social work. The Western aid organisation pays part of his study fees and those of his brothers and sisters. The extra needed they earn themselves. He suggested they do not give their earned money to their father, who would immediately spend it in the pub. His twenty-one year old sister, who left home, will manage the finances in a joint account in close consultation with the children. They will be all right!

His focus on balancing old karma is very strong and intense; everything he does is focused on that. He resisted the temptation to take short cuts, which would only have led him further away from his life's goal. This road fits him like a glove.

When he approaches the age in his life as Robert at which he killed himself, he will be tested for a short while. Many with his kind of background go through such a short time of reorientation on life. He will not have a problem with that now.

16. Suicide

It remains a taboo

Margaret: My research showed that there are still many taboos surrounding the complex subject of suicide. It is not an issue easily discussed. This inner urge to put an end to life can sometimes become so strong that it is difficult to share it with others.

I visited Urmani, the part in the spheres where people who kill themselves are going. During my first visit I met people there who in the meantime are reincarnated in a body on Earth, like for example Robert who is flourishing in South America in his new life. This time I had a meeting with two people and I saw clearly that suicide does not offer real solutions.

What our Higher Self has to offer in terms of lessons will come to us at some point. Once in the spheres and looking at their own book of life, under loving guidance, people see very clearly the meaning of certain aspects of life, of negative events in previous lives. You are the one who breaks down processes of the soul and not a judgmental god who brings hell and damnation, as many people assume.

I know that counsellors like Thea, who receive this book, often get questions about euthanasia and suicide. So many people today consider ending their lives because they have cancer or some other life-threatening disease. When confronted with such a disease, the first thought sometimes is to put an end to life, in anticipation of the suffering that lies ahead. Yet it is exactly that time of illness that offers people so many opportunities for change. Things that used to be so self-evident are suddenly no more. Other values emerge. It is different for every person, but more often than not contain valuable life lessons.

I have witnessed how precisely these periods of human illness led to major transformations. How great love can blossom between people, how people could experience friendship from the people around them that comes straight from the heart. How unexpected miracles can happen in the field of human connections. How facets in their life that usually remained on the surface, suddenly gained new depth and a totally different meaning. How people in such a period learned lessons, which would otherwise take them four or five lives. How people threw off shackles put on themselves and were able to

"

break through self-made barriers that had kept them locked in specific aspects of their life.

Old negative beliefs can transform by virtue of looking at it differently and new beauty can be discovered and change one's entire appearance. How dark colours and obfuscation in a person's energy field are transformed into beautiful, bright colours by such a transformation. It may be that the material body becomes powerless and that it is perceived that way by people around, but from a different perspective the energy field becomes lighter and lighter. The dying person himself sometimes observes the most beautiful colours, unaware that it is his own, brilliant energy.

A man who knows he has nothing to lose looks at life differently, that is for sure. You can enjoy things that went unnoticed before, all those little details that passed you by in your hectic world.

On an energetic level, I witness the change in people. I saw how dark parts of them transformed and how they enjoyed every particle of light that flowed into their being. People who have experienced a process of euthanasia may relate their story here. They are elated that their story can be heard in this manner. Those left behind on Earth have feelings of guilt and doubt, and that is not necessary at all. Perhaps these stories will help us to gain some insight into what is happening behind the veil of our crude existence.

17. Simon

And the white cockatoo with the cheerful eyes

Margaret: Ever since I stayed in the healing chambers, I had regular visits from a very sweet man. He would come and go. I could see Elize and the man were acquainted. On his first visit, he looked at the alabaster vase with white roses in the corner of the healing chamber. It struck me that he paid unusual attention to that. His hands caressed the beautiful roses thinking he must have loved roses very much. His thoughts did not reach me.

Later, when I left the healing chamber for short periods, we walked through the lavender gardens. I found his presence very enjoyable. He told me that he, together with Elize, would be a guide for me in my new life. He showed me around and took me to beautiful gardens. He showed me a hilly area with many birds. At times, a silent small woman accompanied us. I could see she enjoyed the beauty of the wonderful landscape.

The man was full of love and attention for her, but left her in the desired silence. If he stuck out his arm, a bird appeared out of nowhere. A white cockatoo with cheerful eyes and exuberant feathers on its head. The man called this bird 'his friend'. One spiritual call was enough for the bird to appear. The man loved stroking the animal's feathers. The cockatoo walked over one arm and via his shoulder to the other arm, a kind of game only to fly away again. I enjoyed such moments too and so does the little woman. There was a loving soul connection between her and the man. Later he told me that this little woman had been his mother, Anna, in his last life. Anna had had a hard time in those days, with an alcoholic husband.

Ten years after her death she reincarnated in a warm and loving family. There she healed from the previous life and learned to cast off the armour she had put around her. She had a fulfilling love life in which she managed to balance a lot. Love is always the key word. It was a life for her to heal peacefully. Back in the spiritual world, she ascended in her light. My lovely guide often visits her and takes her to beautiful places. She loves the butterflies and birds. The butterflies are big, bigger than my hand, in dazzling colours, like flying flowers.

My guide took me to concerts and told me that, especially at the beginning of his life in the spiritual world, he derived much pleasure from these concerts. He had died at the end of the eighties and his granddaughter, whom he had only known for a short while, was his guide in that beginning. She took him to all sorts of places, just as if he takes others and me now. His granddaughter was Maria in her life second to last and had studied singing at the conservatory in California. She still sang and she took him to places where you could hear beautiful music. This was all so new to him, he said, because in his last life there was no room for music.

This girl, as a younger version of his own daughter, led him through the wonderful world of music. If she performed, he would listen, as did I. I was like a sponge, soaking up every beauty I found. In my last life, I was very attached to music and so was my dear guide. He took me where I wanted to be the most. Sometimes these were small performances, some large ones. I let all that wonderful beauty flow through me. Colour and music, all of such a different intensity here that it is hard to describe. There are concerts given by the great masters of Earth. Especially in the beginning, I was very grateful for this kind of experience. I witnessed that beauty and let the sounds feed my being. Musicians I only knew from radio or record on Earth played their music here just for me, in this supreme beauty.

No need to buy expensive entrance tickets in advance. I just go there. Listening to music is a great, shared experience, and while listening, something happens to you. The sounds are of indescribable beauty. I get absorbed in the music and am carried away by the purity of the sounds. Words fail me.

My dear guide became a good friend. Once I was used to my new life in the subtle world and consciously started on my book of life, I discovered that it was Thea's father. He had not told me this yet, to give me the opportunity to get used to my new life at my own pace and in my own way. Now I understood why he had lovingly caressed the roses I had received from his daughter.

Later I told him all about our special relationship and our desire to make contact. Of course, he already knew all that, but he enjoyed my stories. He knew about the death guidance and our friendship. He knew about the old soul connections that were there. He also told me about his daughter and the periods when he had been very worried about her, and I understood what he was talking about.

Yes, Thea, I now also know that the lovely creature he had described, the girl who had taken him in and shown him around in his new life, is your Eve of today, your beloved granddaughter. You would boast about her and her brother Vincent, such a beautiful couple of light children. Those are life's riches. I know that you are aware of the soul connections with your family, and the different forms in which you have been together with them before in previous lives, that is great! More and more people are becoming aware of these mutual soul connections, making them more respectful of life, and it will let them see the wonders of reincarnation and the evolution of the soul.

My dear guide and friend, Simon, took me to Earth. He showed me his grandson who was on a special soul mission. I saw a young man walking in the Pyrenees, carrying a heavy backpack. It would be a journey of months and Simon was one of his guides. He showed that the young man drew extra strength from his presence. To travel through nature all by yourself, that requires stamina from a human being.

Simon beamed when watching his grandson and I saw how the young man's aura lit up when that love touched him, giving him the feeling he was not alone. I saw the young man put up his tent and cook his meal. Simon said that two regular guides accompanied the young man, a high level of protection needed for such a hazardous trip and a journey of great spiritual growth.

Simon stayed with him on a regular basis to give him extra spiritual support. Shortly after Simon's transition, he began to guide his grandson, who was ten years old at the time. In Summerland, they are often together. Simon fathered him, you might say, in the absence of a father on Earth. Simon knows that his grandson is aware of his presence and spiritual support.

This meeting in the mountains was very instructive for me, and it touched me to watch the way one can care for each other. Even though such a companion is invisible, it was clear to me that his presence and love was felt. We are never alone; someone always takes care of us, no matter how deeply we have strayed into the physical world. Love and attention always protect us on our path. The deeper people descend into matter, the less susceptible they become to it. The concealment and suppression are like thick curtains that hinder the experience.

Children are very often aware of an invisible presence and more and so are more adults. More angels and guides appear in books and films, and displaying an appetite for things that were buried for so long. There is already a new wave of people awakening who explore this, with every culture its own tradition. Even if the form is always different, the essence is always the same.

Children accept their guardians and angels with an unspoiled openness that the average adult has lost. Children can teach us a lot. The mature approach to the phenomenon of 'angels and guides' in a number of books that are published in this area gives people strength to continue on the chosen path of life.

18. Mary

And the karma of Maldek

Margaret: I was a guest in a group of special people who found each other during work in and around the healing chambers here in the spiritual world. One of them is Mary. She was lying in a healing chamber with greens mixed with a silvery energy. Whenever she felt the need, she had the opportunity to look outside, with a view of soft green hills and beautiful multi-coloured flowers. A nurse brought her roses. Mary needed roses. In her last life in the former Yugoslavia, her garden was full of roses. Serbian soldiers plundered her house and set it on fire.

Mary was completely apathetic when she first arrived. She had died of blood loss. She refused to help the soldiers who ravaged her house and they beat her severely. Mary was a non-Muslim woman; she came from a Christian family. The soldiers preferred non-Muslim women. They took her away. Her imprisonment and forced prostitution lasted seven months. Twice she got pregnant and twice she miscarried. Mary received much love and support from the other women in captivity. Religion and ancestry do not matter anymore when you need each other.

Mary lived constantly in the hope of seeing her family alive again. She did not think of anything else. At the time of her capture, she had only been married for a few months. She had her dreams of a family of her own, together with her husband.

They rebuilt her grandparents' old house in the place she so loved. Her grandmother used to grow roses and had always been her great pride. Mary continued this hobby and made sure it remained a beautiful garden.

The garden returned to its former beauty, after a few years of neglect after grandmother's death. Mary spent entire days in the large garden and enjoyed the place where she lived. She did so until the war also reached them and in a relatively short time, her world had changed completely. Muslim neighbours with whom they had always lived in peace suddenly became their enemies. In the sparsely populated region, people had always helped each other like good neighbours with respect for everyone's individuality in terms of religion and way of life. For Mary, the turnaround came like a bolt of lightning in a clear sky. She was never raised to hate, nor was her husband. At best, it would occur occasionally at school. People lived in harmony for a long time before the war broke out.

The dirty war of hatred was an attack on their society. She witnessed how the Serbian soldiers took her father, husband and brothers away without ever seeing them again in the earthly realm. Only in the spheres of light did they find each other again. Her parents are also a couple that want to be together. Mary visits them regularly.

In Serbian captivity, Elvira, a Muslim woman, became her dearest friend. Elvira witnessed the soldiers shooting her two sons in front of their house. The men in her family were taken away and so were her mother and she. Elvira's mother was convinced that the soldiers would not sexually abuse her because she would be considered old at the age of forty-five. The opposite was true. Women of all ages suffered the same fate.

Mary tried to comfort Elvira. She in turn did the same for Mary when she suffered two miscarriages in captivity. She took care of Maria when she became increasingly apathetic. Mary was young and beautiful, non-Muslim and therefore the soldiers preferred her. They had fun punishing her if she refused. Like a ball, she would be thrown from man to man getting raped at times even in front of everyone else. They were often heavily intoxicated.

Shortly after her second miscarriage, and not yet healed, she suffered a heavy bleeding during one of those soldiers' orgies and died shortly afterwards. She had seen her younger brother and she wanted to go to him. He waited for her on the other side of the veil, together with her grandmother. Mary went to the healing chamber.

All the women found each other in the spheres. The group of fifteen sprouted from their spiritual search for like-minded people. They all had the same background, souls of the same monad, the same spark of God, and had all been members of the Family of Light since the time of Atlantis. Souls who in their incarnation are all committed to bring light into the darkness on earth. The 'work' they do touches parts in those who transformed into light in their own evolution.

All fifteen of them shared their story of their own path through the incarnations, in which they once felt hatred for other races and other forms of religion. The hatred transformed in the three long periods of Atlantis. From that moment on, they belonged to the Family of Light and since have always worked to bring light to the places of darkness. These were often heavy incarnations. They are intensely connected at soul level with the light peoples from higher dimensions, who fulfil a similar function on Earth. These women, varying from man to woman in the various incarnations took their karma with them from Maldek. There they were all once intolerant and loveless towards those who thought differently, and they became persecutors in word and deed.

Through the Law of Karma, the law of cause and effect, they learned their lessons. Each of them had to endure what had been done unto others. It required many lives, incarnation after incarnation. They would leave some of it behind for a heavy period of about seven months in this time. Together with souls in the spheres, they did a great job in this period of great purification to conclude life in the third dimension.

As a man, a long time ago in incarnations as a soldier, Mary plundered, set fire to houses, raped and murdered, just as those men did to her. It was a normal way of life for this soul at the time. So many armies roamed the world and that was the only state of consciousness, sowing death and destruction. Millions were victims of this kind of 'life' and history kept repeating itself. In Earth's history, it could take ages for such an awareness to change. In former Yugoslavia, a concentration of people exists, who, for centuries, cultivated a deep-felt hatred towards each other. Some claim that this battle is as old as 600 years, but it goes back much further.

When a human is taught to hate by his parents, family, teachers and immediate surroundings, and keeps on incarnating in the same environment of hatred, a chain of hatred arises that is difficult to eradicate. A soul is attracted to what it is attuned and where that energy can be spent.

Mary, Elvira and the whole group of fifteen women underwent karma. They consciously chose this place on Earth and that specific energy. In just seven months, the experiences they had chosen passed them by in their awareness of what they had done to others. The entire group had balanced this energy perfectly. The Wheel of Karma had stopped for them, and that is possible only through intense cognizance. None of them on Earth had the ability to attune to hatred, not even at the time of their death. Mary and Elvira were able to exchange their feelings, while the perpetrators were unaware of the suffering they caused.

These fifteen women, members of the Family of Light, have deliberately chosen to experience this suffering now and to work out their karma, because the energy of this moment closely resembles that of their actions on Maldek. The explosive end of that planet prevented them, as a group, to feel the same kind of energy at the place they had chosen themselves.

It takes some getting used to the idea that the soul chooses such experiences, but such a lesson balances a lot of karma. For many, the events at Maldek are coming into balance now, before they stream into the world of light that Earth will become. Whilst in the third dimension souls can consciously clean up their entire incarnation this way.

The group of fifteen women chose to work in the lower astral spheres. This way entire incarnation pasts are cleansed and lessons learned. Quite a few female incarnations in the former Yugoslavia were elected by souls who had acted insensitively in many male incarnations. They had tortured raped, looted, committed arson and killed randomly. They did so in war situations, and their sexism towards women had left deep traces in those souls.

Members of the Family of Light, such as Mary, assist these people to read their books of life, together with the light beings. These days particularly, the whole hierarchy of angels is more active than ever in the spheres and on Earth. The aim is to balance every facet of the third dimension period. Those who are clearly not yet ready to move on to the fifth dimension will reincarnate in a third-dimensional world. There is a place for every soul.

Never before in the history of humanity has there been such an enormous inner urge to cleanse what is unbalanced, and the desire to flow along to the new Earth of Light into the fifth dimension is great and intense. The Holy Scriptures will be fulfilled. Master Jesus - or Sananda, as he makes himself known as well - gives wonderful lessons and instructions through gifted, sensitive people for those who want to hear. Archangel Michael and others from the world of angels bring their messages. Great Masters such as Kumeka, St. Germain, Kuthumi, Kumara, El Morya, Serapis Bey, Hilarion, Mary, Quan Yin, Vywamus, Djwhal Khul, and many others let humanity know through their messages that now is the time for the great change. In waves of consciousness, flowing across the Earth many people sought and found their way to purification.

Teachers of Lord Kumeka, all masters of their trade, have taught me and prepared me for the passing on of this book. Partly Thea and I had those lessons together. Some teachers are specifically concerned with the major cleansing processes of, for example, Yugoslavia and areas such as Rwanda. During my last years on Earth, when all this was going on, I prayed and meditated for the people of Bosnia, feeling pretty powerless but I now realise that I am not the only one praying and meditating for the victims of war and areas of disaster.

On Earth there is a strong inner alertness growing that it enough is enough. Also in the countries concerned. The kettle has reached boiling point and there needs to be a stop to it. With that in mind, many people arrive in the spiritual world. The karmic lessons change the perception strongly; the turning point or saturation point has been reached, also according to those teachers. The consciousness of humanity has reached a critical mass. The cup is empty.

In the Hall of Wisdom, where I received my lessons, I repeatedly heard about the 'land of hatred'. This meant the former Yugoslavia. It is such a devastating feeling when you study (as I did) the execution of so much hatred, concentrated in such a relatively small part of the Earth. The soul groups that live there have been fighting each other since ancient times. That history goes back further than the early days of Atlantis, to Maldek and even before that to Mars. A history of constant combat.

During my life on Earth, I might have put it away as fantasy that soul groups from an earlier evolution incarnated here on Earth. The study of soul groups, the effects of power abuse, war and the consequent destruction of life showed me otherwise. In his last period, Maldek was obsessed with the desire for war and hate was instilled, generation upon generation. Although Maldek has also known beautiful times of peace and harmony, it had become a terrible place to live. Maldek went through processes of extreme negativity and was like a magnet for many from all over the cosmos to work out their vibrations of power there. Maldek finally fell prey to what we call the 'black beam'. Maldek exploded and fragments of the planet were flung into the cosmos.

A collection of souls and soul fragments were taken to Earth to start a new phase in their evolution. Earth was still young then. They went to the bottom of the oceans in spiritual cocoons. Wise beings of Sirius, the dolphins evolved tens of thousands of years further than man, helped these souls to heal from their terrible traumas. The scale of such processes and the insights they provide fascinates me. We have arrived at the end of a long cycle of 26,000 years at the same time the end of an even bigger cycle of several other eras. It is a turning point in time

Earth also has begun cleansing itself on a large scale at the end of this very long period in the third dimension. Thanks to the added eighth ray of Lord Kumeka, it takes place at an accelerated pace. The transition from the Pisces to the Aquarius era is rapidly bringing about a change of consciousness. I can see that very clearly from here.

Ancient Relationships:

Ohan took me to a department of the Hall of Wisdom where people come together to transform very old processes. This 'faculty' are dedicated to certain periods in the ancient history of the Earth, such as the thriving period of Egypt, or of Peru and Mexico. Here one busies oneself with specific periods and the cultures thereof. The study group I attended focussed on the millennia before the Christian era in Egypt. The negative vibrations from those early periods are worked out in a group or individually. Masters from the highest spheres supervise the group processes. Earth submerged in deep darkness and a lot of karma was accumulated. In order to transform and go into the light, people let go, bit by bit, of the old vibrations of the past.

On the one hand, this period brought a lot of pain, while on the other hand extraordinary spiritual growth was achieved. The duality was very strong and the differences were virtually irreconcilable. Time does not exist on this side and therefore does not apply to these issues. When we talk about the purging of 26,000 years of three-dimensional life, it is immaterial which period it concerns. Personally, I have known many lives in Egypt. Some were very constructive and joyful; others meant deep valleys of pain, devoid of love.

Together with Ohan and Leviahnarah, I made my own incarnations from that time visible and healed part by part. Overall, I had few negative experiences, with the exception of a life of oppression in a temple in Karnak. I was forced into activities of the spiritual kind. I had to perform spiritual 'tours de force' that the black priests in that place could not cope with themselves. When my own limits were grossly violated, I refused and I got the death penalty. I became a guide - from the spiritual world - for others who lived in these same situations.

Together with Ohan I made contact with a group of people who are still connected by negative ties. Despite all positive inspiration from the spiritual world, there are souls who cannot let go of these ties indefinitely. They are not prepared to tell their story and still too busy balancing their old vibrations, and even rekindling their old negative vibrations. It is an organic growth. They are busy on Earth with awareness and spiritual growth. We may attend their meeting, without telling personal stories. That is not necessary. Ohan talks about these processes. Most of them are still alive on Earth and the meetings take place at night. Their Higher Self is working very hard on the purification of all fragments. It concerns mainly their 'Egyptian' past.

They are active in areas of 'New Age' in their physical life on Earth but unbeknown to them, they reactivate old vibrations of control and greed. Especially these days groups are formed that concern themselves again with the things that have brought them to a high spiritual level in Egypt bringing about a quick and complete purification. It can also go in the opposite direction and rekindle the negative vibrations that caused heavy karma in those times. They get together with souls from those days during everyday life. One can balance energy with each other in multiple ways.

Ohan told me extensively how this works and showed me the energies that are involved in these short or long encounters. Some meet in the passing on the path of life, others work and live in closer, more sustainable relationships. Within what we call the 'spiritual groups', the fiercest issues are worked out and there is a conscious search for their most recently developed talents from the past lest they be forgotten.

For many people, the structure of the purification process gets increasingly subtle and sophisticated. Veils are thrown off. This is inevitable with the higher energies that flow to the Earth and it started several years ago. By now, the first wave of the children of the new age have reached the age of thirty or forty, sometimes fifty. They are the new adults, who will not be deceived. A very different and shocking picture is revealed.

Some of the older people, who underwent a certain development, are starting to see through the masks. Their guides assist them in how to deal with that in a wholesome way. People may say beautiful things, words that give hope, demonstrating high spiritual insight and could be a demonstration of their life blueprints. In order to express a certain negative aspect someone may develop a lifestyle and behaviour that exudes hope and positivity for the world to see. In this way, a person lives entirely according to his blueprint and the desired experience.

It could also be a disguise and the opposite may be the case, and that discovery can have a shock effect. It can obscure old vibrations like control they had over others, the need to have it their way. It can hide intense jealousy and greed with regard to the spiritual talent of others, or strings of domination they held over souls at earlier stages. These kinds of connections sometimes literally draw all the energy from the other.

Most people do not know this or do not know the phenomenon, and certainly don't expect it from spiritually highly developed fellow human beings. One of the signs could be when an exchange with someone else is extremely exhausting for you. That such an encounter confuses you and makes you doubt whether you are on the right track in your growth process and how you are doing it. That you doubt your good work. That you feel disharmony in any form. This can also occur after a meeting with an entire group whereas a union, a meeting between people, should be nourishing.

There is no reason to steal energy from someone else, or for them to tap into yours. It is better to stay in one's own energy and replenish it through the Original Source. Unfortunately, some are so cut off from the Source that they take necessary energy from others. They attach lines to another human being in order to obtain the energy of the desired frequency at every moment it is required. If we could look in the etheric and observe the energy exchanges between people, we would be shocked by all those connections that exist energetically between people. Sometimes even over the phone, in letters, even via email or whatsapp, a certain energy exchange can take place. Threads can be spun by giving gifts. The greater the sensitivity at that point, the purer the intention, the sooner undesirable connections will belong to the past. Only sincere actions, coming from the heart will bring growth for both parties.

A heartfelt gift will be pleasure to use, or will be a pleasure to look at. A gift given with a second agenda will not miss its influence. Subconsciously, people can suffer from this, but once such a 'gift' is removed that indefinable feeling of disharmony disappears. When a child makes something for you, just for you, you can feel it. It gets a place of honour and each time you look at it you can feel some of the heart-energy that the child has put into it. It makes you happy. However, if someone gives you a gift with an ulterior motive, either to dominate you or control you, to apply energy threads, then that energy is present in the gift. After all, it is all about energy.

Thea: I want to give a very common example of the influence of negativity in material objects. Once a family member promised me an antique closet. Not until years later, the cupboard came into my house. That was a nice moment because it was a beauty. Friends admired the cupboard, opened doors, opened drawers. Everyone agreed, it was a beautiful cupboard. Those same friends came back a year later for my birthday. They walked around the cupboard and again words of admiration.

When my friend helped me set the table, she spontaneously walked to the cupboard in the corner assuming she would find the tableware there. She was stunned, that the cupboard was completely empty except for a few of the children's belongings. Only then did I realize that I did not want to use the cupboard. I did not want to put any of my own things in it. When we talked about the cupboard, I called it 'the box of disputes'. My friends thought that I was referring to an era, some kind of style. I did not give it much thought, not busy with that kind of thing.

However, the cupboard proved to be a wise lesson on my path. I could not really put a finger on it, like with so many things in my clairvoyance, but I did not doubt my 'feeling'. It was part of life then, in many things still so unconscious. It was not until much later that I discovered that ever since it was in the family, it had been cause for much quarrelling.

Margaret: Many people who become more sensitive start cleaning up their house, throwing things away with unpleasant memories. Energetically it gets cleaner and cleaner, not lastly because it is often goes together with a thorough scrubbing. Tidying up the attic is like tidying up your own upstairs room. It is therapeutic to get rid of all those devouring energies in your home and energy field. For as long as we live most of us do the very same thing. Spring-cleaning when it comes to relationships and energy connections with other people is a different matter. Distance is of no importance, as energy cords are not distance-bound. Light exercises have already helped many people to remove old, non-beneficial energy cords, without judgment, with love. They may have served you, no matter how negative such a connection was. It might have made you very strong and you do not need it now. All it needs is to call upon your spiritual helpers, the angels, the masters, and ask them to help you to intentionally break off all non-beneficial energy connections in the here and now.

Diana Cooper described some very simple exercises to disconnect these kinds of unwanted connections in a conscious way. It makes you aware of things, which can make your field of life cleaner and purer and greatly simplifies the task you have set yourself to achieve total purification.

Ohan: 'The group where we were guests receives help from the Angelic sphere. There is help and assistance at every conceivable moment. Unfortunately, they breathe new life into old, very negative energy they generate together. They do this unconsciously and it is obvious why. Within the group, there is spiritual jealousy, envy and greed. These emotions are very old, but are revived in order to achieve purification. That jealousy, greed and envy is not necessarily obvious in the physical realm, but can be disguised nicely. I say this mainly to make people aware of situations like this. A group never comes together without a plan; it is inevitable because coincidence does not exist.

When you recognize a situation like this, you have to stay very close to your feelings. Do not let anyone take you out of your power. This time is mainly to purify old, negative vibrations only to fully recover your own power. That goes for everyone. When we are back in our own power, we can enter the new era with a higher frequency, smoothly. When old, negative vibrations purify, there is room for positive facets of life. More and more people experience this already in the material life and learn to enjoy every moment of wholeness. If you have gone through profoundly bad times, you appreciate the peaks that lie ahead. Happiness can be found in very small things.'

Hate and Love

In this world, hatred will never combat hatred,
Only love;

This is an eternal truth...

Conquer anger with love,
Conquer evil with good.

Conquer the scrooge with generosity,
Conquer the liar with the truth.

Buddha

19. Shadow Spheres

Margaret: My visits to the healing chambers are very instructive, but only when I was ready Jasmine took me to the lower astral spheres. Being there was tough. Especially the first time I was quite upset. I did not have much to do myself, except connect with Jasmine. A cocoon of light protected me.

Jasmine was dressed in a very simple tunic. She did this mainly because the man we wanted to visit hates everything that remotely resembles a 'clergyman' with a passion. Bernard also visited him many times, but did not manage to contact him. Jasmine felt she was getting somewhere with him and paid him as much attention as possible in his consciousness dark with hate.

While we were talking to the poor man, a whole group of souls in that sphere attacked us. Even the man we came for turned against us. In the blink of an eye, a large group of men and women surrounded us. Their faces were so twisted with hatred I will never forget them. They attacked collectively. I had a hard time staying connected to Jasmine. One moment, we were standing there in chaos…. in a flash, we returned to our own sphere. Jasmine took me to Elize, my guide, who reassured me by telling me that I would get used to it. One never does get used to anything so awful.

Thea, I now understand why you told me about these things and asked me, when I was still alive on Earth, if I still held an unresolved hatred or resentment for something or someone. Do you remember how many times we talked about that? It helped me look back into my life and take stock. It is very useful to look at that consciously and to solve those feelings when necessary. We always talked about it in general, without you asking me about details or specific events. You yourself were always very honest about such aspects of your own life, and the vivid experience you carried with you from your life immediately before that. I have always found your openness about these connections to be a good and telling example.

Resentment is insidious and hatred hides. Sometimes they emerge like invisible droplets of negative energy. An insignificant word, unobtrusively woven into a conversation, or even into your thoughts. These droplets become a stream and the tide is unstoppable. Most people are undoubtedly unaware of the miniscule doses of poison they are administered. It is insidious and they would be shocked if they knew.

Thoughts and words are energy, and once you realise that, you can see what even the smallest drop of poison can do. Some thoughts, such as thoughts of hatred, start to live their own life. Then they become elementals. This also applies to compulsive thoughts, circular reasoning that keep coming back stronger and stronger.

After my experience in the sphere of hate, Elize took me to a silver healing chamber. A beautiful, soft silver energy encircled me and went through me. There is no time here, but measured in earthly time I spent an afternoon here. Healed and completely refreshed, I left the healing chamber. I had asked for a visit to the lower astral spheres, because I wanted to gain every conceivable experience for this book and returned later to these places several times under supervision. It is important to mention, because they are also part of the totality. However, things will change here too especially after the major Earth change that is now taking place. After that, everything will be different. The lower two spheres were made redundant a number of years ago.

20. Alcina

The lost light rediscovered

Thea: In this End Time, the end of a series of cosmic cycles, we are balancing our old karma from previous incarnations. We heal old karmic processes. Many are busy doing this very consciously. The following story is one of a karmic experience that brought about a transformation. A long history.

Alcina: 'I want to share some parts of my book of life with Leviahnarah. By telling my story, it can provide insight with the reader. Moreover, many consciously or unconsciously, carry this with them as spiritual luggage. I came to Earth with a large group of souls who had lived on Maldek. I am a light-bearing soul, serving light and human, animal and plant-friendly. My spark of light encapsulated the moment I chose to serve the darkness. A process that grew slowly. Let me start at the beginning.

At some point, an extremely evil Reptilian race attacked Maldek. Beside Earth, they terrorized at least another fifty planets in our part of the universe. Most of those planets are liberated by now. By virtue of the growing awareness of humankind, Earth is busy with its liberation with the help of light forces.

It was a very evil Reptilian race. An egocentric, self-serving, life-extracting breed. Real energy robbers. Even though I never saw them, they dominated all the nations that lived on that planet. A positive human- and animal-friendly civilization slowly turned into a severely hardened society. We were energetically encouraged to create a society without love. From a world where there used to be compassion and empathy, it turned into an unyielding one. Many, out of self-preservation, opted for the prevailing darkness and thus only served those who controlled the planet. Slavery is the best description for this. It may also be comparable to the billions of people on Earth who are stuck in their jobs; who work to serve the relatively small elite. An example is the clothing industry in Asia, or the banking world, the political world, and so on.

A relatively small group on Maldek deliberately chose to serve the darkness. On Earth, you say, 'selling your soul to the devil'. Well, I was one of them. The dark rulers thrived on the low frequencies that people and animals emitted because of their bad circumstances: fear, pain, hunger and hatred.

I became a powerful man in an administrative position there. My power was a real pitfall, because it was extremely addictive. This had an effect on subsequent incarnations and it was extremely difficult to get rid of. In later incarnations, I chose again to sell my soul and to get me out of that darkness became almost humanly impossible. Now properly free, without ties to those who serve the darkness is a precious freedom that I now cherish.

Energetically I stumbled badly on Maldek and later again on Earth. I was totally encapsulated. At some point, people on Maldek began to wake up though. Impulses from the light forces reached those who were ready for them. Since I served the darkness I did everything I could with my team to prevent that from happening. The moment people woke up and realized what kind of prison they were actually living in, without any freedom, they started to move away. Under the guidance of a number of light masters, they were taken through the woods to an extensive cave system with a dematerialisation space that had existed for eons. The rulers would never occupy that area, because it contained a very high light frequency scaring them off. They could not tolerate so much light and love energy.

Many were able to leave the planet in this way, with the help of light beings who provided material and subtle help to those who had fled. It was expected that the increasing darkness would lead to an explosion of the entire planet, which later actually happened. The result was a fragmentation of the soul.

In my position of great power over many people, I have committed huge crimes. Every refugee we could intercept was used as an example, by killing them in front of groups of people causing terror with victim as well as with spectators who were forced to watch. That fear was energy food for the rulers.

This behaviour towards their fellow men was the norm for those who wilfully made the switch from light to darkness. So darkened were they that could not see the light any longer. Veil over veil. I saw in their behaviour how addicted they became to their serving darkness. Every time I intercepted a number of awakened people on their way to the forest, it was euphorically rewarding.

When we read our book of life and look back, I see a psychopathic sadist with a sense of lust in his actions enjoying power. It was very heavy negative burden on my soul. In the end, as more found their way to the caves in the forest, I ended up in a kind of weird insanity. I was under pressure from the rulers. The dehumanisation that I had helped to deliberately create was based on fear, also transmitted to me. After all, no matter how highly I thought of myself, I was a puppet and all I did was carrying out the orders from above.

I have knowingly experienced the destruction of Maldek.

Light is never lost, that is a fact. My soul fragments were taken to a particular area since my being was veiled and my God-awareness severely obscured. A sphere or dimension for exact such darkened souls. To me, an area where only those souls lived who literally had sold their souls to evil. Not a pleasant place. We had a very low frequency without much light. Souls that were spiritually similar in many ways because of their actions. I stayed in that dimension for a long time and regularly experienced what I had done to others. Think of it as a dream state where you have re-occurring nightmares. What I had done to other people in the negative sense kept repeating itself.

A large group of which I was part was taken to the Earths' oceans in cocoons where the dolphins took care of us. They healed our soul, our higher being. I was not aware of this. So little consciousness did souls like us have at the time. Later again we incarnated as people of the Earth and were admitted to the temple schools that the Pleiadians had founded in the early Atlantis period. These wise people from the Pleiades took care of our education and we learned about a loving society, empathy, and care for the planet and everything that lives on it. I did not have any memory of Maldek at the time. This Temple School became my base that brought me much good. A new beginning under optimal conditions.

In the three Atlantic eras, I built up my energy, my frequency, life after life. It was only towards the end of the third period I was tempted again to serve the darkness, which was building up strongly during that period. It may seem unfair, but that way through that temptation, I could try to balance my Maldek crimes. Perhaps I could not remember the events of that time. The universe is just and fair in all respects. Sometimes our spiritual guidance put us to the test: we chose either for our lower lusts or with inner certainty chose to stay in the light.

My talent to work with groups of people came to the notice of those who served the darkness. From their satanic order, they received a lot of secret knowledge, built up one grade after grade and observed my talent. That is how some of the higher grades discovered my crimes on Maldek. The seduction that followed was very subtle and went almost unnoticed. The charisma of those who served the shadow world was (and still is) great. Huge rewards were presented to people like me and promises made. Their proposals with their ego caressing vocabulary began to appeal to me. I attracted it like a magnet. It triggered an old resonation with that shadow world and they knew that!

In the end, I chose to influence large groups of people in an administrative position. Serving darkness as I was, I really had no inkling of my action and the consequences. The power I had been given was once again very addictive. A hard period within a feudal regime helped me to shape it.

It was another trap; my frequency was getting lower and lower. I did not shy away from anything, carried out every order that was given by the High Command, no matter how cruel the task was. I also became very greedy in many ways. A disease that resembled today's Aids was artificially created to eliminate the light-bearing people, the ones who wanted to keep the light alive and all were empathic, loving people. With wars and artificially created diseases, beautiful groups of people and entire nations were exterminated on Earth throughout the ages. The people infected by the virus were evicted from their homes, all their possessions confiscated and violently thrown outside the city gates with all their possessions and goods. Few survived hunger and thirst.

I have experienced the total destruction of Atlantis. Another immense trauma that I had helped to cause. I was drawn back automatically into the lower dimension. No place of light, so much is clear. In this last stage of a cosmic cycle by the way, many people all over the world have incarnated and are currently working out such old karmic, spiritual baggage, precisely from that last period of Atlantis.

In the early Egyptian era, I incarnated as a girl. My parents were the same souls of the Pleiades that once, so long ago, offered the fallen light-bearing souls of Maldek a new beginning in their temple schools. Life after life I lived in which I learned a lot. My dominant traits were occasionally there, but fortunately, they did not take on any negative forms. They taught me how to work on my qualities to work with groups of people in a positive way. Among other things, administrative tasks that I enjoyed carrying out.

In later times, again the elements of the shadow world gained ground systematically and, I went in that direction yet again almost unnoticed. With their immense black occult knowledge, they recognize the weaknesses in people. Mine, too. Now in a male incarnation I was a servant again of what was not of the light. I ended up in a Reptilian temple and became a powerful man again grossly abusing my power.

In a subsequent incarnation, during the beautiful reign of Pharaoh Akhenaton, I belonged to the black priesthood. They were all men of great power. I saw Akhenaton, like so many in Thebes, as a danger to our power and way of life. Do not forget that light can cause pain, a lot of pain even. At one point, I was part of the group that did everything in its power to ridicule Akhenaton, fully convinced that we were doing the right thing. We wanted to frustrate his initiatives to build a large city, El Amarna, with facilities for health care, education, clean and spacious places for everyone to stay who came to live there.

We managed to picture Akhenaton as an insignificant, delusional leader and he was consequently rubbed out of the history books and we killed his son Tutankhamen.

When I look back on my long and turbulent journey through incarnation, I see my veils. I see the dark-infested beliefs that caused us to destroy a beautiful city of light and to cause a great deal of human and animal suffering. However, the light planted there by Akhenaton still exists and I see it gaining ground in the present time.

After having taking that spiritual dip again, I was sucked into incarnations that made clear to me what I had put others through. These often very difficult experiences changed me, but whomever sells his soul connects himself in such a way that it feels as if strings pull at you. You have to get very strong to cut yourself loose.

I finally managed to free myself in lives that passed me by like a rollercoaster. It was incredibly hard work. It took until the twentieth century for me to disengage completely.

I incarnated in ancient Greece, where I lived through beautiful incarnations. A strict upbringing by wise sensitive souls who took in people like me as if we were children. It was in ancient Greece that I thrived and created beautiful, constructive things, alternatively as a man and a woman.

Poverty

In the various lives of experience in Egypt, I had endured poverty. I felt what it was like to work for a pittance or to be fired for the slightest offence, ending up without shelter or income. The poverty I suffered meant that I focused on material possessions in later lives. That is how, in a life as a woman, I developed this great desire for material matter. I married a rich man, manipulated him and got everything I wanted.

In the spheres, after my last incarnation in England, I was in an exchange group. This was my own choice. The communication in the group was very open; we shared what our karmic baggage contained and how we had balanced it. Extremely fascinating and instructive. One of the people in the spheres in that exchange group said that she had once been a very rich and powerful woman who had become rich by the exploitation of others. She treated her workers very badly. Besides corporal punishment, which was all too common, she also sent people away for the slightest misdemeanour. Workers who lived there with their entire family could end up without income or roof over their heads. Her power was immense. She was consciously busy dehumanising people and that had taken on outrageous forms. In this case during the colonial period on Java.

In the group we discussed our old luggage and learned a lot from one another's difficult paths to the light.

It was also in that beautiful place in ancient Greece that I created a new addiction. My husband, a militant high-ranking gentleman, loved big parties. Plenty of food and drink. In the end, this grew into proper bacchanals, with all the trimmings. It was not a sudden addiction; it had built up over time. In that life I often found myself in the company of quite a group of warmongers. Every victory was celebrated exuberantly and without limits. Eating without limits, emptying my stomach in between to then start all over again. I drank so much I was delirious and later on drugs entered the scene.

It was previously mentioned in many books that wandering entities, which had succumbed to their drinking addiction, look for a person with a similar need. These aura lifters find their comfort in their host, who usually starts to drink and eat even more.

No matter how neat and proper our family would seem from the outside, with great power and prestige, during the bacchanals I often lay drunk and comatose on one of the sofas and the same would be the case for the others. I finally died of the consequences of my eating and drinking addiction. I had become so fat I could hardly move.

I took this addiction to the next incarnation as a girl. This was also the case in ancient Greece. I married a governor I had remembered form previous incarnations during both the end times of Atlantis and of Ancient Egypt. We both made a positive start, with in our blueprint the desire to balance old negative energy. The society that was built with so much positivity over many centuries was infiltrated by darkness, like it happened during many eras. Society hardened again and we went along with that. Now, looking back, we went along out of self-preservation, but there is no denying we were attracted to the power we were offered including the countless beautiful promises. We gradually joined a cruel and increasingly hardening society once again.

We again sold our souls and became servants of the spreading darkness. I became a cruel and despised woman. Slaves who took some food from our copious buffets I had beaten without mercy. Few were living in extreme abundance many more were starving at the time. Overindulgence exposed itself again.

I treated the slaves who served us extremely badly, without exception. I had spies who made sure that the slaves did not take any of the food with them. These spies were allowed to take the leftovers from the buffet as a reward and so I divided and ruled.

This old thing had led to my addiction to power on Maldek returned despite my good intentions at the beginning of this life. Opportunities came along to do the right thing but I enjoyed my omnipotence the way people feared me, and so I became a very cruel woman who caused a lot of spiritual and physical misery.

For example, I enjoyed my regular visits to an arena where fights took place with death as the goal. I loved that violence. I continued visiting these kinds of places where the energy of the event satisfied my deepest yearnings. My husband also shared my need to attend these man-to-man combats.

The deep resentment people held for us however led to an assassination attempt after years of extreme rule. We were both poisoned causing a long painful death that was not unusual in those days.

During various incarnations, I had possessed this kind of power and seriously abused it in many instances. I bought staff and slaves and treated them very badly and all this led to difficult lives with karma that had to be balanced.

In the middle Ages, I incarnated in a Hopi community. Also the original inhabitants of America took in souls with a background like mine sometimes. I received an education and training that was very important to me. I have been incarnated with them no less than five times. In certain lives, I learned to steer my then 'innate' leadership in good, positive directions. I also learned to recognize false light and to see it for what it was. It would be of great benefit to me in future lives.

There were also lives of experience as a slave from Gabon to America. As a servant or slave in an old European noble family in Scotland and in England. They were hard lives. Later also a life as a girl who was sold by her father as a slave. A life in which I experienced just about everything I had done to others.

At the beginning of the 19th century, I began to find my long lost light again. In a number of very different lives, I had gotten rid of my addiction to food and drink. I gradually unbound myself from the attraction to the darkness. It had elected to take a bumpy road. I went through a couple of wars and started taking care of people. This was the beginning of a string of nurse's lives in places where human care was urgently needed. Many that I had once treated cruelly, harshly and without empathy in another life crossed my path.

I balanced my energetic baggage in the places where there was a lot of human suffering. Living and working compassionately. A tough lesson was during the American Civil War. I was a black man and astounded at how black people were belittled and considered inferior for so long. I concluded that this divide and rule mentality had caused indescribable suffering. In the period just before that war I was whipped and beaten for the slightest offence. They were sadistic supervisors who took everything out on us

My next life was as a woman in England, where I and many other women and men stood up for the workers in the dirty and sickening factories. Thousands of people were thrown out on the streets without any care or money because they had contracted serious illnesses or suffered injuries. At the expense of hosts of workers, the modern slaves of the time, the small elite became filthy rich.

It took me a long time to see the world for what it truly was. Without all the glamour of the tiny elite, worshipped so much in that country, then but also now. During the Second World War, I worked in hospitals in London. I developed my administrative talents again at a fast pace because the air raids in London caused great chaos. As a head nurse, I organised places where the wounded from the daily bombings could be cared for. I worked in the London Underground, where shelter and care was co-organised by me. I remained calm under these circumstances and oversaw the bigger picture. It was remarkable how some sort of order could be created in the chaos of those days.

The law of attraction meant that many of us did this work together, without ego, and with great compassion. This period was pivotal. I came across many with whom I could balance old negative energy. I eventually died in an air raid.

At the end of the forties of the last century, I incarnated once more, this time as a man in London. This gave me the opportunity to use my managerial qualities again, but now to the full. At a young age, I was committed to making the necessary improvements in London, which had become very impoverished. First in a trade union, later in politics. I have worked with heart and soul to improve the wretched housing, the poverty, bad education and massive unemployment. I worked with a goal-orientated team. Our commitment and our efforts were rewarded with satisfactory results. My drive turned me in to a workaholic and I died of a heart attack at work and went into the light. A life of 52 years of total dedication to balance what needed balancing.

In the spheres I work with people in a group that, like me, once belonged to an elite using extortion. It is hard work. Fortunately, most are beginning to see that it was our choice to live in an energetic captivity so we could fully indulge our lowest desires. The work to get out of the stranglehold of those serving darkness is an often gruelling and long way. The numbers who find their way back to the light are forever growing.'

Art of living

To live is a privilege,
To know how is an art.

Toon Hermans (Dutch comedian and writer)

21. Help

Help from the spiritual world and New Age children

Margaret: We should be rounding off even though there is so much still to talk about. I hope that I was able to give you some insight into the human processes and the cycle of the soul. My intention was to provide insight into this side of existence, in a period of enormous change in the cosmos. A lot will and a lot has changed, albeit not always visible to most people. So many struggle to process the accelerated release of karma bringing them chaos and unrest and for some the fears accumulated over several previous lives come to the surface.

I would like to dwell for a moment on the colossal intervention and help offered to humankind by the many light worlds. Whole legions of light work in the problem areas, and a growing number of people are aware of that help. One only has to ask for it.

Earth is a planet of free will. If you want to take on the role of the victim, you will get to play it. Going on without help is a choice that is always respected. During my journeys through the spheres, I met many people who never asked for any help. It is lectured in many religions that you should never ask. Pray to God or Allah, but never ask for anything for yourself. It is praiseworthy to ask for help, light and love on behalf of others and for their benefit and to be of service with all your heart. I came across so many who are of the belief that one should not ask for anything for oneself, but should only accept the suffering. As if suffering alone brings salvation.

People who understand how it works asked me to clarify this once again. When you wake up, invite an angel on your shoulder and ask him to help you with the things that come your way. Invite this energy, dare to ask for assistance or help when difficult processes lie ahead. Do this every day; make a habit of it. Not for nothing so much was written about help from other dimensions. So long as the light worlds keep stimulating these kinds of messages people will start to use them automatically.

As a human race with a free will, unprecedented opportunities will present themselves; there is no doubt about that. With that same free will dare ask for help from the realms of light and it will be given. During my illness on Earth, I prayed a lot for other people, my heart went out to people who needed help. I was well aware that my meditations and prayers were being heard and

I gained the necessary experiences with that. I never asked for help for myself until, slowly but surely, I learned to do so during the period of death guidance together with Thea. She remarked on that hiatus and encouraged me to ask for help. Her supervisors also passed on things about this to me. A principle is hard to change, not like pressing a button. I learned to do it though.

Sometimes I felt guilty when I asked for help for myself, even though the reservoir of light and love is inexhaustible. Children remember this; they ask for help in the evening before going to bed and address the realms of light. An ever-growing amount of children is born with a high level of mental attunement. They come with very specific love tasks during this special time of transition of the Earth. They surreptitiously make use of their inner knowledge. They see nothing strange in meetings with light apparitions that communicate with them and, if necessary, reassure them. In this way, these children use their communication channels to the spiritual world in a very natural way and find it very natural to see a guide or an angel. One of the reasons that few children will divulge this, taking for granted that everybody is addressed in this way. It belongs to their normal world of experience.

Thea: I was very clairvoyant during my childhood. Especially now that I am older and looking back, I see that even more clearly. I found it very common to see colours around people and animals. I saw it in nature too, and that made it extra nice outside. The beautiful colours around trees and flowers were a fascinating spectacle. I well remember the bike rides with my parents and enjoying nature. Only later did I understand that my parents did not see those same colours. It took quite a long time before I realized that not all children saw what I saw. The fact that my parents could not see it was the first insight I had in this area. I felt somewhat lonely.

In the evening, in my bed, I asked for help just for myself. The light people who appeared to me were familiar to me. I have worked with Leviahnarah for years and he gives me the material of books of life. He was just as familiar to me as my father was, so very ordinary. Leviahnarah only came when I needed it most. His appearance alone was enough to reassure me. Most of the time I saw a friendly woman in light clothing. She spoke to me and told me that not all people could see what I took for granted. Many people would not see that until much later. I know now that she spoke of the present time.

When I was eight years old, I was admitted to hospital for observation. Weeks of tests followed. I always felt pain everywhere and especially the last few weeks my tummy aches got worse. The doctors could not find anything. I was clairsentient, but nobody in our vicinity had any idea what that was, let alone our family doctor. It was 1955 and who was familiar with it at the time?

My mother was terribly upset about it. On birthdays, I embarrassed her. I was often sick from people visiting, feeling their pains and fears. My parents were already in their forties when I arrived so my family consisted of (at least for me) mostly older people. During such visit, nothing but their pains and ailments were the subject of discussion, and the one was worse off than the other was. Nothing else seemed to be worth talking about and I just sat there. If my uncles had had a drink and I sat next to them, I would get such a strange feeling in my body. Not a pleasant place to be for a clairsentient child.

At the hospital, I was next to a girl with a heart condition. I remember the dent in her chest on the left. She told me her heart was on the other side. I do not know if it really was, but she was very sick. She was afraid to die, she told me. Across the hall was a child in great pain. I remember so well, because I felt that pain too. I snuck out of my bed and went to sleep in a big wheelchair in the bathroom. They kept finding me there only to put me back in my bed. When I told them I was not in pain in the bathroom, no one understood of course.

I felt great sorrow. I started to feel all kinds of pain in the hospital that I had not felt at home. I asked for help, and my angel appeared before my mind's eye. The one with what I called the sweet appearance who always came, my guide. I cried and she comforted me. "You feel the pain of other people," she said. I asked for help for the sick girls in the room. The girl next to me, with the heart condition, was so scared. I told her about my angel who always came when I called her.

In the days that followed, I told her a lot, more than I had ever told any other child. She did not laugh at me. With big eyes, she was looking at me. She calmed down. One day her mother told me not to tell her daughter such strange stories anymore. Later the girl told me that her parents thought her illness was a punishment from God. They kept telling her that. She was a little older than I was and believed what her parents had taught her. One night she cried and was very scared. I lay down next to her and asked for help. A lovely creature appeared, consisting of light mostly. Looking back, I know that for a moment I could be an instrument to help transcend a deep fear. The sick girl saw what I saw, lying in my aura. In the days that followed, it was our big secret.

Something had changed and she began to perceive the other world. Whispering I sat next to her bed, I listened to her stories and every now and then, a smile appeared around her serious face. Then, one day, a creature of light appeared in a blue robe near her bed. It was the middle of the day, the girl saw her. She looked at me and she knew I saw it too. Tears flowed down her cheeks, I will never forget that, but she was not scared any longer. She radiated a kind of happiness I had not noticed before. We did not say much more about it, except the exchange of looks of understanding between us from time to time.

The girl died that night. I remember the curtains that went down and the buzz in the night. My guide was there, reassured me and said: "She's going home". I knew she was dying and everything was fine. It all went very fast. For an instance, I saw her, just before they wheeled her out of the hall. She looked peaceful and I shall never forget that image. My guide reappeared later to reassure me and I knew they were not just empty words, like grown-ups when they reassure a child. I felt it really was okay.

Once discharged from the hospital, the severe abdominal pain started again. Shortly afterwards my brother's appendicitis turned into a peritonitis and was rushed to hospital. He was in very bad shape. He must have suffered from his appendix for a long time before it was diagnosed. Two operations followed. I had learned a lesson I would never forget and more than a year later, I decided to lock my inner world.

I had come to understand what was happening to my clairsentience and sight. My uncle, who turned out to have the same 'gift', spoke to me and that helped. I did not want to feel the pain of others around me anymore. I asked for help, and for a long time I was spared those experiences. What has always remained is my discernment of the subtle world, my inner eye. Like a precious treasure, I carried it with me, and I kept quiet about it. Only years later, after the death of my second child, did all of it come back, like an avalanche.

It is wonderful that the children of today, when they bring certain talents into their lives can talk about it. I enjoyed talking to kids about their multi-dimensional observations. How they described their guides and how I could see from their faces during the description that they enjoyed the memory. Stories of children talking telepathically to their guides 'in their heads', just like I always did and still do. What a wealth. It is wonderful to see that people learn to make contact with the unseen world and can draw strength and courage from it. I have also seen people 'see' through the third eye, how it opened up in their meditations. Others developed a deep inner knowing when spiritual help was present. Some have sensations of feeling, for example experiencing heat or a flow of energy through their whole being. I saw how their inner confidence increased, and radiated outwards. They actually felt support after a request for help. We are all given the ability to develop it.

Margaret: The children of the new age will teach us what is so obvious to them. Changes are gradual and we can see in the family lines of these children how the frequency builds up. Parents and grandparents with their own experiences in this field will appreciate the children for who they are. With their own inner knowledge, they will guide these wise souls to their ultimate task. They arrive on Earth with great wisdom and those who appreciate their wisdom can sometimes be very surprised. They do not derive that from books, yet from their pure soul's wisdom.

The schools in the Hall of Wisdom are filled with souls that incarnate in this time of change and chaos. Beautiful beings, with a high frequency of light, wise souls. Their presence on Earth is important. Their 'presence' alone, brings about major changes in the large human collective. Their charisma is uplifting and they radiate love. Therefore, it is important that we protect and guide them in their presence on Earth. They do not need a pedestal, but to be incorporated into everyday life. They do not belong to the elite as they have a function in society. They head the many more beautiful souls to come.

The process has been going on for decades and started as a small stream that will continue to grow and turn into brooks and rivers. Many pioneers ploughed the necessary fertile ground that was required for their talents to take root. People who did not have a particularly easy time of it in their past lives and now often play a (grand)parental role for these children. This process took place in silence and we reap the benefits. It goes with the territory that everything novel is suspiciously checked out by the masses.

Unlike some people may think, these special talents can no longer be ignored. This stream of souls will find its way into a rapidly changing world. Their values and standards are different. They are not, like many people on Earth, bound to and focused on matter. They will work for a more humane life on the planet, for alternative energy sources such as the inexhaustible cosmic energy. Energy that costs little and is harmless for the environment.

There are children born carrying the expertise to generate inexhaustible energy resources. The souls of Nicola Tesla, Lakofski, Rife, teach those who go to Earth to reintroduce what was stopped by the ruling powers. If Nicola Tesla had been able to do what he had come to do in the first half of the twentieth century, there would have been no need for oil now, and cars would run on an inexhaustible source of energy and it would have heated our homes, as it once did in Atlantis.

Medicine would have taken a completely different direction if Rife and Lakofski had been able to find acceptance for their inventions and equipment. Scientists are trying to pick up the thread of their inventions where it was left off to make us independent of the power the oil-producing countries hold. I say this as simply as possible, but a very complex world order is involved.

A lot has to change and that is definitely unstoppable when you see what beautiful spirits have incarnated now and still to come. The old world as it is today cannot be sustained, the silent streams of light souls, the help given by the surrounding light worlds, high-level incarnations, clearly show that what has been sown by thousands of invisible souls, can now take root.

Scientists are busy searching for extra-terrestrial life. They have trouble finding this life because part of it can only be found in higher dimensions. The arrogance of many people that Earthlings are the only intelligent species in the universe is of course ridiculous.

The light worlds closely follow events on Earth. This planet of free will is apparently the only one of its kind. From that area of free will, huge leaps in humankind's growth have emerged, as well as profound, unloving misery. Look around and check out what man has done with his free will. Unfortunately, the negative is considerably more obvious than the positive and the media pay much more attention to it. According to the media, good news is no news. The tabloid press has become a great 'success'.

Those scientists who are so focused on finding intelligent life in the universe would be surprised to see how many thousands of 'extra-terrestrial' souls of light worlds have already been incarnated here. Souls who find it a great honour to help this beautiful planet in its birth process. In fact, this is literally a 'heavy' choice, because they had to descend deeper into matter than they were used to. Especially at this time, when humankind is sinking deeper and deeper into matter. Some of those incarnated are outstanding teachers in every conceivable field of innovation; others 'exist' only in quiet, inconspicuous lives. Together, these noble souls are holding a certain frequency of light, which is necessary to help Mother Earth through her birth. They all carry and maintain a high vibration of love. They spread that vibration, by writing articles and books and in their dealings with people.

Some use their voice that carries that love vibration; others make paintings with that high vibration or are builders or musicians. The wonderful thing about it is that one would never look for that vibration in the unobtrusive places where it is located. In ordinary life in every conceivable form. Simplicity is the hallmark and the living example of the Master who preceded us two thousand years ago in the ascension to a higher vibration of the Earth and humankind.

The children and adults of the new age, whatever their lineage of soul, are all one, just as everything is connected to everything. Souls that went through the Earth evolution connected to souls that come from other galaxies. A star-spirit is also part of All-That-Is. Insights in larger settings, in larger totals, will flow in and more and more people will adopt these visions.

Future visions as outlined in the series 'Star Trek' make people familiar with a larger spectrum of 'existence'. The Earth is already a great cosmic experiment if you look at the many kinds of souls that are gathered here on one planet. People are already struggling with the outer characteristics, and racism on Earth still seems to be growing. However, when you realise that we all come from the same source, the embarrassment makes you blush. Duality will disappear and those first steps have been taken. With the increasing awareness of the bigger entirety coming from one source, man's actions will also change and the 'I' era will submerge into a great 'we' consciousness.

As you grow to a higher consciousness, it will become clearer that the importance of the whole is also in your individual interest. I hope with all my heart that the children of the new age and all those pioneers, who become discouraged at times waiting for the big change, will achieve their high goals. At a later stage, they will familiarise us with life forms other than the earthly ones, like themselves.

I attended a meeting on the silver island, a wonderful place where people discussed things that affect us all. There were a number of blue people present. People like you and I, but of such great inner and outer beauty that my eyes were constantly drawn to them. They have been connected to the evolution of the human races on planet Earth for eons. They are an old and high quality breed from the Andromeda system. Their number on Earth has always been small and of all the souls who incarnated from the stars throughout this period, they were always a minority. They especially brought great love and togetherness, like in tribal life in ancient times. In groups, their life lessons were taught and shared. They represent mainly the female, soft energy. They lived normal lives in an ordinary earthly, material body, and we reap the rewards of their legacy.

I admire souls who dare to choose for an incarnation on such a primitive planet in order to contribute to its evolution. They usually incarnate in a certain lineage, so that their mother and grandmother were of the same soul-decent, or the solitude would have been unbearable.

The Andromedans are like teachers in our midst and I thought it was such luxury to know this. Speaking of help. They often are new-time teachers who relink the lessons of ancient times with the times of today. Much like the high-level being who teaches the Mayans now in an unobtrusive way, living in simplicity. The genuine masters live a life of simplicity and in unity with the All-That-Is. They consciously serve the bigger whole.

So forget about scary creatures that want to take over the Earth. Oh, for sure, cosmic wars were fought out over this planet. There have been periods in history when such external influences have penetrated our atmosphere. The collective consciousness provided the space in their hanker for power, domination and war. That is why it is so important that the human consciousness on Earth changes and allows for other values that serve the greater good and therefore also themselves. It is important that people transcend the ego consciousness and no longer pursue self-interest and personal, material wealth. The course of change cannot be diverted any longer. It may not be very visible on Earth yet, but believe me; we have crossed that Rubicon for quite a while. The old way of thinking keeps rearing its ugly head, but eventually it will disappear and transform through all chaos. No halting it. The New Earth will be reborn into a higher frequency and whoever wishes to do so will flow into it. Those are immense processes, which take place at a higher soul level.

Most people do not know what is playing but huge cleansing is taking place in their earthly lives and if you have eyes, you can see it going on in your vicinity. Let us try to flow along with all those beautiful souls who deliberately incarnated on Earth to make this birth easier for humankind. Let us try to appreciate every small improvement for the better that we notice, even if partly obscured. Support the children who will be true signposts. I think a time will come soon when many people will become aware of these changes, the many small and large miracles that will take place before our eyes.

In the greater realm of events, let us have the courage to ask for help, when we find ourselves in a difficult situation. Invite the sweetest angel to sit on your shoulder in the morning to help you with the small and big challenges that come your way. Connect with the energy that gives us love and warmth, an energy that has compassion for the special time that we, as humanity, go through.

All and everything is connected, be aware of this. That includes the help from the realms of light. We have been trapped in negative patterns for far too long, dictating us what is good what not, what should be and what should not be. Connect with your own power, take control of your own life, take responsibility for it, and join the growing number of people who consciously create their own reality.

22. Tobias and Elah

About cats and vibrations

Margaret: A man and a woman invited me to a sphere just above that of my attunement. Ohan accompanied me and he created a cocoon of light around me that would protect me until I was back in my own sphere. It became a very wonderful experience. I can travel freely through the spheres and to Earth, and the further I rise in my light, the greater the area I can cover. Without help, you can never get to a sphere that is above your own attunement. You could not tolerate that much light without a protective cocoon of light.

We arrived in a wooded area at the edge of a quiet lake. A tall man with half-long, reddish-brown hair was waiting, dressed in a simple, white tunic and next to him was a somewhat smaller woman with very long, blond hair. The two slender appearances presented themselves as Tobias and Elah. We walked to a place that could best be described as a scene straight from a fairy tale. Beautiful in all its simplicity. In the middle of the forest was a 'glass' structure, with the spherical shape of a soap bell. Colour wise it completely blended in with the surrounding nature. On the side, the spherical shape continued in a number of smaller spheres. Elah took me inside and again it was like being in the middle of nature. One of the smaller bells was opaque.

Elah: 'This is my workspace with a holographic screen and where I have access to 'technology' with which to communicate with the light worlds. We are teachers and guides for people on Earth.

We have not been incarnating for a long time and we serve groups of people who are waking up. Tobias works with channels on Earth, transmits messages and lessons related to the change of the Earth and guides people in their search for ascension. He works very closely with the Galactic Federation of Light Worlds. The work is now in full swing.

Many people open themselves up to the incoming light and from a growing inner awareness they work on the dark facets that surface. Every phase is highlighted and where there is light, there can be no darkness. Tobias travels regularly to different places on Earth where he passes his lessons on to channels. He is totally committed to the wonderful work he does. The more people take up his lessons, the more he shines.

I too help people to open up higher senses, such as clairaudience, knowing, feeling and seeing, and help them develop their telepathic abilities. I have known most of my students for a long time along the whole line of incarnations on Earth and they always only have a temporary need for my help. I am well trained in my job and I have been doing this for a long time. Also in what you call 'ancient times'. Moreover, people are less scared of a friendly female voice. As soon as they have thrown off their old covers, the personal guide takes over again. My work is especially enjoyable because people are letting go of their old fears, and become receptive of their higher capacities.

It is a time of great fortune. We live in the quiet place we prefer, surrounded by nature and natural beings. There are many of us and most of us choose a quiet living and working environment. Exchange takes place through the holographic screens and now and then, these spiritual teachers come together. Always nourishing and joyful gatherings. We travel to the various light worlds and light cities and feel connected to everything. Tobias has his own workspace with a holographic screen and means of communication.'

Margaret: We went to the living room and I noticed several chairs each in a different, delicate colour as if made of an illuminating substance. Carefully I sat down in a soft blue one and felt how it took on the shape of my body. This clearly can also be done with thought power. I sat upright, then again stretched, experimenting carefully with the delicate shape. In the end, I used it as an armchair. This kind of 'play' still amuses me and I am like a child in a toyshop. I realized it was like a Barbapappa House and saw the others adapt their seats to the requirement of that moment. It looked as if they had fun watching me explore.

Tobias was talking to Ohan, which gave me the opportunity to take a quiet look around. In the corner was a painting with lots of blue, water, sky and clouds. I found out the 'painting' is alive. White horses on the waves that roll in and out with gently moving clouds above. It is an image of a sea on Earth. It was so rapturous and fascinating that I kept looking at it.

Elah put down a tray with small glasses, filled with a white drink with gold specks. Above the small glasses was a haze of golden energy, miraculous. It was a very pleasant sensation to feel it running through my body after I took a sip. There was a light shape moving gently outside the living room and in a flash the entire front of the room was open and the light moving shape approached

Elah. She looked pleased and two more such light forms joined and I wondered if they were devas. The shape gracefully floated around Elah, stroking her hair. She radiated happiness.

The three light forms took on the shape of a cat. The first became a white cat as big as a panther on Earth. What a beauty, that gorgeous head with amber-coloured eyes and a soft white coat. The hair is softer and longer than that of an 'earthly' domestic cat. The other two took on the shape of a red and a black cat, as big as the white one. They were sitting and lying around Elah and I saw four radiant creatures now.

The chair immediately adapted to their shape after the black cat walked up to Tobias and settled down with him in the chair as big as he was.

Elah: 'These are creatures that have soul parts on Earth as cats. They are the greater being joining all parts, each with its own tasks. The characters of these three creatures are very different. The black one with Tobias is a powerful creature and his soul parts who incarnate on Earth as a cat, are protectors. He is strongly connected to Ahnahtah who incarnated on Earth as Akhenaton. As a panther, he was Akhenaton's personal guard. He often warned of danger. That danger could be the food (poison) or posed by nearby family members who had doubtful intentions. Akhenaton and the panther were very connected beings and could communicate freely with each other. Akhenaton's wife, Nefertiti, was connected to a soul part of the red cat, present in various soul parts as a lioness that did not leave her side.

The white cat has connected many lives on Earth with protection and passing on the love vibration to children. Cats neutralize negative energies and generate the vibration of love. They choose to be and remain 'free'. As cat lovers on Earth know, they like to be independent. If people in the spheres long for their cat or cats, the cats will manifest themselves. However, they will not attach themselves to someone for long in the spheres, as dogs are known to do. More so than on Earth, they will come and go. That is why you will not see cats around people as often as you will dogs in the spheres. To put it simply, their service does not go that far.

For the people living on Earth they have almost everything to offer, but these beautiful creatures find it unnecessary to do the same in the spheres. Beings of the realms of light, they are very much at the service of the evolution of the Earth to the fifth dimension. Their 'being' is considerably larger than the shapes you see now. Tobias and I have always been fond of cats and they represent a lot of love we experienced in our lives on Earth. We love it when they honour us with their presence and consider it as such.'

Margaret: Her hand petted the head of the big white cat, which enjoyed this exchange of love with its eyes almost closed.

Elah: 'Anyone who radiates the intention to meet his cat or cats will see them appear at any given moment. Either as one facet or as the whole being. We know all their parts separately and love the whole. It has everything to do with the consciousness of the person concerned. So they are not always there, but when they are, we have 'quality time' with each other; moments of high frequency.

They come regularly when we put our work down and feel the need to be together. They are not our property. In a number of spheres as well as on Earth, we tend to consider our dog as our property. Here on the other hand, we enjoy our freedom and theirs. They share and generate their love with more people. On Earth, they represent the love energy and are important for people.

Now and in the past century soul parts of a much larger whole, found their way to those who needed healing. To this end, they come to the right people. These animals were persecuted during long periods in history. The dark forces had a certain amount of knowledge about their background but they were blocked from feeling their love at that moment. They saw and knew however that cats generated energies and protected the people of light. Hence, they persecuted these animals for many periods, as they did the people of light. Especially during the Inquisition and the centuries thereafter, but also in the more darkened times in Egypt.

The healing of these parts of the soul takes place amongst people on Earth. Many have been connected for eons to the same group soul of the cat. It is possible that the same parts keep reuniting in incarnations on Earth. In preparing for life on Earth, it is a given you do this together. The same with dogs. Choices for a mate are often made before incarnation.

There are also group souls of the cat who have a task to people in the current context of awakening. They generate certain energies and purify the environment of that person as much as possible. Cats constantly perceive the subtle world, so their experience is much broader than that of most people, as goes for dogs. Very special are the cats that specialize in neutralizing anxiety vibrations in certain places. Their connection to the realms of light enables them to be of great service, even if there are soul groups among them that are more advanced in their evolution than others are, as is the case with humans. Their connection is focused on the love vibration; they never choose or chose for duality, for darkness. They are like the angelic hosts that serve the light in very various ways, in many forms and from many places in the cosmos. It is not surprising that the ancient Egyptians who served the light saw the cat as a sacred animal.'

Margaret: Elah put her seat in a different position, it became wider and on each side of her was such a beautiful cat creature. They enjoyed each other's company.

We took a stroll together to the shore of the forest lake. The cats transformed into a flowing energy form again. They danced around us like white energies that move freely. They touched my heart and I feel great love for these creatures. Ohan laughed aloud at something Tobias told him. Their merriment was contagious.

Elah: 'I wish that people on Earth would give up their very serious view of the spiritual world. There is plenty of laughter here and we love sharing a good joke.

We do not sit on a cloud being 'holy', as many on Earth might think. Holy is a fine word, because it means 'whole', Even though we are not sitting on a cloud playing the harp we are healed.'

Margaret: Tobias and Ohan's laughter and their merry sound were clearly audible, albeit a little further away from us.

Elah: 'Margaret, you know hard work is carried out here in all light spheres as well as in the areas above. Especially now at the end of a 26,000-year cycle and transition from the Earth to the fifth dimension into a new era in a higher vibration and energy. Through channels on Earth, we try to express our humour. Fortunately, more and more people are picking it up. Those who reject contact with other dimensions always find reason to ridicule everything. Many still stick to the old holy books and ruminate every word as if it were the absolute and only truth. They do not hesitate to accept the supernatural inspiration and truth of these ancient writings, but reject the channelled messages from today.

Unfortunately, in a number of places that old setting is resuscitated, for example, the Old Testament, with an avenging and punishing God who predominates without vibration of love. The rise of fundamentalism all over the world, in whatever form of religion, stems from deep fear, from a lack of love. Still, in the name of God, there is persecution and murder. There is so much fear of change.

Within such communities you see very few or no cats! Nor much humour. Think of it as the last convulsions of this last phase of an era. From the light worlds and spheres, we work with great dedication in those areas. Help is offered from all domains of angels, especially for the reception of those who move from these problem areas to the subtle world.'

Margaret: We walked silently to Tobias and Ohan, who sat on a large flat stone in the water. We found a place next to them. I could see how the two of them were clearly having a good time. We sat together silently and enjoyed the beauty of the lake and the surrounding forests. It reminded me strongly of some images of nature in Canada, that kind of unbridled beauty. Everywhere I saw birds and butterflies in countless colours and shapes, some as big as two hands. The butterflies land on your hand or arm if you invite them to do so. This wonderful encounter has awakened deep feelings within me. I can only feel joy when I realize that growing in the light continues. From a particular level it seems to go faster and faster, as if the light multiplies at an increased speed. Much goodness is released and I would like to retain that awareness and cherish it as an inner treasure.

Hold and release

Write down the bad things that were done to you in sand.
Engrave the good that happened to you in marble.

Kahlil Gibran

23. Adrian

Leviahnarah: 'People who are in the final stage of their physical life often see animals. When they do so, it is usually on their sickbed and they are not always taken seriously. It often is attributed to the side effects of the medication. Similar to those with a near-death experience. Both doctors and nurses rarely took it seriously whereas experiences such as these can be so valuable for those who are about to depart from material life. Here is the story of Adrian.'

Adrian: 'Animals surrounded me for my whole life. From my early childhood until late in life. I had several dogs and many cats. They were my mates. When my wife died, my animals were instrumental in my grief process. They knew this very consciously and missed her as much as I did. My two Newfoundlander dogs helped me, not least because I had to walk them every day, which I forced myself to do so. My tendency to shut me off from the outside world was immense. I increasingly turned inwards and started to analyse the life that was behind me. I believe that people in their seventies seem to do this. It is important to scrutinize what you have made of your life.

I found a type of inner peace that was new to me. I could sit for hours with the dogs at the waterside where they could run around and play. The newfound inner peace was a great gift. My wife and I had lived a busy life, running our own company with little time for ourselves. My wife's illness prevented us from enjoying our well-deserved retirement. We had so many plans. On the way home from the beach we, the dogs and I, had a serious car accident. The dogs sadly did not survive the accident and I ended up in hospital with severe physical injuries with multiple bone fractures.

I instinctively knew I would not recover. I accepted it, knowing life would not end after death. The last three days before my transition, I started to see subtle people. Just for a short moment or rather, that is how I perceived it. They were obviously my guides. I had dreams about my wife and our reunion on the other side of the veil.

One day I 'saw' the eldest of my two dogs, subtle but without a doubt it was he. Newfoundlanders are not small dogs, no lapdogs, but on the last day of my life, he was lying next to me. I put my hand on his subtle body and I felt his trusted energy go through me, I felt like carried.

That night I died in my sleep. There was no fear in the days before, just a great desire to go home. I have not consciously experienced my transition and 'woke up' in the healing chamber. In terrestrial time, I spent about five days in a kind of hibernation. When I woke up, I found myself in a spacious silvery room with shreds of pink, shades of delicate opal and blue. Such a great experience is hard to describe. I was on a floating bed that shaped itself to my preferred position.

When I first woke up, I thought about my badly injured body and the car accident, the many broken bones. I realized I was not in hospital anymore. A loving male presence told me that those injuries belonged to my physical body and I had now passed into my subtle body. "Lift your arm," he said. My first reaction was that I could not lift anything because my arms and legs, my pelvis, everything was broken. He asked me to let go of my conventional thinking and to lift my arm. That went without a hitch. I looked at an undamaged body without plaster or bandages.

Next to me sat my wife, my lover. She looked so much younger than her 67 years at her time of passing. She looked like she was in the midst of her life. All traces of her illness were gone. Merely thinking of her brought her back, how fabulous.

When I was able to leave the healing chamber also my father visited me. When I arrived, I had the attunement to the third light sphere and read my book of life with the help of angels and guides. I had a holographic look into my life blueprint with all aspects of that past life. A sweet mother who was caring and made my childhood pleasant. However, she herself always had to be careful not to upset her husband, my father. She always looked after him and me lovingly, though.

Very cautiously, my father made himself known. He had died at an advanced age but now he looked like he did in the pictures of his youth that I knew. We had not been very close, he was a quiet grumpy man, unable to express kindness or make friendly gestures nor show any emotion whatsoever. He quietly came to visit me occasionally and my wife (telepathically) informed me about his way through life. I listened quietly and began to appreciate the life of this much-damaged soul. From the age of five, he was sexually abused for nearly seven years.

His father and grandfather had been members of a secret society, one a lawyer and the other a mayor of a small town. When I heard the story, I understood why he had not been able to show any kindness or emotion. Not so long ago it had passed through the veil and for a long time it was located in a special part of the spheres in a healing chamber. Something had snapped in the little boy abused by his family for years since he was a five-year-old. This was not just about paedophilia but also about black occult rituals.'

Soul Split

Leviahnarah: 'During the abuse, his soul split and the boy would leave his body in order not to have to feel the pain. To make matters worse, his grandfather was also a cruel sadist.

He turned into a very quiet and barely approachable young man. His parents forced him to go to university. He had no choice in the matter. Just like his father and grandfather before him, he had to and would become a lawyer. It was not until college that something started to change for him when he met my mother.

Eventually Adrian left the Netherlands for his maternal grandparents. They had a large farm in the middle of France. During a long vacation, he did not return to college and ended up staying there for a few years learning about farming. By working on the land and caring for the animals, he was able to balance things. He still could not talk about it, though.

In the 1950s, there was no room for discussion about incest or paedophilia, even though people knew it existed. That period in France helped him move on.'

Adrian: 'I was born in the Netherlands where my father was able to work on a farm owned by his mother's family. We lived on a small farm with animals always around. Father kept me far from his wicked family. Although unable to cuddle me, his son, or show any emotion, he taught me the love of nature and animals. At a later stage, we looked at his and my life together. Finally, he managed to talk about it. In the context of the End Times in which we find ourselves, various confrontations were organised. With me, it was merely one man who crossed my path in several past lives. A real service-to-self man, a pure opportunist. He disadvantaged people for his own benefit, but there were also lines of deceit and great lies.

In one of my past lives, he had been my business partner and reduced me to poverty through lies and deceit, even though he was very wealthy. In my life as Adrian, he returned. This time, he helped me to make my company a success. In order for him to balance what was energetically wrong, his efforts were considerable. The imminent end of a 26,000-year cycle, entices us to get rid of our old luggage. We succeeded. Every now and then, we meet up in beautiful areas with places where you can have a good time. We talk about our ego, our selfishness that caused so much harm to people in countless lives. We discuss competition and how that can lead to ugly excesses, like with us.

The Group

My father and I spent a lot of time together. He had joined a group of people who all severely damaged by incest and paedophilia, among other things. I went with him. We now shared things that were unconceivable during our lives on Earth. The exchange was extremely instructive for everyone who attended these meetings. For me, too.

There are many such groups because child abuse has become a true disease on Earth, a real pandemic. This still occurs on a large scale in various religions not geared towards the light, as in all kinds of black orders and secret societies. It was always kept under wraps but it is coming out into the open everywhere in recent years. Nothing will remain hidden due to the incoming light from the Cosmos.

We create our own home in the light spheres. Both my father and I chose a farm. My wife, who had been on the other side of the veil before, showed me this beautiful place when I had left the surgery. She was all-radiant when she told me about the work that could be done here. We work from the spirit here and the farms are small farms, scattered and not the large farms as became increasingly common on Earth.   There I saw my dogs again. Two big dogs came running at me. I held them in my arms and thanked the greater of the two for his guidance during my transition.

My father, who had taught me so much love for animals, showed me different places where dogs lived together. Between the trees, I saw a group of dogs of different sizes and shapes. A striking appearance between them was a huge longhaired dog. He looked a bit like a rugged Irish wolfhound and it was very clear that he was the leader of the pack.

My father told me that there are places like this where animals can be healed. His stories were very interesting but, as with people, not all positive. There are countries where these beautiful animals are eaten and treated very badly before they are eaten. Countries where all animals are treated very badly. Loveless behaviour.

Just as people go to a healing chamber after their transition, so these animals go to a sphere like this, where extremely loving people and angelic creatures take care of them. It has a healing effect for both sides. For the maltreated animal and healing for people who choose to do this work.

Father was in his element showing me the different places. Between groups of trees, I saw a huge transparent ball with dogs in it. Just as relaxed as dogs can be. There was some wandering back and forth, in and out of the sphere. A place like this is similar to the healing chambers for people, just the shape is different. The frequency is also fully adapted to these animals.

My father showed me several such spheres. Each with its own energy, necessary for the soul healing of these animals. One of those spheres, I saw, was made of a golden transparent substance. The dogs in it are not approachable for the people who work in this environment. Only after a period in this loving golden energy can they start a follow-up phase. The suffering inflicted on them by humans was too great. There are fortunately angels, beings of light, who take care of them, not with a human form but like strings of beautiful energy that are around them. They are in good care. Dogs usually flow straight back into the group soul after their transition. Just the severely damaged animal souls go to places like this. There is a multitude of places similar to these where the traumas can be healed.

It was such a gift that my two Newfoundlanders could be in my vicinity. They in turn work together with the people who heal damaged animals. Some damaged animals flow back to the group soul after their full recovery, others long for loving human presence. People like us do the preliminary work. There are also veterinarians with a great deal of knowledge of the soul essence, doctors who opted for this work after their transition. With a lot of patience, we see big positive changes of these once so damaged animals.

There are people who long for an animal in the healing rooms and beyond reminiscent of the loving connections they experienced during their lives. There are specialists here to ensure that such wishes are fulfilled. Animal and human are energetically attuned and together they find their path to healing. The vibrations and the love that flows to each other are always healing. After that they take their dog to the next dimensions in their ascent to more light.

There was a man here who arrived in the spheres badly damaged by the war. He had spent a long period in the butterfly garden and following that, he had little or no need for human companionship. We saw him with his three mates, huge wolfhounds. After his healing, he joined the group and is now cooperating. The dogs chose his company voluntarily and go about their own way.

The animals help this man to leave behind several incarnation experiences of wars and he helps the animals. He usually works alone and knows how to make contact with animals that are difficult to approach. Eventually we see him playing with these animals in one of the large meadows between the trees. They need to learn to play with each other, the man and the animals, sometimes with three dogs at a time. His own three dogs assist him in his work with animals that are problematic.

Horses

The man went on to tell us he had worked with horses in several wars. His deepest traumas come from watching the suffering of these animals in several wars.

From a long line of incarnations, he repeatedly ended up in wars often through family lines in following military traditions, as was so often the case in those ancient times. Still a choice, even if under pressure. Horses on the other hand had no choice in the matter. The emotion of these experiences with beloved animals had not completely healed. Wherever possible he used his weapon to put an end to unbearable suffering on the battlefield, except when he himself was mortally wounded. His last war was in Afghanistan.

There are people and angels in another dimension who work with these damaged animals. Now that his own process was flowing systematically towards more healing, his great wish was to work with horses as well.'

Leviahnarah: 'The souls of horses go to a higher dimension. At those various levels, all horse souls heal. The heavily traumatized animal souls go to a separate area. As described in the section about the dogs and their spheres, the spheres for the horses are similar. They are fields of light covering a special area in which they reside temporarily. The colours and vibrations are tuned in to the damage done to the animals living there. The horses that served in wars often faced great pain and fear at the front, enduring both their own fears as those of the other animals and people around them. They went to this special dimension with dedicated vibrations for such a trauma.

They were like tidal waves of fear in which they ended up during those wars. These were useful and much needed for those for whom fear was energetic nutrition. Horses nowadays are no longer required to take part in wars, but there is a lot left to be desired worldwide in the unloving way people treat their animals. These highly sensitive beings feel the pain and stress of the people who work with them. The need to go for a ride when they feel very stressed so they can relax is not always good for the animal.'

Slaughterhouses

Adrian: 'To get to know so many beautiful things with my father and because we had worked with animals all our lives, we gained insights into the care and healing of animal souls. There are dimensions where the animal souls go. For example, there are areas where chickens go, whole collectives of animals that died in an extremely stressful way. The mass slaughterhouses cause major damage too. The fear and stress of these animals, including pigs and cows, is in the meat that people eat. These frequencies of anxiety are not healthy for those who eat it. Entire animal collectives are hurt and are healed in groups. There will come a time when people will transcend the barbarism of the mass slaughterhouses. Ever more people no longer tolerate this form of food, physically nor energetically.

Recently Henrike arrived in the spheres, someone who adopted and cared for animals on Earth. She concerned herself mainly with cats and dogs. When she came out of the healing chamber, a whole group of cats welcomed her, she told us. Her guides led her to a large garden near the healing chambers, where a number of cats welcomed her. She had devoted herself with heart and soul to these cats, finding a loving new home for them. In our telepathic transmission, she showed me what that meeting was like. She was sitting there in a field surrounded by a number of cats. It was a wonderful thank you.

She now works with us with dogs. It is amazing to see how she makes contact with them. For some time now, she has had her own animal company, two longhaired dachshunds. Where you see her, you see the two dogs. It is beautiful to watch. Light-footed, with the appearance of a very young woman, she strides through this area and a pleasure for everyone to meet her.

Many people are worried about their dear animal friends after they die. Just like people who pass, each one of these beautiful light souls is taken care of.'

Leviahnarah: 'Both dogs and cats can return along incarnation lines. There are sensitive people who feel that a familiar animal has returned to them. Thea, for example, is aware that a line of cats returned to her life, repeatedly. That reunion is beautiful. It is wonderful that these light forces can be with people, often with a protective function. In this End Time, many millions of (domestic) animals support humanity and the planet in its ascension.'

Goodness

We are not loved because we are good.
We are good because we are loved.

I believe that goodness is the basic condition
And badness is the deviation.

We are made for joy and goodness.

Desmond Tutu

24. Leviahnarah

Leviahnarah about the spheres

Leviahnarah: 'It is impossible to give a complete picture of the spheres in this book. The spheres form an area many times larger than the Earth, and who manages to describe the Earth in the scope of one book? I can only describe some parts of such a place. Luckily, there have been many people who, from an inner source, have described the spheres in detail. Nevertheless, for the sake of clarity and a better understanding of the situational sketches, I would like to give a little insight into the different layers and levels of the spheres.

It is assumed that there are seven lower astral spheres and seven higher light spheres. Between each sphere, there are transitional areas. Between the seven layers, there are three twilight spheres, each with its own transition areas to the next sphere. Much has changed in the last decades of the twentieth century. There are accelerations taking place, entirely in the spirit of the great change.

The Earth is flowing to a higher dimension and for some the dimensions have already intertwined. They can perceive other levels and are therefore ahead of the masses. They syphon their knowledge into everyday life and it thus flows into the light network of people. People's accelerated awareness is causing change everywhere. Not always visible, but it is there.

Much also changes in the spheres. In the context of the great purification on Earth during this transitional period, the souls that lived in the lowest layer of the dark spheres incarnated on Earth under the guidance of the light worlds. Those souls had sometimes been stuck there for eons and ended up in this place and the result of the choices they made during their lives. As part of Thea's awareness and education, I took her to all spheres years ago like to the lower, dark sphere.

I encapsulated her in a light cocoon; otherwise you cannot be there. Such a visit makes a deep impression on a human being, the sight of which can never be forgotten. It was an impenetrable darkness where souls remained in a state of total unawareness of the light. This sphere is now resolved. In the 1990s, this was completed. For the souls who stayed there, there were two options: reincarnate on Earth or proceed to a galactic recovery facility. The realms of light completed these works. No soul is ever lost. The souls who incarnated on

Earth ended up in places where they could undergo rapid learning processes. This group of souls made progress towards the light. Some of them did so relatively quickly during a period on Earth that was optimally suited for that purpose.

Every astral sphere above the seventh layer is a bit lighter, but there is still darkness. Now, in the new millennium, we see that the sixth lower sphere is also dissolving. Parts of that sixth astral layer are already gone, no longer necessary.

There are souls who opt for a galactic healing facility when, after their incarnation from the seventh layer, they return to the spiritual world. Many have gone through a life of purification, assisted by the beings from the realms of light. These can be angelic beings, or souls that once lived on Earth and could grow to a higher state of being through their own incarnation path on Earth and do not have to incarnate anymore. These masters are a great help on the path of those souls who incarnate from the dark spheres on Earth. They usually know from their own experience what a person can go through. When people on Earth, within certain religions, talk about 'damned souls', they do so out of ignorance. No soul that is originally a spark of the Great Light is ever lost. However, the path can be longer and more difficult for some than for others and this has everything to do with the free choices a person makes on Earth during his journey along the golden thread of incarnations, but this has nothing to do with 'damnation'.

The major shifts that take place now are possible partly by virtue of the transitional laws. One of the most important aspects of these changed laws is that every soul that arrives in the spiritual world is obliged to read his or her book of life. Before that, there was a choice not to do so. Because of the free will on this planet, it could therefore happen that those who refused to look back on their past lives, piled up karma on karma in their consecutive lives. Refusing to look at yourself and your actions is a certain state of consciousness. That is how many people built immense dams in the stream of their lives, until the flow obstructed.

These new laws were introduced in the late 1980s and early 1990s and from then on, every human being has to read his book of life. We do not mean watching the 'movie' that every soul sees at his transition, but rather making a conscious study of the book of life and watch what was and what it had come to. To consider the cause and effect of one's own life stream. Without judging.

We have to keep coming back to the words 'See what is, without judgment'. In this 'evaluation', every human being gets the best possible help, no matter what the past may look like. We see countless people cautiously acquainting themselves with the laws of cause and effect. We see how they begin to understand it when they watch events of their lives pass them by in great clarity on holographic screens in the spheres. Since this process also occurs in groups, the masses are beginning to gain insight into how things could have happened in their lives the way they did. The working in groups in the spheres is precisely what is productive. Together they observe how that wheel of karma kept continuously spinning. Old convictions and negative ideas kept winning from the positive impulses given throughout time. It is a moment in time to abandon old dogmas. This happens on Earth, but also in the spheres, exactly because one reads the collective books of life and examines them together.

The world shows us how difficult it is to let go of old dogmas. The time in which we find ourselves today will energetically encourage us to consider, release and transform old beliefs that no longer serve humankind and do not provide food for the growth and awareness of humankind. Notwithstanding today's impulses given these days by the spheres to let go of old dogmas, large numbers will resist the energy that comes to Earth. They will stubbornly hold on to old habits, forcefully breathe new life into them. They will fight the new by condemning it ferociously if need be, as they did for many incarnations.

This reactionary power can become very strong and make many people doubt the innovative path they have taken. This movement will reach a critical point to follow the new stream into which humanity is directed. For the sake of clarity, even people living on Earth in a material body read their books of life when they are out of their bodies at night. Everyone, both upstairs and downstairs, is doing the same great job of purification. Every human being on Earth.

This happens under the inspiring guidance and light of Lord Kumeka, Chohan of the eighth ray of purification. This brings about the waves of consciousness going over the Earth that have great influence on social life. Look at the presidential elections in the United States since 2000. An immense process of accelerated awareness took place. These waves are swelling and continue to flood the globe. It is not always obvious; a lot happens at a level that is not directly visible to the masses. The discerning spectator however notices the changes. Changes will manifest themselves quicker now that every human being has begun reading his or her own book of life. They are beginning to identify the results of (free) choices they made in their life field and around it. They are shocked when they realise, that for centuries, they had actually been part of a group and dragged along in the group spirit.

People will make conscious choices, making themselves heard and not necessarily according to the groups' expectations. This also applies to those who have always remained neutral, life after life piggy riding on what other people started. They turned right when the majority turned right and vice versa. Neither personal opinion nor a clear sense of choice. That will clearly change. During these huge processes, the angelic worlds offer a lot of help. Overwhelming feelings of guilt will be part of the process, when they look back on many of the lives they handled in a particular way, or not handled at all, looking away. Lives lived on the side-line, watching things happen.

Without that intense help from above, the Earth would be flooded by waves of guilt and that could well be contagious. During the night, we work hard to transform those released feelings of guilt that are the result either of an awareness or as a result of what happened during those lives. In groups particularly, it often solved problems and brought light.

The lower spheres could as such be emptied in the last decades of the twentieth century. Souls with karma so heavy that they remained in a self-created darkness and The Councils of Karma, with all the assistance of the light worlds, helped to guide their processes. To assist these souls on their way back to their light, people incarnated on Earth from higher light regions. These are acts of love, for it is certainly not easy to assist souls who incarnated with the attunement to the lowest spheres. This could have been anywhere on Earth, but it is not fitting to mention areas where these souls lived in high concentrations. The very lowest sphere became obsolete by these acts of love and it is fortuitous that all those light beings who dedicated themselves to this, have seen clear results of their work.

The 'sphere of hate' has long been a popular hiding place for many, and every assistance imaginable was devoted to this sphere as well. Floods of souls who were stuck in that atmosphere for a long time were fully committed to reach those people with every fibre of their being. They were experts who knew how difficult it is to get rid of feelings of hatred. They were ideally suited to help transform old rigid convictions.

The same applies to the huge amount of people on Earth that were in the grip of some kind of addiction of literally any form imaginable for a long time. Drink, sex, drugs, medicine, compulsive behaviour, power, money, you name it. With addiction, we mean 'not being able to do without', a total dependency and repetitive in different consecutive incarnations. We do not mean enjoying a glass of wine with a meal or with friends, or using stimulants without being mentally and physically dependent on them.

Quite honestly, many are instrumental in this change but unaware of it. As part of everyday life, the change may not be spectacular, is simply taking place in the family and friends' circle or in the professional sphere. Here too we see how many people, from the spheres as well as on Earth, are trying to help each other. Experts assisted by the angelic worlds and the light beings, do a lot of work. Some people are waiting for a real 'task' within that great turning point, but we are all busy with it at present. There are already so many invisible processes in motion. Hats off to all those silent workers who, in their existence and on their path, make choices with their hearts and to the best of their ability. Head and heart together are capable of achieving beautiful things.

Let us go back to the seven lower astral spheres, where the lowest is completely discontinued and those directly above are now in the process of being discontinued. On the subject of the lower astral spheres, without light, love, and encapsulated in more dark layers, I would like to make a comment. The insistence of some people to make contact with the Beyond through occult games; they do not always attract entities of light. It is not surprising that man was urged by various religions to leave the dead alone. Due to ignorance, insufficient knowledge and insight into the different spheres, there was always the danger of attracting entities from the lower astral spheres. Depending on the attunement and intention of the contact seeker, this could lead to dramatic occurrences.

Why do people do these things? They might have unconsciously drawn in entities from the lower realms, sometimes with disastrous consequences, by 'spinning a glass' or playing with an Ouija board. From aura lifters to a complete possession by an entity that gratefully nestles itself in the host's life field. Children of these players have often been the victims of this. These age-old warnings contain a deep foundation of truth the origins of which date back to a time when there was a much greater knowledge of the spheres. We, in the spiritual world, have always been grateful for the warnings of well-known people, like Jomanda – a famous Dutch medium in the eighties and nineties - who, in television and radio programmes, attracted the attention of viewers and listeners and pointed out the dangers of 'turning a glass' or playing with the Ouija board. It is playing with forces you do not know. Mediums in other countries gave similar warnings.

These messages seem to have hit home, because the number of people engaged in this kind of activity, like a true addiction for some, has since decreased.

Each subsequent sphere or intermediate sphere contains a higher frequency of light. Every soul that ascends in the light, in its light, can handle more and more. Much good trapped for too long is released collectively. That positive energy can multiply rapidly. Light can multiply fast and turn into waves of light. It can also lead to an increase in polarity. The distance between those who anxiously cling to old dogmas and those that are ready to let go and purify. It takes trust to follow your heart in a world that makes it feel like the downright opposite.

Heed impulses that come to mind, very short and concentrated, exactly as they present themselves. How they manifest themselves, as feelings or thoughts, dreams or visions, is immaterial. It will help you later to interpret these telegrams of light. They can be valuable signposts on your way. Trust is a very important in this. To rely on intuition is for many people like dancing on a tight rope. When you dare to listen to your feelings more, you develop confidence and start to see the wholeness that lies behind this process. That way you will be more confident to rely on your own wisdom. It makes the path you have to go easier. Asking for help from the spiritual world is one of the things that are important. Ask and you will receive. Put a sweet angel on your shoulder every day, and know that you do not have travel the road alone.

All over the world, children that are born are familiar with the different dimensions. There is now a future for such children, because a number of pioneers have quietly prepared the Earth for this. The world was not ready yet, but they ploughed the fields for the innovations of our time. This allows the seeds sown to germinate. Many are the pioneers in the here and now who wait for their task on Earth to be revealed. In their meditations and prayers, they asked the question: "When will my task become clear within the great plan of change of the Earth?" When that sign finally comes is something many brood over.

The answer is simple: They are already busy doing what they came for. Be your own 'light' there where life brings you and deal with the tasks. To be. For those pioneers in this period in time, this becomes more obvious. They discover it in their meditations and prayers. Everyone contributes and that it does not always have to be spectacular or visible on the outside becomes more and more evident to them. Many silent masters on Earth have carried this process together for some time all over the world as simple and inconspicuous people. Now the Earth is ripe for change, and it will gradually go through its birth process.

The children who incarnate from higher light areas do so out of love for Mother Earth and humankind, a selfless act that is (almost) incomprehensible on Earth. These children of the new age are in danger of being placed on a pedestal by well-meaning people. That is the last thing they aspire. Their wisdom is great. It is also true that the average school system on Earth no longer functions for these children. To the conscious mind, this also is a sign that human systems, as we know them, are no longer functional, cumbersome and ineffective and past their expiry date. This applies to education in general, but also to other sectors of society: health care, the legal system, administrative structures, etc.

People have incarnated and will go on doing so during this era, capable of bringing about positive changes. These incarnating souls of light carry a great 'we' consciousness with them. They are aware of the responsibility for the whole and they communicate this, already as a child. They transcended their ego and have all come a long way through many incarnations to get this far. Most were teachers in the higher spheres of light where they taught people the love for life and creation and how to care for each other. Fears that cause so much misery on Earth do not rule these souls. Fears that you come short, fear someone else will get a better job than you, fear of death, and all those negative aspects that are the most important motives for many people. They started with a few drops after the Second World War, slowly turning into a wave of souls who contribute to the growing light in this time. They do their work unobtrusively, governed by the quiet and the inner peace within them. They live their light and anchored deeply in Mother Earth. They form a human network all over the world in which they feed each other and their environment.

These pioneers of the first hour and the new children carry each other. From our spiritual world, we enjoy the beautiful spectacle that the growth of this human light network offers us.'

What is Time...

In the spiritual world, there is no time concept
Like past, present and future,
Because they contradict each other at the moment of the present,
The moment that life really lives.

Past and future go hand in hand with the present moment of light
And this right now moment,
With everything it contains,
Is not something to ponder over,
...because that too goes on.

Daisetz T. Suzuki

25. The white-golden mains

By Lord Kumeka

Kumeka: 'Since June of the year 2000, the white golden network around the Earth was completed. This protection was achieved thanks to the work of numerous human light workers on Earth. They have formed the pillars of light that are now deeply rooted in Mother Earth and it would not have been possible without all their effort.

The eighth ray of purification can therefore do its healing work and help people on Earth to put an end to duality and separation. The energy of this white-golden netting, also the colour of the eighth ray, enables people on Earth to make their processes run more smoothly.

'Good', positive energy will not go lost any longer and all shall be balanced. The positive energy between the Earth and this net will remain powerful and external forces can no longer use their influence. The network is also a permanent source to tap into. It consists of higher light frequencies and is tuned to and co-designed by the light workers on Earth who have made its anchoring possible. They laid the foundations to hold this structure of the spiritual world.

This source of white-golden energy will be the marker to aim for in the coming period. Many were unable to balance the opposite energies of their own accord and waited for this opportunity. Because of the now anchored energy, everyone who chooses to go up to higher frequencies will know how to behave without the fear of relapsing. Cleansing and transforming will now be possible, and for many a period of renewal will begin at a faster pace than is thought possible.

Through this white-golden network, spiritual development can be nourished directly and dissemination can take place directly and effectively. Wait and see how many will unexpectedly open their hearts. The descent of the light of Christ can now take place with unprecedented openings to light and love for all those who are ready to open their hearts.'

26. Joanne

Friends on both sides of the veil

Thea: My friend Joanne Klink died shortly after a big party she organized for her 90th birthday. We worked together for a long time in this life. We used to joke about contact after passing. A while after her transition I wondered if I would hear from her, to find out how she was…

Joanne: 'Hello dear Thea, it is wonderful to make contact with you in this way. It was a big wish. This has to do with the clans of souls, their frequency and the message and communication.'

Thea: I want to ask you a thousand things.

Joanne: 'I understand that. Leviahnarah filled you in briefly about my path after my transition.'

Thea: I knew you were fine after your transition. It was all in readiness and your path was set out. At your party at the castle, you had the look of a radiant young woman lying in that big bed. Quite a few people noticed it. We felt like you were close to departure.

Joanne: 'Yes, it was over and it felt that way to me. It was so good to see all those people, dear friends and acquaintances. The harmony was great and very pure. There was no struggle but surrender to a new beginning. I could not have imagined a couple of years ago that I would feel ready to start the journey to the other side in complete capitulation and acceptance.

My mother and my sister had been with me for a couple of days. Upon seeing them they made me think of your words. I had a near-death-experience at the hospital, like a gift. I believe that many dying people receive such a gift so that they can surrender to the transition wholeheartedly. It is as a pregnancy and birth, as you so often told me; surrender to the waves of contractions. Become the wave.

I experienced my transition as if I was the wave. My mother and my sister were my midwives. They look so much younger than when they left the mortal life, around thirty-five to forty-five.'

Thea: This is what you look like now, around forty with soft half-long light brown hair.

Joanne: 'Yeah, so you have to see that through Leviahnarah. I can tell you that a human being suffers a lot from years of fear of death. I had fearful images, at times complete scenarios. No need for that at all. So many angelic creatures and companions who take you to your next destination. To the healing chambers. There are many of them and they are very diverse.

During my last year on Earth, I read my life blueprint during the dreamtime when I was outside my body. Many now choose to do so, which greatly shortens the period in the healing chamber. Insights in all gradations of 'being' come past, you process it in your last life phase. The help here is overwhelming. When we encounter our own deep negative actions and we read the book of life, no one is judging. The guides and angels never judge but help you to see what was and how to deal with it.

I have 'seen', 'read' my book of life of all Earth-lived lives, thus experienced, and felt it. If you hurt someone, you will go through the same thing! You yearn for restoration, to balance the energy. Reading the book of life is a wonderful process. You see your negative actions and when you actually execute your intentions to balance energy, you see the positive effect, how the good deeds multiply. To observe how goodness is rewarded in all its facets. Occasionally, when you want to balance things, goodness becomes boundless and naïve and people go overboard and trample you. How many times did you warn me that this could happen? I have seen it with my own eyes now.'

Thea: I knew no boundaries in the dedication to my work. You often notice it with others before you notice you do the same thing.

Joanne: 'It is extremely interesting and instructive to read all the lives lived on Earth over the past 26,000 years in the book of life. The missing pieces are suddenly all there and the beautiful puzzle falls into place. Now I understand my feelings and inner attitude towards my mother in my last life.

We had to balance things together and that was a difficult process. We did our best, more than that we could not do. On many levels, an understanding arose and the wholeness of the whole was beautiful to see. I learned a lot in my last incarnation. I am still working on it a lot.

After my material transition, I arrived in the third light sphere and went to the healing chamber. I did not consciously experience the transition itself, which was good. I woke up to a soft silver-pink energy, lying on a bed.'

Thea: Without legs, it floats...

Joanne: 'Yes, without legs. It was a very pleasant environment. I saw several large vases against the 'wall', with roses, many roses, including a bouquet of garden roses from you. Spiritual flowers, beautiful. You visualized the roses that grew so abundantly in my garden. How wonderful to wake up in your next life, realizing that you have known dear sweet people who greet you with flowers. It is such a beautiful recognition by those who know that life continues after the material transition.

After a week, earthly time, I left the surgery with my mother and sister. I did not meet my father, he reincarnated years ago. We walked through the rose and lavender gardens. I could get used to my new life. I looked at my arms and legs a hundred times, away wrinkles, away spots, flexible and young. Gone was all the pain and discomfort. It literally felt as if I had taken off my ninety-year-old coat. Later, when I 'read' my book of life, I thanked that old body with which I had worked out and transformed very old matter.

At some stage, we saw a woman come out of the healing chamber, together with two supervisors. She looked around the wide glassy hall in front of it. At first, she walked down a path slowly in between the lavender to a slightly undulating open field. With her arms high up in the air, she strolled into the field, looked around and started running. Like a young foal in a meadow, she ran around. Her companions smiled as they watched her. Later I became friends with her. We walked together through the gardens and beyond and told each other about our life on Earth. She had died of A.L.S. and became more and immobile ending up totally paralysed. Her inner self was rich and got richer. A very tough road. I have always been interested in reincarnation and the how and why of things.

The period in the healing chamber and the gardens have been very educational so that people interested can read it. Especially to take away fear. We share the same passion.'

Thea: Your wish was to write another book when that was no longer possible at all. Now that could be your story from beyond the veil. It feels good and nice to hear your voice. I enjoy working with you.

Joanne: 'You must let the feeling of our first contact sink in first then give it a place in peace and quiet. Writing in your own courtyard with vegetables and flowers is a new experience for me. Its energy is a delight to the eye. The devas and angels look after this place. When you listen to the blackbird with your eyes closed, I see energy light up around the heart. When the cats come by and you stroke them, the same thing happens. Light lines and small light explosions, puff, puff. Here I understand with every part of me what nature means to man. The love for animals and plants is a wonderful energy. The black cat looks at you radiantly.'

Thea: Last year, when I spent five weeks in the south of France finishing my book, this cat was angry and indignant. Upon my return, he sat with his back to me for a week. We eventually made up.

Joanne: 'I once gave you the book 'The Secret Life of Plants'. It changed your awareness of the energy of plants drastically. '

Thea: So you remember such moments?

Joanne: 'Yes. When I feel the need to, I reminisce by such precious moments of friendship as we had. I had training in the city of light once I had moved on to the sixth light sphere, like how to write with you. When we are in our physical body, we have no inkling about our attunement, our soul frequency. I consciously worked on my spiritual development, an exploratory road full of humps and bumps. Now I understand that when people assume things they often stray, make detours. I spent some time here with a group of people who were educated in the field of deceitful light. Meaning captivating words in a beautiful ambiance, listening to a person who considered himself as enlightened with a look that impressed us. This teacher's truths were so convincing that we never learned to turn inwards and look for our own truth.

In the city of lights, I met Mahlah who, like Margaret, passed on so much material to you. A deep-felt wish to pass my material onto you was fulfilled. Leviahnarah accompanied us with a number of other spiritual teachers.'

As announced by Leviahnarah I am here to write with you again. After the period of the healing chamber and subsequent journey through the spheres to my own home, it was not difficult to pick up where I left off. The urge to write as was my work and passion in my earthly life was back.

While reading my book of life, I saw how we worked together before, each on one side of the veil. The veil that is presently getting thinner and thinner. During my life as Joanne Klink, I was intensively involved in unravelling the spiritual world. In the many conversations we had, at times on a daily basis, you taught me a lot in a very natural way about what is strange for many or does not even exist at all. So much fear is instilled by the many religions and cultures. Those who 'know' and get more and more insights do not usually exhibit this. It is a subject much ridiculed, mocked, and hushed up for centuries.

Those who are born with special gifts are conscious of the fact how the outside world can react to what is called the paranormal. You always told me it is normal.'

Thea: Don't we all have this natural gift to feel and know?

Joanne: 'Yes. You know that centuries of ecclesiastical power made people scared of the spiritual world and the natural connection to light. That was the way to dominate people, to rule them. A relatively small group managed to keep the masses out of the light and their unsavoury acts are described in thick books. People became isolated from their nature-religions, from their connections of light, with Earth as the living body, from the deva's of nature and how to experience God in a natural way.

There are still populations far from 'civilization', who live with Source in a free and natural way and respect all that lives and grows on Earth. They were handed down the tradition of plants from ancient wisdom and how to administer them for the treatment and the cure of diseases.

I am very aware of the contamination of earth people and animals. During my life, I endeavoured to eat organically as much as possible avoiding chemicals and hormones. No meat, with the occasional piece of fish.'

Thea: I know how you bought your food at the shop 'Het Sterappeltje' and the delicious bread. What fun we had when we had an occasional dinner together on the mountain eating fish, joking about UFO's I recall. Lovely memories.

Joanne: 'Yes, that kept me very intrigued then. I could not talk about that with many people in such a light-hearted way. You had seen them. In the light spheres, it is a perfectly normal subject. They are stunning vehicles specially built for the great change on Earth.'

Thea: Joanne, how did you experienced the process of transition may I ask?

Joanne: 'The last few years of my life Gertie took care of me lovingly and professionally competent. She made light and bearable what could have been very heavy. She was like a light angel to me.

As I approached ninety, my wish was to see many people again and organised the celebration in the castle in Wittem. That beautiful old castle was the right place for me to say goodbye to the people who were dear to me, like yourself, and it was perfect. A few days before the party I broke my hip and was taken to hospital in Heerlen where I had a near-death-experience. I met my mother and sister and went through my entire life blueprint. I observed that where karma was, people had balanced it. It was finalised and everything I had planned has been accomplished. The days after were a continuous party for me, despite the physical inconvenience but they were made as pleasant as possible under Gerties' care.

The ambulance took me to my party and you were all outside to welcome me. That party in the castle was still very much a physical experience of being together, eating together, laughing and talking. I loved it. It felt as if I was carried during those last days of my material existence. There was no fear of death, yet a complete acceptance of what was. I longed for the light and the loved ones waiting for me. In your death guidance, you described it like this:

'You stand on the platform with your (spiritual) luggage and wait patiently for the departure.' That is what was it was like for me.

After my party, I gradually let go and entered into a kind of intermediary existence. The physical, crude world drifted away from me, the subtle spiritual world came ever closer. There was no sorrow or mental pain. I went in my sleep unnoticed by me. Only after I woke up a couple of days later - in Earth time - did it dawn on me that I had passed. My mother and sister were with me when I woke up in the healing chamber. A silver-lined pink setting like a radiant haze. I needed that energy to heal and enter the new life.

For me, the castle party was my farewell party. I did not reflect much on Earth. I was totally wrapped up in my new life. You and so many sensitive souls wrote and talked about spheres and the passing and that life started to unfold as my own.

The unspeakable joy to learn that unity, beauty, love, as you described so accurately, was all there. It was 'to be' in silence; loving and genuine. The entire disharmony that was ever there, big or small, had disappeared. It was not until later that we started talking more with each other.

My sister was my main guide in the new life. My mother was otherwise engaged but paid me regular visits. Her spiritual attunement was in the sixth light sphere as was my sisters. You can descend to spheres below those of your attunement but not to those above your frequency. It is a growing process, together with reading your book of life. I eventually attuned to the sixth light sphere. We cannot go straight there because we would not be able to withstand that light.

The natural telepathic contact returned as a matter of course. During the past years, first my mother and my sister helped me go through the transformation of old processes later on followed by my spiritual guide. Here we are so acquainted and familiar with each other. I remember quite logically who he is and in relation to whom he was in previous lives and our respective roles.

I have not felt the emotions in the materialistic earth-like sense of the word. It no longer drags you down to a lower frequency. To read my book of life was emotional, at times even painful, but it does not drag you down into a lower frequency. It is Seeing What Was and What Is. It was enlightening and disclosed the reason of my actions. The results of the intentions I had for my last incarnation slowly unfolded before me and it is good to see how the intentions were implemented. One more smoothly than the other. Human choices always involve two or more people making choices with their free will. If someone refused to go along with working out together what we had intended to work out before our incarnation, the flow would stagnate. This could still happen at a later stage in a new set of possibilities. There are always several opportunities and possibilities to balance old energy. To develop intentions anew and actually realise them.

The year before my transition, I did a lot of work in dreamtime in the ashram of Lord Kumeka. Cleansing a life of 90 earth years. As I did so, I found inner peace and that calmed me. The unrest that was always part of me faded until it disappeared completely. That was a great gift, especially when you were used to the inner turmoil.

The cleansing of our field of life is like peeling an onion. Eventually we arrive at the white core. In my quiet way, that final year was extremely precious, balanced with the inner peace.'

Thea: At your party I witnessed this serenity and inner peace, as did quite a few other guests. I told you at the time, you looked like a young woman. Therefore, we see skins falling off during the material life too. A true transformation.

Joanne: 'I really sensed it there already. Here in the spheres, that peace is complete. We form a conscious unity with the One, the Source; that is so wonderful. I received education from a dear old friend in the Hall of Wisdom. He was Jacob Lorber during one of his former lives. We were colleagues in one of our previous lives when we worked together in a large library in Florence. I realized how much I read and studied beautiful old books. He quickly helped me to train my (dormant) ability so I could start writing with you. That is what happened.

There are those who arrive in the light spheres, read their book of life or life blueprint together with friends and angels, and proceed to work in the twilight spheres. Depending on their luminosity, they will busy themselves there with work with souls who need help. They usually are of the same group. In this End Times, a whole range of cosmic cycles end and everyone is committed heart and soul to the whole. Speaking of unity.

Much help is given to those entangled in old dogmas and a lot is done and exchanged with each other. This concerns all religions and their dogmas. For me, this is important because many are ensnared in religions where power was used to intimidate. Within these groups, much has already been balanced. In this way, everyone seeks the work that suits his or her spiritual knowledge. At least I am not sitting on a cloud doing nothing, like our little joke, back then when I was busy writing.

I look back with love and respect to what I accomplished during my last life. The books, the lectures, and the many interesting people I have met.'

Karma

A bad person
Will want to do evil to the virtuous,
Spitting at heaven.

But the spit,
Will never touch the sky,
But will return
And come down on himself.

Virtue cannot be destroyed,
While evil inevitably destroys itself.

Buddha

27. Yan

Story of a family

Leviahnarah: 'When one searches for the solution to one's problem, one's guides and spiritual counsellors will do everything in their power to provide it. A cosmic law is: 'Seek and thou shall find'. You pose it as an intention, as a heartfelt desire. It is linked to a path of wholeness, creating balance. Where solutions emerge, we see well-being. Not always in a way, we expect.

Yan was born into a family with four children, three boys and a girl. Yan was the eldest. Prior to this life, he deliberately chose for his parents. It provided a karmic way of learning, a way of trials and possibilities for healing. Choices; it is always about choices. His father was a man of few words; his mother was caring and loving. His father had a tendency to drink too much and become belligerent, even violent. Before Yan was born, he took out his anger on his wife. He would abuse her and rape her. Their marriage had nothing to do with love, respect or care.

Mary, the mother, had engaged in a karmic connection with her husband. It was the desire of the soul to balance old energy. A circle of lives with violence, disrespect and sexual power. At soul level, she chose this man and these children. Together they would try to balance old negative energy.

Yan was a quiet, self-conscious boy. Father's raving terrified him and ranting and he would hide whenever it occurred. His two younger brothers were a bunch of noisy troublemakers. The youngest, the girl, was a light child, a star child who chose to recover their lost light-love connection. This girl was able to neutralize negative energy with her spiritual light. In many incarnation patterns, we see how the star seeds do heavy and difficult work in places where negative frequencies, behavioural patterns and negative thoughts prevail. This girl used her light to bring out the best in people. Neutralizing was her job.

The dominant father determined everything for every family member and checked everything and everyone. The family was terrorised. Yan got a beating for the slightest mishap. He was a desperately unhappy boy. He despised his fathers 'drunkenness and unbridled fits of anger and the violence resulting in the mistreatment of his mother and the siblings. He saw how his father threw household goods around and destroyed things.

The youngest one, the daughter, spent a lot of time with Yan and he protected her. When she was 12 years old, his father tried to rape her. However, she managed to escape. Yan then found her outside in the street and took her home.

Yan, now 16 years old, confronted his father and mother with this incident. Mother wanted nothing to do with it, afraid of another violent outburst from her husband. She did not defend her daughter but lived in great fear. His father repeatedly attempted sexual contact with his daughter and the pattern could not be broken. It escalated three years later, after yet another attempt by his father to sexually assault Yan's sister. Yan took her to a friend of his who helped her with her education and later on with her studies. His younger brothers, a bunch of troublemakers themselves also ran away from home. In the end, their, father's violence became too much, even for them. One took to sea and the other joined the military. Yan moved into a student house occasionally visiting his parents in between studying and working to foot his bills.

One day he got a call from the police to tell him something serious had happened. When he arrived at his parent's home, he found a smoking and smouldering ruin. Both parents were killed in the fire. He learned from the neighbours that there had been a lot of noise. It turned out to have been yet another violent outburst from his heavily intoxicated father. The police was alarmed, but arrived too late.

In that life, Yan became a doctor. His great passion was to help people balance their lives. Those who actually found themselves in similar situations as his had been. As a result, he took great interest in psychology and psychiatry. He worked in several countries in rehab clinics to help people get rid of their addictions. Some were forced to seek help; others came out of their own free will. During his work in the U.S., he met reincarnation therapists. He learned a lot from their experience.

Yan learned that he had been an alcoholic and violent man in a few previous lives. He relived a few of his experiences and began to understand on a different level why he was so disgusted by his father's behaviour. He never touched a drop of liquor, not even in his college days. It became his great passion to balance old energy and his work gave him that opportunity. Completely committed, aware of his own past lives, he put his knowledge into practice by helping others.'

Freedom

Nothing is more important in the world than freedom.
Freedom is worth making sacrifices for,
It is worth losing your job for,
It is worth being in jail for it.

I would rather be a free pauper than a rich slave.
I would rather die in dire poverty with my beliefs,
Than to live in wealth without self-respect.

Martin Luther King

28. Marianne

Marianne: 'I came to Earth as a Pleiadian in the first Atlantis era. Although each of us had consciously chosen to do this, it was occasionally very hard. We came from a higher dimension to the third dimension of the Earth. This adjustment was in itself very gradual. The Pleiadian Temple Schools that were built had rooms on the one side where we could experience the vibration of 'home'.

Most of us had brought some precious possessions, including musical instruments. I owned a golden flute and a trained voice. In my time of habituation on Earth, this musical instrument and my singing voice were extremely important to me, as was the case with all of us. There were people around me who sang with trained voices, alternatively accompanied by flute but also often without. Music was used for entertainment as well as for healing. At the place where we came from, we knew different forms of polyphony. Healing sounds that were adapted to what was essential to balance energy. Within the Temple Schools, in addition to all the other knowledge taught there, music lessons were an important part of the education. Sound as a healing instrument both spoken and sung.

I often sat at the waterside with my students and we sang or played together on different flute instruments. In my first period on Earth, music was my main subject. I taught my pupils the power of the voice and the sound of musical instruments. It would be an extremely important foundation for these souls on their journey of incarnations.

There were many pupils that we guided life after life to the very limit of their abilities. For example, our work in the Temple Schools was one of many earthly years and several lives of our pupils. Like that, we guided about six incarnations. In that period, we reached the age of some 600 to 700 earthly years. The ancient writings that mention people of very high ages speak the truth.

We carefully preserved each student's writings together with their important personal belongings. Every time they incarnated again there came a moment when we handed over a box with these old belongings. A solemn transfer, accompanied by a celebration in a small circle.

There were disciples who we foresaw could bring great blessings to the Earth in difficult times. We carefully developed their curricula for this purpose. In the early Atlantis period of our earthly stay, which for me would last about 12,000 years, our seers foresaw an ever-growing darkness on Earth. One of our tasks was therefore to neutralize negative energy.

The Earth was an immense challenge. A planet of free will where so many different peoples would live together. We came to Earth from the realms of light, such as the Pleiades, Arcturus, Andromeda, Sirius and so many other star systems. Our task and intention was to neutralize the energy of negative populations who had come to this planet and were still to come. They could be self-centred egotistical beings that would use humans as convenient tools to suit their purpose or the light-energy robbing creatures because they lacked the light. They came from the dark realm of Anchara.

The Pleiadian mystery schools have been of great importance in this earthly tour. Especially in the first period of Atlantis, they laid a solid positive foundation for later periods that were anticipated at that time. At every level of education provided during that period in time and important information was conveyed the spiritual development was high.

Brilliant minds emerged from that era, who in turn became motivated teachers in every conceivable subject in every subsequent time. To this day, these people form the basis for keeping the light alive in what we call End Times, the end of a series of cosmic cycles. All the star seeds that came to Earth from the realms of Light, together with all the previously mentioned, form a powerful foundation to keep the light going and neutralize negative energy.

The three epochs of Atlantis were a positive instructive period for me. Although the counterforces became stronger and got a chance to influence people in their typical way, the basis of light was strong. At the end of the third Atlantis period, however, I longed to go home. Society was veiled in darkness by the power that prevailed at that time. Small elite wielded power on the masses. Anyone focused on the light had a tough time. We see the parallels with the end time of Atlantis and the last decades of our own time.

In line with the process of this End Times, everyone who had made severe karma in the Atlantis period now had the chance to balance it. Many people actually did this, but a relatively small group of them lapsed back into old behaviour, consciousness that was never healed. It is of all times that people who consciously serve the darkness, become more and more addicted to that negative power in many incarnations and sometimes become even more self-serving souls than before. The dark strings and the darkness, with which they were once connected, pulled them in a direction of self-centred and psychopathic behaviour repeatedly.

During the late days of Atlantis hundreds of souls made severe karma by creating a so-called 'makeable society. It was synonymous to creating a slave nation that was subservient to those in power. They got the opportunity to balance that negative energy they so consciously put in place at the time. In this socially engineered society, you could think of the robotisation of people or the far-reaching experiments at the time with genetic manipulation and bio robots, serving pure darkness. To create a vast slave race, serving only a relatively small elite. If that sounds familiar, history is indeed repeating itself.

In an ever-on-going flow of positive energy from the cosmos, we see these power-hungry weaken. The Light hurts them. An ever-discerning humanity is aware of human- and planet-unfriendly developments and the negative trends. Due to this, everything not based on light loses power, faster and faster.

Between that positive beginning and now in the end of a 26,000-year cycle there are many incarnations in which we tried in many ways to keep the light alive.

When at the end of the third era of Atlantis the continent disappeared into the ocean I was taken to a mother ship. In the seven years leading up to this traumatic event, the star seeds already managed to bring a great deal to safety, including writings, equipment and instruments that could have been used by the counterforces to cause harm.

I longed for home with every cell of my being. I had a contract for about 12,000 years with the group I came to Earth with. During the great conclave on the mother ship, it appeared that a small percentage of our people had made karma in the last period in which darkness prevailed. That was partly the result of passing on too much knowledge and consequently misused to the detriment of the planet, humankind and everything that lived on Earth. A unanimously decision was made to all stay. I opted for a rest period in the mother ship of 200 terrestrial years. Some kind of stillness period. Only much later, did I return to ancient Egypt where the various star seeds had unfortunately passed on knowledge that caused the downfall of Atlantis.

At that time, some 20,000 new star seeds came to Earth and we incarnated with them as their children. A part in Egypt and other areas of the Middle East; a part in the Americas with the indigenous peoples with an origin of the stars. I then incarnated with various peoples, such as the Hopi, the Maya and the Dakota people. It was a long period for me during which my old knowledge of the use of sounds was passed on. The many original peoples of the American continent still carried that knowledge of sound in relation to neutralizing negative energy.

For me, these were the times when the white people from the east did not yet colonise the whole continent with brute force, firearms and alcohol. We sang our sounds on the Leylines, the master points and vortexes of the energy web of the Earth. We thanked Mother Earth who fed us and thanked the animals we took to serve as food with our sounds. Our society lived in harmony with nature.

In later times, when the white armies of the East took possession of the continent and the Catholic religion took over everything that was sacred to us, we discovered that they also built their churches and cathedrals in power places with positive energy but managed to turn it into negative energy. This, by the way, took place worldwide, like so much since then was consciously and carefully reversed.

The awakened man now knows of all loveless acts that brought domination and control globally through the ages, directed by a relatively small group of people. I have experienced the struggle that led to the extermination of the original inhabitants of America. I was one of them.

I then incarcerated in a black community of slaves in the southern part of the United States of America. A beautiful area in Georgia. It was a life of terrible hard work as a slave. The plantation owner was a man I knew from the late Atlantic period, a man who at the time also used slaves, albeit artificially created slaves, for his own gain. An extremely violent man hated by many for his unloving and sadistic attitude towards the black people.

Sphere of hate

It was easy to be consumed by the emotion of hatred, like many of my people, black people. After the transition from this life, people go to the sphere of their attunement. The sphere of hatred still existed in that period of our recent history. Once sucked into that sphere of hatred, lead to many lives of incarnation for people to rid themselves of that hatred. The spheres of hatred were fortunately dissolved in the last decades of the 20th century. The many who now die with feelings of hatred go to a galactic healing chamber. More light flows to the Earth since the lowest frequencies were abolished.

Our grief at what happened to our people was great. I incarnated four times in the same place as a girl who always sang. When life was hard, I used to sing. By the way, we all sang. We balanced negative energy that way. During work on the field or sitting around the fire together in the evening. We sang when one of our people died, often as a result of extreme violence by the slave owners. We sang because that man was free from a hard life in slavery. We sang together to guide his soul safely to the spiritual world. We sang when a child was born, in this case very aware that this could be a hard life. A sad sounding song often. We sang in our churches and many black people still do. Healing sounds.

I incarnated a few times in a Quaker community where we consciously worked to neutralize negative energy as a group. Those in power cautiously built their structures in the most crucial places on the Leylines e.g. government and administrative buildings, churches and cathedrals and so on.

I often contributed to the heightening of energy in the groups that kept he light alive, witnessing the growing darkness. My various incarnations during the last years were often very heavy. Again, I did so using sound. Music was my passion. I had lives in which I used my voice as a healing instrument. As a black woman, I could do a lot with my voice, not only for the black man but also for everyone else who wanted to listen to it. Many star seeds recognized my sounds intuitively. I know, for example, that Thea, who receives this material, listened to my voice in a previous life of hers in the 1920s.'

Thea: That was in the last life before this one, in Sydney Australia, in the nineteen twenties and thirties. I liked listening to the radio, especially to the music of the black population. It was an unconscious recognition on different levels. Her voice pierced to the depths of my soul. A little later, we got a gramophone, the wind up one. Her music helped me to balance myself in a very sad time in my life. There was an unconscious recognition of the soul of a sister of the Pleiades. We worked in the same temple that first period of the Atlanteans period. Soul-level recognition.

A couple of years ago someone dear to me gave me a CD of this singer. What happened then was bizarre. Sitting under a wooden lamp covered with fabric and a U-shaped radio next to me on a side table listening to her voice threw me back in time. That was an emotional experience. What had caused great disharmony and sorrow in that life is I am sure healed. Every now and then, I listen to it again, grateful for that music that helped me partly to heal in a very difficult period.

Marianne: 'When you look back at the past life after your transition, you can see in detail what has become of the intentions that were in the blueprint of that life.

I died in a major car accident. Dear friends came to pick me up. They sang to me and accompanied me to the other side of the veil. I went to a healing chamber and recovered from that last life lived in the southern states of America. My voice was doing much good, just as many people from the black community did good to me at the time.

My greatest wish for my subsequent incarnation was to experience changes in relation to oppressed people. People in general, black, white, red or yellow, that did not matter to me. We all come from the same source. In the light spheres, there is a way to discover unity in diversity for the many who were racists during their lives. Depending on their mental baggage, they will usually choose karmic options to rectify this.

In the period before the following incarnation, I joined a large group of about 120 people, all of my own soul group. We started doing tunnel work, helping people who died in the Second World War. There were more such groups and we took turns. When we were exhausted, we would go to Ahrill, a green planet in the Andromeda area, where we could recharge our batteries energetically, so to speak. I have always been able to do that there, just like all the star seeds of different galaxies that came to Earth.

The work we did was hard. With three of us, we could pick up about 15 souls and bring them to a safe area in the spheres. A dimension where they were welcomed and cared for. We worked in the concentration camps that were located in many places on Earth, not only in Germany and Japan, but also in the United States. My work was in the European camps and above the cities that were bombed, such as Gdansk, Rotterdam, London and Dresden. Once again, I was able to use my voice, this time to collect people. Shortly before their transition, people would hear us sing. Sick, exhausted or wounded as they were, it helped them to pass over.

Others worked on the battlefields such as the Normandy coast, the Japanese islands, Stalingrad, Berlin and other places of military activity. Still others picked up the people from the sinking ships and from the submarines. The likes of this war was worse than anything Earth had ever experienced, had ever witnessed, with massive blood sacrifices on both sides of the war to what use? Much is coming to the surface of late, as to who directed them and why? The responsibility of slightly light-deprived loveless people, badly in need of the energy of suffering.

I incarnated again in America and this time on the west coast of California, as a white woman in a musical and artistic family. Each of them had experiences with 'red' or 'black' incarnations. It was 1947. I grew up with a lot of love and attention, to have respect for every human being, regardless of his or her skin colour. My father was an artist and made music. He was a teacher for children at a primary school. My mother was a singer with a classical education and taught at a conservatory. My grandparents from both sides were Quakers who taught me a lot about non-violence.

During the fifties and early sixties, race riots in the United States were widely reported by the fast-growing mainstream media of the time. Aggression levels raised everywhere with feelings of hatred at a large scale, often instigated. I started singing again in that life. My parents taught me and later I got a personal teacher. It was a ruling passion. I sang in the school choir and there was lots of singing going on at home too. By my fifteenth, I sang in a band.

My family followed Martin Luther King and his movement. We travelled miles to hear him speak. I was 16 years when my parents took me to the huge demonstration where King gave his legendary speech on the steps of the Lincoln Memorial. "I have a dream". He expressed his hope that someday people would be judged on their behaviour and not by the colour of their skin. It made a deep impression. The power so many people can exude all gathered to listen to King and I understand the power of his words now too. Those were adventurous trips travelling in our van with sleeping places for my wonderful parents, my older brother and me.

Later I joined a group of young people called hippies. Our passion was unity in diversity; that was our soul frequency. We saw what was wrong and sang about it. The peace movement that arose then was supported by many light people from within but was infiltrated by those that served the darkness. This is something that so many great initiatives have experienced over the years. The opposing forces made it difficult for us. The way they infiltrated those groups of young people who wanted peace for all people was literally poisoning them with alcohol and drugs. The leaders of such movements were lured away from their path with promises and ego caressing words. False light obscured them.

One of my friends went down on booze and drugs. Once addicted to those terrible drugs, there was usually no way back. It destroyed entire groups of young people. The whole infiltration in this community that genuinely focused on light and love was like the 'Pied Piper of Hamelin'. So many people were distracted from their light path in those years. All imaginable means were put in place to this purpose.

The peace movement to which I belonged has been able to reach many people, partly through our music. I was 22 when we went to Woodstock in our vans with the whole band. A lot of positivity showed in places like this, at the same time destroying a lot through the negative infiltration of drugs and alcohol. It was evident on all fronts that the infiltrators deliberately created the decline.

It dawned on me that action had to be taken and I disengaged myself from the hippy world that, because of my changing consciousness, no longer matched my frequency.

My father was a member of an organization, the Underground Railroad. This organization helped young people who actually had to go to Vietnam to fight, flee to Canada. Waking up and choosing not to go was a difficult process. So many families who had served as soldiers for many generations and regarded it as an honour and the highest sacrifice to die for their country. The daily TV coverage of the unloading of body bags from the military planes were very poignant images and numbed people in to a sense of apathy after a while. Those daily images on the news brought the frequency of the whole country down.

I joined the Underground Railroad. Together with my father and grandfather, we brought many people to Canada. My grandfather, a non-violent man, financed a large part of these activities. It was intensive work on both sides of the long border. Returning was not an option, as it turned out later, because their children were not allowed to go to university. Through the Underground Railroad organisation, projects were started in Canada, to help them with all the possibilities imaginable for education and for building a new and safe existence.

When I was 27 years old, my father and I were killed in a car accident. The years had been tough, but I did it with heart and soul. In the light sphere of my attunement, I became aware of the enormous damage a terrible war had caused yet again. Not just in Vietnam, but in that vast Asian area. These young men, the victims, often went to a sphere described elsewhere in this book: 'The Butterfly Gardens'.

I joined a group of souls who worked with sounds. Singing, alone or with a whole group. One of the men I had known well was killed in Vietnam called our singing 'angelic singing'. The vibrations of our singing were healing. Up and until the end of that terrible war, I did that work in the different spheres.

At the end of that war, I incarnated for the last time in 1975, again in America, but now as my brother's daughter. The line was continued. All were star seeds of the same lineage and group. It was a life to heal what I had experienced on my long journey of almost 26,000 years.

There were parts from the life of a black singer that were not healed. The racism and everything related during my lives as a black slave, the brutal violence, and the abuse that was still in my cellular consciousness as vibrations. It all needed healing. There were old wounds from the car accidents and from the persecutions during the Indian lives. What we do not have to go through as a human being…

I got cancer. I refused the chemotherapy that the regular doctors prescribed as a matter of course. In my family, there were doctors, holists with a different perspective on health. I lived in a big city in the east of the US and worked at a music school after my studies. Not a very healthy environment. The enormous stress that I experienced in my education and later in my profession as a teacher was not exactly suitable for healing. Frankly, my environment horrified me. The towering blocks of flats, the hustle and bustle of such masses of people. A person sensitive to that cannot cope so well with all those triggers. I sought and found a way to heal, largely intuitively. Gentle nudges from my dear guides and spiritual counsellors. Regression therapy became important to me. I learned a lot about my previous incarnations that way. It brought insight into my long journey of earthly lives.

When I got sicker, family members took me to a clinic in the Southwest of America, where they dealt with health from a holistic point of view. Grown up in a harsh urban materialistic society in which almost all diseases were treated with chemical medication, all this was new to me. It turned out that my eating habits were unhealthy and lived in an unhealthy environment.

With one of those doctors, I felt a soul solidarity. As soon as I arrived there, I trusted him completely. He drastically changed my diet. We opted for organic food and non-toxic therapy. There were experts who gave regression therapy, which helped me to understand and heal my old injuries. We made jokes about my different singing careers. No matter how sick I was, I started joining a singing group. Healing sounds, singing the upper tunes. Listening to solfeggio frequencies. They worked with the vibrations of plants, beautiful herbal remedies tailor-made for my bodily needs. As well as blossom remedies. My body and soul began to heal very slowly. I was coming home to myself. With what I learned from these passionate people coupled with my own academic music education, I started to sing again. The knowledge I had brought with me when I came to Earth entered my consciousness again. So here we were working together to get back into our own. Receptive people described extra-terrestrial civilizations. They accepted it. My body and mind healed.

They offered me a job in the same centre where I had arrived as a very sick person. We exchanged knowledge with researchers in the field of healing vibrations, which was a true voyage of discovery. For years, I have worked with sound, the power of the voice, to help people heal.

I died at the age of 39, killed in a car accident for the third time. I died instantly and did not notice a thing; so hard and so fast was the collision. I went to the third light sphere. I read my book of life of the past 26,000 years, first the last life backwards, along my earthly curve. I moved on to the sixth light sphere and started looking back to where I had come from before I came to Earth. Instead of 12,000 years, I stayed the whole cycle and experienced the intense times that people currently call the End Times. The end of a long cosmic cycle.

We have been preparing for the new era for so long. The old that no longer serves will no longer be able to exist in the higher frequency. Those who still need war, violence and all that is of lower vibration will go to another 3-D planet. People who, in their last lives balanced old karmic energy are preparing themselves in the various spheres for the new era that is dawning. An era in a higher frequency.'

Everything of value

Our country is worth more than money.
As long as the sun shines and the water flows,
This country will be here to feed humans and animals,
That is why we cannot sell this land.

The Great Spirit has put it here before us
And we can't sell it, because it doesn't belong to us.

Before the invasion of the white 'civilization', it was customary for Indians to give away food, clothing, horses, often their most beloved possessions. It was important to them that everyone had enough to live. The obsession of the whites with the accumulation of material goods surprised them and led to the apt remark of Sitting Bull, the famous war leader of the Sioux Indians:

The white man knows how to make everything.
But he doesn't know how to share it.

Sitting bull

29. Elisabeth

Leviahnarah: 'In the different spheres where people come together to exchange ideas about a certain subject, it is often said that they lacked joy. These moments of exchange are valuable, instructive for those who attend. These meeting by the way are voluntary and are 'heard' as a telepathic call or for making an appointment to work things out.

One of the participants, talked about her last two lives as a woman on Earth.

Elisabeth: 'At the beginning of the 19th century, I incarnated in Friesland in the Netherlands, within a small farming community. When it came to religion, our family were alternative thinkers due to the experiences of older family members who had to deal with loveless expressions of the Roman Church. Messages from other Mennonites who had moved to different areas in America and Canada prompted us to make that decision.

We were skilled farmers and cattle breeders, convinced that we could build a new life. As a child, I was taught how to make cheese. I was married off to a young farmer from another Mennonite community. His name was Lucas. With many of us, we immigrated to America where we ended up in a community of distant relatives. Through hard work, we built communities that still exist today.

I landed in a community where elders imposed guidelines on all of us with a firm hand. These extremely dominant men took the joy out of everything. Natural laughter and fun the way I remembered from my early childhood in Friesland made way for a rigid attitude to life, pressure to show the right attitude as a woman. Only in the cheese dairy did women and we girls feel a little freer. We had lots of fun in there. It better not be noticed by certain men, or we would be strictly admonished. Our behaviour was, of course, sinful in their eyes.

In a short time, I had two children. They gave me joy and I could play and laugh with them, but especially indoors. As a woman, you had no voice and like most women at the time, we mostly worked a lot performing our domestic and marital duties. It was a much stricter community than I was used to in

Friesland. Every time we laughed or had fun, we were punished with texts from the Old Testament.

My husband soon took over, copied the behaviour of the elders. He made a habit of quoting long biblical sentences, generally with a loud voice. All these men were cruel and unloving. My husband turned out to be a gloomy negative man, very judgmental and as strict as the elders were. Unable to give love. You realize it is risky to get married off as a young girl. Some women and girls learn to love their husbands in the end, but I did not.

You leave much behind once you are married and moved to your husband's community. For me, that was the warmth of both my parents and my brothers. I came from a loving empathic family, without any verbal or physical violence. My husband's family was of a hard line of faith, unloving and very woman unfriendly. Corporal punishments were common. To the outside world, they were all religious people, impeccably behaved, but a hypocritical family at that. Later, when I read my life blueprint in the spheres, I 'saw' it all very clearly. Some of them, including my husband, I knew in earlier incarnations. They volunteered for this incarnation to balance old loveless energy with others and I was one of them.

These intentions were not realised; on the contrary. Old rigid thinking that had manifested itself before during the various incarnations and had led to severe karmic baggage was rekindled. The Mennonite community in which I was born preached non-violence, refrained from all acts of war and all forms of violence. It was a hardworking, peaceful and empathetic society. The community I had ended up in through my marriage represented exactly the opposite. I therefore wrote letters to both my brothers, who lived near my parents, in a more northerly area of America. Writing letters to my family had to be done secretly. Unfortunately, their answers never got back to me and that made me very sad. The elders and my husband intercepted their letters.

My husband got violent. It started with clips around the ear but soon I was hit hard, downright manhandled. Bruising stayed hidden under my long clothes and hat. He was constantly telling me how I should behave, in his view and in that of the elders. In his eyes, I was a pagan. He always spoke in a chiding way and behaved like that too.

My third pregnancy was the result of very unloving acts of violence and rape by my husband. I was very reluctant to give birth. In our community in Friesland, a gifted midwife prepared girls for marriage, pregnancy and childbirth. In this way, the new residents of our community always received a warm welcome. I was lucky to experience that in the year before I got married. It was also good to hear the stories of the women around me who had children. I was never afraid of it. Of course, our society was based on love.

It was a wonderful process to give birth to a child, to receive a new family member. Is that why childbirth was so much easier? The faith in a good midwife, the love that surrounded us?

When I had my child, the whole process of pregnancy and birth meant to be one of suffering. That is how it was supposed to be according to them. I had to listen to similar words from other women in the community on a regular basis. They were proud to have had their children in great suffering. Nothing was made comfortable and texts from the Bible quoted all the way through as a kind of mantra.

One of the older women handed me the letters from my family, she had found, all opened by her husband, the oldest elder. It was an emotional breakthrough to realise this act of love. For her to give me all those letters from my family and the consequent punishments she risked was not a harmless thing to do. She obviously realized I was abused badly.

My brothers wrote that I had to leave my violent husband and the loveless group of people. They indicated how I could do that and how they could help me with that. At that moment, I understood that several times a trader from another Mennonite community had been along giving me signals that I could go with him. I also suddenly understood why I was guarded and separated from the others. The words my husband spoke as punishment for a 'disobedient woman' was in fact his fear of losing face. I processed this information, calculated my possibilities, and decided to leave as soon as the opportunity presented itself again.

During an exchange of two young brides from elsewhere with two young men from our community, there they were again, those men with their wagon. One of them wore something on his clothes that I recognized. A message from my brothers, I thought. I did not recognize the men after so many years but they turned out to be both my brothers. The oldest on the wagon, the youngest on a horse. They brought the brides to us, with their dowry. The girl to be married off was always taken to the future husband's family and that meant that people of the community where I lived did not know my two brothers.

I was not allowed to attend the wedding ceremonies and they wrapped my two children in blankets and put them in the car. I snuck out of the house and left with my brothers and my children, away from my husband, the elders and everyone in that community. No one had noticed.

The journey was long and not particularly comfortable for a highly pregnant woman. After a three-day trip, I had contractions. My brothers sought and found help from a small indigenous Indian community. These indigenous people from that great American continent temporarily took us in. Both my brothers appeared to have an exchange in their own community with an indigenous Indian community in the vicinity. They were therefore able to make themselves understood. There were Mennonite communities that maintained intensive methods of exchange. Trade was one of them.

I was in a bad state and looking back at that life I saw that the baby had been injured by my husband's mistreatment. He had kicked my belly and used negative verbal expressions. I saw how damaged I became during all those years during that arranged marriage. For the first time in years after leaving my parental home, I experienced human warmth and love. The Indian women saw my bruised body and took care of the wounds. A sweet old woman petted my head, hair and hands. It was like the nightmare of that loveless, violent marriage slipped away from me. She was a shaman who helped me to heal.

The baby was born deformed and died after three days. While reading my book of life, later after my transition, I saw that these wise people understood that the child could not have developed normally because of the flow of violence. I lost a lot of blood and was too weak to move on. My eldest brother carried me to the place where my baby was buried in a beautiful place in the wilderness during a loving ceremony, wrapped in a blanket that I had made myself. These experiences have brought both my brothers and my children something that was unthinkable in our world. The beautiful songs, the loving care of our group. Both my children changed forever. The joie de vivre that they found in this place made a deep impression on them for the rest of their lives. Both my brothers agreed that I would stay with these people, together with my children, until I had recovered. They agreed to pick us up later.

My children, who had always walked around in tight black clothes with socks and riding boots, were now walking around barefoot in the clothes of our hosts. In no time at all, I saw them turn into cheerful and happy children. In the teepee where I was I heard their cheerful voices. We were to be picked up after the summer and in retrospect, it was a great feast of being together with a special people.

I came from hell into heaven. The Old Testament god disappeared completely into the background and I enjoyed the rituals to honour our environment, Mother Earth, the Sun, the wind, the water and the animals. I taught my hosts how to make cheese and from them I learned how they did it. Once recovered, I helped with all the housework, just like all the women. How respectful the men were towards their wives. How the elderly were cared for and honoured for their wisdom. I learned how to make medicines from plants and I taught them the natural remedies we used. I enjoyed the gathering of the men and women around the fire. Although men and women had their own groups, the meetings by the fire were wonderful for me. It was a new experience for me that friendship could develop between men and women.

A very warm friendship developed with one of the men. He was ten years older and father of two daughters. His wife had died in childbirth at the birth of their third child.

As autumn approached, I became quiet and gloomy. I realized that no one would want to have me anymore, especially in the community of my family. I was going to stay alone and serve the community. After all, I was 'damaged goods'. A woman who had left her husband, serious in that religious community, quite simply unacceptable.

During the months of my stay, I had learned the language of the Indians and I understood that I could never get pregnant again. The shaman explained everything to me and drew it in the sand. They asked me to stay and take care of the motherless little girls of the man together with my two sons. However, no one put pressure on me here, as I was used to in many ways in the strict religious communities of the past. I carefully considered my options. I was reluctant to be squeezed into that straitjacket again and most likely to be rejected by people. A woman was not meant to leave her husband and that is exactly what they would encounter. A healed woman with her sons. Intimate matters such as marital violence was never talked about. Only in the direct circle of family, parents and brothers, one would know.

Autumn came and I was faced with the hardest choice in my life. My oldest brother came to get me. His wagon loaded with sheepskins, food and natural medicines and so much more. He was amazed to see his sister in the simple clothes of the indigenous people next to a couple of very happy children.

He also told me that my husband, Lucas, had sent people over the past few months to find me and pick me up with the boys. No one knew where I was. Just my two brothers. Lucas had come looking for us then. He saw us as his lost property and suffered loss of face and incredibly angry about our leaving.

My brother stayed a few nights to discuss things. As a woman, I had to conform to his wishes in every way. However, he saw how balanced I was with my two boys and those two little indigenous girls. He heard about the suggestion for me to stay with these people. This was all very different to what he was used to, but he agreed with the elders of the tribe that we could stay. He could not (yet) cope with the idea of mixing, but he was told that I could not have children anyway. My brother knew very well that if Lucas knew that I had gone to live with my brothers, he would immediately claim 'his' sons.

Looking back, reading my book of life, I saw the joy, the pleasure that I experienced from that moment on. With the father of the little girls, I formed a warm loving bond. We remained each other's best friends and partners until old age. My sons found their way in a time of great change, a time of the advancing aggressive whites. They did not regard them as white people because of their native clothing, attributes and hairstyles.

My grandfather in Friesland was a mediator between people and groups of people. A peacemaker. Reading my book of life, I discovered that he reincarnated as my first child. Both my sons have become mediators.

After reading my book of life, I did some tunnel work in the period before I would reincarnate with people who were my parents before. Together with many others, I did this work with heart and soul; especially in the period of the First World War, we brought many home. The places where organised blood sacrifices took place, such as during that terrible war nourished the prevailing darkness. The theft of light and soul; the energy of suffering was their nourishment.'

Leviahnarah: 'The tunnelling that many people from the immaterial world could do together was of great importance. The bringing home safely of so many souls was done by many immaterial people.'

Elisabeth: 'In a next life, I incarnated in Friesland. The parents of the previous life, which ended in America for our family at the time, were again my parents. Loving individualists. We had to learn lessons together. My father built sailing boats and together with his brothers, I spent a lot of time sailing the waters of the Frisian lakes. The feeling of freedom that I experienced was wonderful. My father in particular was my role model. We did not belong to a community of faith in that life. It was striking that my mother was caring but never organised my life. She allowed me the freedom to find my own way that I had not had in the previous life. She was a primary school teacher. Mother taught me to spin and weave with the most beautiful furs of the sheep of the province. She belonged to a circle of women who worked with textile moulds. A group of people who once belonged to strict religious communities in previous incarnations.

The skills that I had learned during my life with the indigenous people of America came back to the surface little by little by working with this group. My creativity developed rapidly. Whilst weaving my knowledge I acquired at a soul level in that earlier life, revealed itself.

I enjoyed the flow I was in. I went to the academy for visual arts where I mainly painted. The amazing thing was that I started drawing and painting indigenous people. I could incorporate my love for these people into my paintings. The love and joy I experienced there I had carried with me. Life with Lucas was healed. There was no need for therapy, as so many people might do after such a violent marriage. The indigenous shaman in combination with the loving environment had healed my damage in that same life.

I went to Amsterdam where I continued my studies. The free spirits in the art world were pleasant to hang out with except for the disturbed artists out there. I managed to shift the wheat from the chaff. The way of life with the indigenous people taught me a lot in this area. I intuitively knew whether I wanted to connect with people or turn away in silence.

Still, I came across Lucas again in that scene. Reading my book of life later, I 'saw' that his dominant violent behaviour had already been present in several incarnations. After his life as Lucas, he experienced what he had done to others in a karmic way, because of his great need to dominate people by force. There was so much more than just that incarnation in the Mennonite community.

We had met before, a long time ago, where he was a slave driver. I was sold as a slave. He saw himself as a servant of god and country within a very orthodox religious community. Devout, going to church on Sunday, but every other day of the week a very violent slave trader. Without any self-reflection, he considered himself to be of the highest standard within that society.

Back again, crossing my path. While going out with my art friends, I met him at a party. An arrogant young man, telling anyone who would listen, he belonged to the 'higher' circles. Possibly that was the way he attracted attention he craved in other circles, but my art friends didn't want to have anything to do with this arrogant gentleman. He clearly felt superior to other young people. I felt a strong aversion to him. He used to show up every occasionally in places where our group gathered. His attention went out to me.

He wanted to 'have' me. I was not aware of our past lives, but in a marriage like the free-spirited girl I was, I did not want a relationship and certainly not a marriage, as some around me did. He started stalking me, at first inconspicuously but then it became annoying. He figured out where I lived. He was like a small child who did not get his way, not violent but pushy and annoyingly insistent. Once he had regarded me as his property in a marriage, as his slave, he now wanted to possess me again. He did not take 'no' for an answer, but I wanted to be left alone. He played the role of victim to me from time to time. However, his stalking behaviour upset my studies and work.

One of my teachers at the academy subconsciously recognized this man. Their paths had crossed before. Together with five other students, we left for Ibiza. My teacher had a house and a guesthouse there. We gave drawing and painting lessons to enthusiasts and with a little pocket money, stayed there with board and lodging. We had a wonderful time. Many artists were looking for places like this to live and work in complete freedom, far away from the tightly organised society in their country.

Once more, our paths crossed in this last life. Lucas found me again on Ibiza but by my teacher and his family removed him from the property. In the meantime, he had become addicted to hard drugs, a scene I did not want to have anything to do with. We heard of his ridiculous utterances and what he would do for the art world. All empty promises.

He disappeared from view and I settled permanently on Ibiza to live with my beloved, who had also returned on my path: the man of the Indian life. We had a daughter together. Life in our self-created free society was wonderful. I dedicated myself to my creative expressions and he was a builder, a designer.

A few years later, my teacher from my academy days told us that Lucas had died, apparently of an overdose. Sad, very sad how old, unsolved cases from previous incarnations worked out for him. I am convinced that every human being has every opportunity to heal what is out of balance. Seize those opportunities when they come along.'

30. It is accomplished

Time for a party

Margaret: Ohan and Elize accompanied me to a meeting of a large group of people. They were a little secretive. We arrived at an open and spacious place, a large square where a whole crowd had gathered with an air of expectation. I immediately noticed that everyone looked so cheerful and happy. Until now, I had only been invited to participate in situations related to processing and purification.

A tall, black man received us. His motions were flowy and supple. He was dressed in a long tunic of a deep purple fabric, with underneath a smooth pair of trousers of the same fabric. His clothes were beautifully coloured on his dark skin. I was struck by the feeling I had before, that these dark races are of an extraordinary beauty, and it is completely incomprehensible that people on Earth are persecuted for their different skin colour or seen as unequal or inferior. He introduced himself as Leonard.

We walked over the large square, lined on the one side with low bushes and large trees behind it and on the other side the square flowed into a naturally sloping landscape. The square was elevated and the view was wide. I saw a small, golden pyramid, in the distance shining as if it was made of glass. Small structures blended in organically with the surroundings in between the green. As if they had grown there. A little lower was a large, low building, looking like a star seen from above. It resembled the same glassy substance as that golden pyramid, but with a kind of colour mixture of blue and green. The effect was a bit like a bubble in which the colours intermingle. It looked like a community centre, with many people walking in and out. The whole atmosphere was imbued with a strong, white-gold filled, sparkling energy of love and peace. A wonderful place to be.

We joined a group of about ten people. The group was engaged in a busy conversation with bursts of laughter. In amongst the adults were four children, and one small and two large dogs. The children separated from the group of adults and ran with each other across the large square. I saw how two were hiding behind a wide rose quartz flower box. The bin was smooth and opaque with benches of the same material around it. Large, flowering plants hid the children from view. The other children ran around in search of the other groups of people and disappeared into the crowd.

I enjoyed watching this spectacle. Clearly, these people had left the healing chambers behind. The searching children wandered further afield, into the main square. The small dog ran to the flower box behind which the children were hiding. Yapping loudly, he circled the children to lure the seekers to the hiding place. Once discovered, they all ran to the edge of the large square and the sloping field, where they tumbled over with a lot of laughter and excitement. The two big dogs leisurely walked there and tumbled along with them.

A man disengaged himself from the group and said that he would call the children. Not producing a sound, he called them telepathically, as communication here usually goes. The children reacted immediately and walked back to the square, dogs in tow. Pulling, pushing and playing, they returned to the group.

Leonard invited us to go with him and we walked to the star-shaped building. The groups on the square were moving into the same direction. There was a path down, paved with irregularly shaped rock crystal tiles. The entrance to the building was like the opening of a large shell, natural in shape, wide and welcoming. I saw two young women walking with a musical instrument under their arms. Their long hair danced on their backs.

We entered into an immense space, but it felt as if we were just standing outside. The blue-green colours were not visible here. Everywhere small groups of people were talking to each other. In the middle of the star-shaped building a long figure with a noble face appeared. As he walked, his softly curly, blond hair moved half-long to the shoulders. Immediately I knew: this is Lord Kumeka, Chohan of the eighth ray of purification.

Here and there, he stopped to talk to people. Close to him, I saw little angelic creatures, nicely and gracefully built, no taller than about one meter fifty. Beautiful and at the same time so ordinary. They wore a kind of plateau with an opaque dome on it.

It got quiet. The plateau was placed on a square block of Lapis Lazuli, with white flowers small and large, arranged together. Also on the ground were vases with beautiful white roses. The angelic creatures placed the bell on the stone and it got quiet in the hall. Those present began to sing a song without words. Like a wave of beauty, the sounds are streaming together. At the edge of the space, I noticed different kinds of angels, large and small, together. The singing subsided and when Lord Kumeka removed the bell, a deep black crystal appeared. It was beautifully shaped, like a pinecone, with many layers. I guess the crystal was about a meter high.

Leonard stood next to the crystal and directed some people forward. One by one, Kumeka touched them. Leonard conducted several people forward. Men, women and children. Some groups had a dog with them and a hand was laid on each creature. All the participants radiated pure joy. When everyone had passed, the angels formed a group and began to sing. Wonderful sounds flooded my being and brought me into complete harmony. I am not even going to try to find words for these sounds, because it is impossible to describe the sounds that were actually waves of lights. The entire space filled with this light energy. I noticed that the dogs, as far as I could see, had been lying stretched out. Children stood still and full of attention next to the adults.

In the middle of the hall, next to the crystal, a few more figures appeared. All with the same physique as Lord Kumeka, with the same noble appearance. I knew that Master Jesus stood there and next to him Lord Makhimsih, on Earth known as Buddha and next to him Lord Rahaal, on Earth known as Raphael.

I knew this was a very special moment, and I could hear the message offered to the whole community telepathically. Ohan sent me the following explanation:

Ohan: 'This meeting is a group transformation and initiation to a higher level of 'being'. All participants belong to the same group of souls. They have individually and with this large group as a whole, released all earthly karma, and have brought it to light. This meeting is a ritual in the light worlds. This group is so special because none of them lives on Earth anymore, all of them have returned. There was a lot of hard work and lots of suffering on Earth, to be able to go through these karmic processes at an accelerated pace. They will dedicate themselves to world peace, to the care for Mother Earth. They are strong as a group; each individual has become stronger through series of lives of learning and undergoing. People who belonged to different races on Earth, but are one as a group soul gather here. Leonard was an inspired governor in an African country; his search for light and purity eventually brought him death. He was not to be bribed and therefore a danger to the incumbent government. A man of great wisdom.'

Margaret: I watched the miraculous spectacle by the stone in the centre. It had become very quiet by now. All of them knew what they had gone through in their many lives, before they could reach this level of light again. Ever, they were this light, before they connected to matter in a series of lives with each other. A long journey was completed. None of them had to incarnate if they did not want to. Many would serve from the ethereal area, to inspire people positively who are still in matter. Some would return with special assignments that they would take on.

A girl came in with a goblet of light. I thought it was a beautiful sight. The goblet was completely transparent and the contents consisted of pure light. It radiated out far beyond the girl. Everyone followed her with their eyes. She was very beautiful, almost a child. A white girl with long and blond hair. Another girl came in, with another goblet like that. She had a supple gait and her black hair was tied together in a multitude of braids with silver ribbons. Her skin was black and she had the same slender build as Leonard. With her head proudly raised, she walked down the aisle. Behind the black girl followed a Hindustani girl, and behind that a small one with a Balinese appearance. Twelve girls passed by, each with a different race characteristic. They were beautiful to see. They placed the goblets of light on the stone of Lapis Lazuli, around the black crystal. The girls formed a circle around the Masters.

"It is accomplished," said Master Jesus, "you have learned to live with each other, sometimes under very difficult circumstances. It was tough. As a group, your task has been accomplished and all your negative vibrations to each other and to Earth have been worked out."

The Masters stood around the stone. Around them it became brighter and brighter, until their appearances dissolved into the light, and became one in that light. It was just one pillar of light and shapes could no longer be distinguished, just light. The angelic creatures began to sing in fluent sounds. It was as if caught up in that light and became one with it. They were still singing when the pillar of light slowly dissolved and the Masters became visible again. The black crystal was completely clear.

There was an almost imperceptible sigh going through the hall. The ceremony concluded with the singing of a song that I could not compare to any other piece of music on Earth. The music of the spheres is of a beauty that cannot be captured in earthly words, but that vibrates through your entire being and is in harmony with your own frequency.

The children present came forward, very orderly, and each picking up a white rose and put it on the blue stone, next to the now transparent crystal like a wreath around the stone. White roses for a new beginning. The Masters walked into the hall and talked to groups of people here and there. The solemn atmosphere now became cheerful. The people walked out, back to the main square. There was a party the likes of which I have not yet experienced here. A white drink, a mead, was served. Everyone was happy.

My eyes were always drawn to the Masters, who moved among the people and had conversations. There was a lot of laughter. Lord Kumeka also has a task in the great process of purification, to bring humour back to Earth. His soft curls waved around his head when he was dancing with the twelve girls. The little girl reached out her hand to Master Jesus and pulled it out into their midst. What a new thought to see him laugh and dance, while most people know his effigy from the crucifix in their room.

Soon everyone was dancing and I really enjoyed it, because I took part myself. There was folk dancing and whoever felt like it, joined in. Best of all, I found a circle of black men, women and children. They showed a traditional dance from the country they last lived. Their colourful clothing and the flexible movements they made were very contagious. Three Balinese women danced in a straight line next to each other, their beautiful arm and hand movements were a feast for the eyes. Such graceful movements.

Mr Makhimsih walked up to them afterwards and made a slight bow to the dancers. He walked onto the square with the smallest woman in the group, his arm around her shoulder and chatting busily. That scene touched me deeply.

It feels a bit strange for me to write about 'the Masters' who celebrate a big party, dancing and talking with groups of people. I loved it and began to understand some of their simplicity that is so typical to them and that we on Earth find so difficult to understand. I thoroughly enjoyed this feast of light.

A joint greeting sounded from the field where the children and animals were playing. I saw the Masters dissolve into light and leave. Some people walked in again to look at the group crystal, perfectly clear on the stone. I also took another look.

Leonard came to me, flanked by two little boys. He thanked me for coming. He spoke to Ohan, whom he seemed to know very well. The stone was taken to a special place, where it is preserved as a symbol for this large group of souls. I went to see Elize; she danced with a whole group of men and women.

I have never been aware that they could party here like this. In the sloping field, there were groups of people sitting together here and there. There were snacks and drinks everywhere. Everyone was beautifully dressed. Children and parents found each other again.

Most people did not look older than about forty years, or any imaginable age below that. There were many grandpas and grandmas but they all looked the way they had felt the most powerful in life. Funny I found a black man who looked like he was in his fifties, with grey hair and a beard. In his role as head of a family, he found this age to be fitting. He was amidst a whole group of men, women and children. He saw me look, beckoned me and told me this. The people I meet seem to know that I pass on these experiences for a book. Every time I talk about it, I get approval.

Slowly everybody left to return to his or her own place of residence. The ceremony I just described largely resembled the initiations that I went through myself. The Masters are always present, and those experiences are dear to me. There are parties every time, but each one is different. They are important events when people individually and as a group transcend earthly karma. Together they build new, positive changes for the Earth and its people. On this occasion, the dancing of these different ethnic groups was so special, the individuality of a certain facet of life. These souls, who incarnated in different races, had worked out very old, negative patterns together. This meeting was an example of 'unity in diversity'. Many here keep the dream alive that it could also be like this on Earth.

I went back to my place and found peace and quiet. On Earth, I was never very fond of meetings and parties with lots of people; they tired me out. The feast I just experienced though was balm for the soul. The peace and quiet I was looking for this time therefore was in order to process all these impressions. I had the vivid images of the dancers from different cultures dancing in one large, homogeneous group, dancers from the same group of souls and monad.

Nothing short of a miracle when compared to how things go on Earth between peoples. Apparently, there is hope yet to be at peace with each other simultaneously working out very old karma. During that hectic life on Earth, processes apparently take place that are not immediately visible, but that clearly show their effect here in the spheres.

May the joy, peace and wholeness of human groups like this, have their effect on many. I carry this experience of peace and wholeness, crowned by the Masters, with me as a precious treasure. I will continue to cherish it, in the knowledge that the light on Earth will come through and will shine forever.

Thea Terlouw

Thea Terlouw was aware of a world that others could not perceive since her early childhood. The burden of 'being different' kept her from developing these talents as a child and young woman. She initially studied visual arts. In addition, she trained to become a yoga teacher like the study of Jnana Yoga philosophy. Thea worked as an independent artist for some time as well as a yoga teacher. For years she worked with groups of people, in schools with children and gave pregnancy yoga for pregnant women.

During her life as a visual artist, however, her special talent began to develop again. When she had a near-death experience (n.d.e.) because of an accident, everything gained momentum for her, partly under the inspiring supervision of her guides. This resulted in close contact with and work for the Merkawah Foundation, co-founded by Pim van Lommel, physician-cardiologist and author of the bestseller 'Consciousness Beyond Life'.

The care and counselling of people with a near-death experience and the counselling of dying people were the logical consequence. In the many years that followed, she helped hundreds of people with examining their past lives and to identify the root causes of diseases in close cooperation with therapists, doctors and psychologists.

Many then asked her to write down her experiences. Thea had doubts however, and it was mainly thanks to the encouragement of Joanne Klink and later Bram Vermeulen, that she wrote two books on the topic: 'De Cyclus van leven en dood', (The Cycle of Life and Death) and 'Een Cirkel Doorbroken' (Breaking the Circle).

At the same time, Thea also worked a lot with children. The exchange with Henri de Vidal de St. Germain was in service of that work. Together with her work as a yoga teacher and pregnancy yoga, you might say that in this way Thea has become an expert in 'transitions': to be born well and to die well has become a true passion for her.

After writing her first two books and giving a great number of lectures on the subject, she decided, in the context of her own development, to 'retreat from public life', as she herself put it, for a number of years.

She stayed there until the end of 2017, when she felt that in the light of the Great Awakening it became more necessary than ever to individually and collectively face and complete the greater reality of our countless Earth incarnations. This is not an easy process, neither individually nor collectively.

However, Thea knows that we do not go through life alone nor do we have to. She is very aware of this because of her telepathic contact with her spiritual guides and teachers. For most of us, that contact happens unconsciously. Preconditioned as we are, we experience life as if it were something on its own, completely denying that greater universal reality.

The main purpose of this book is to let go of the fear for death. Reincarnation lies at the heart of our lives on Earth. Dying is merely a transition to a greater reality, one in which we prepare ourselves for a next life. There is nothing to be afraid of; besides, we have done it so many times. This book also aims to encourage people to renew, engage and develop contact with the spiritual realms. An extremely important and necessary step in the spiritual development of all of humanity and our planet. Slowly moving forward in our processes. This is necessary, or at least helpful, to become as whole as possible. Help is available to achieve this. Moreover, the so-called 'Heelkamers' (Healing Chambers), which became the title of her third book, can and will heal our often heavy experiences as physical beings in countless incarnations on our planet.

As people wake up and become aware of the precarious state this beautiful planet Earth is in, it is time to 'come home'. At home on our planet, at home with each other and at home with our brothers and sisters from other realms in the universe. Places we also know as 'home' and that many of us long for after our wanderings on this free will planet.

The main message of Thea is that although we do not always realise who we are and where we come from, together we can create brilliant Fields of Light Consciousness over the many unloving aspects of global society on Earth. After all, we know - we feel - what we want to change and in many cases we even know how. It is blatantly clear to all of us, that much of what is not based on Love has recently become prominently visible in the incoming flow of cosmic Light. This allows us to change and say goodbye to what no longer serves us.

Literature

- Eben Alexander, *Proof of Heaven.* Little Brown UK 2012.
- Masaru Emoto, *Hidden Messages in Water.* Atria Books 2005.
- Masaru Emoto, *Secret Life of Water.* Simon & Schuster 2011.
- Masaru Emoto, *Messages from Water and the Universe.* Hay House Inc 2010.
- Joan Grant, *Winged Pharaoh.* Abrams Press 2007.
- Joan Grant, *Eyes of Horus.* Ari'El Press 2010.
- Joan Grant, *So Moses was Born.* Dawn Chorus 2010.
- Hazrat Inayat Khan, *The Inner Life.* Shambhala 1997.
- Bruce Lipton, *Biology of Belief.* Sound True Inc 2006.
- Pim van Lommel, *Consciousness Beyond Life.* HarperCollins 2010.
- Joel Martin and Patricia Romanowski, *Love beyond Life.*
  HarperCollins 1997.
- Elisabeth Kübler-Ross, *On Death and Dying.* Prentice Hall 1997.
- Elisabeth Kübler-Ross, *Life Lessons.* Scribner 2014.
- Lynne McTaggart, *The Intention Experiment.* Simon & Schuster 2008.
- Lynne McTaggert, *The Field.* HarperCollins 2008.
- Raymond Moody, *The Light Beyond.* Ebury 2005.
- Raymond Moody, *Life after Life.* Ebury 2001.
- Raymond Moody and Paul Perry, *Glimpses of Eternity.* Ebury 2016.
- Melvin Morse, *Closer to the Light.* Random House USA 1992.
- Michael Newton, *Journey of Souls.* LLewellyn 1994.
- Ian Stevenson, *Where Reincarnation and Biology Intersect* Abc-Clio 1997
- Colson Whitehead, *The Underground Railroad.* Little Brown UK 2017.
- Roeland van Wijk, *Light in shaping life, Biophotons in biology and medicine.*
  Meluma 2014.

To be published Autumn 2019:
Thea Terlouw, *Breaking the Circle*, Obelisk Boeken.
Thea Terlouw, *The Healing Chambers,* Obelisk Boeken.

The Cycle
of Life and Death